To Dean Knapp
with my best wishes
René Défourneaux

6-13-01

ICA ✸

Publication Services by
Indiana Creative Arts
5814 Beechwood Avenue
Indianapolis, IN 46219

René Défourneaux
Circa 1945

Dedication

This book is dedicated to Vic Calvat a genuine Free Frenchman who still believes in justice; to John Taylor an anointed archivist with a remarkable memory; to Mia Waller for her help in my search for documents; to Henri Michel, a rare individual whose knowledge of Vietnam was tremendously useful to me; to Michel Bloit for his guts and role in the defeat of Germany; and to all the brave Carpetbaggers who supported OSS and SOE Operations during WWII; to my friends, Dave and Fran Richards, who transformed my "franglais" into a readable manuscript; to Jeffrey J. Stenzoski for his title suggestion and to Larry Muncie for his help and for his cover creation and without whom you would not be reading this, *The Tracks of The Fox*

Contents

Prologue - Before Memory Fades iii
I Thought You Were Dead 1
Forty Years Later 3
Second Trip to Europe 7
Third Trip to Europe 13
Surprise! 15
Fourth Trip to Europe and More Surprises 18
Capt. Dubois Recollections 24
Leon's Report 54
Buckmaster 60
Fifth Trip to Europe 65
Space-A Party, Salinas CA 66
Beginning of an Earnest Search 68
England, Harrington, Scotland 69
Getting Warm 74
NARA Again! MR Discovery 82
The Sitting Duck Pub 94
The Official Report of Operation Licensee 96
Comments on the Notes 109
Comments From France 113
Kiki's Mission 16
Searching For the First Tracks 125
Vic Calvat AKA Captain Dubois 129
The Trials and Tribulations of Capt Dubois 132
The Return to the Alleged DZ 154
Pierre Bon 169
A Tough Little Guy 171
A Vietnam Story 176
The Defection of Nguyên-Dinh-Tan 193
Reflections 199

Suggested Sources 204
Acronyms 205
Index 207

ii

Prologue

Before memory fades

There comes a time after the years have accumulated when the past acquires a greater significance, when it becomes a driving force difficult to dismiss. The older one becomes, the more urgent it is to remember and to make known. Saturated with this feeling and encouraged by my children, 10 years ago I sat before my computer and filled its window with memories. As I retraced my life from the earliest age I discovered the wonder of the brain and its uncanny accuracy. When checking other sources about past incidents of my life, it was amazing how untainted was the information I retrieved from my gray cells. The result of my efforts was the publishing of *The Winking Fox*, a 380-page autobiography.

In the process I also discovered that there were many facts I did not know, many incidents that were never explained, many people who had vanished from my mind, and all those who had failed to reenter. No doubt WWII had been the most significant moment of my life because it had been a matter of life and death. Because of luck, divine intervention, or perhaps predestination, I had survived three years of peril.

But what about those who had shared the same risks? Those brave Maquisards of France? The few who never accepted defeat from the very day of capitulation? What about those airmen who dodged the German ack-ack and their nosy searchlights to drop me in occupied France? They believed that they had reached their destination, but did they return safely? Are they still alive? Perhaps they are wondering what happened to me? Most were my age, even younger, but others were much older.

It took almost ten years to complete the manuscript entitled: *The Winking Fox*. In retrospect I should have been kinder to some of my war comrades and should not have included the parts that dealt with my personal life as it adversely affected and alienated some members of my family. My purpose in writing this book was to make known that the activities in which some of us were engaged during peace time was not only physically risky, but emotionally disturbing to the families of those involved. Unless the agent had a spouse who understood the importance of secrecy, and was willing to play the "game" as her husband, the family would invariably suffer.

The Winking Fox left many questions unanswered. It seemed almost hopeless to continue on my quest but my insatiable curiosity edged me on.

The following pages describe my efforts in learning about the past, the successes and the failures in my research.

I Thought You Were Dead!

Glancing through the mail, I noticed an official looking envelope from the Finance Center of the U.S. Army at Indianapolis, the installation where I terminated my military career. Unlike other official correspondence I had previously received from that organization, my name and address had been written by hand! Opening it, inside I discovered a smaller envelope addressed to *Major René Défourneaux c/o The Finance Center, Fort Benjamin Harrison, Indiana, U.S.A. 46216*. The envelope covered with French stamps indicating its origin pricked my interest. The return address was from *Vic Calvat* a name unknown to me. Opening the envelope, and extracting a small handwritten letter, I was dismayed by the first few lines which stated:

"I believed that you had died in Vietnam because I never received the box of chocolate which was to reassure me that you had survived. Quickly confirm your resurrection and the address that was given to me."

When I left France in 1944, I remembered vaguely telling Captain Dubois, the chief of our resistance group, who wanted to accompany me back to the United States, "If I come out of this war unscathed, I will send you a box of chocolates. Because of my probable activities my name may not appear as the sender, but the chocolate will speak for itself. You will know who sent it."

I read further:

"The remaining few of us remember you well. Reply quickly, no doubt with your many questions. Fraternally."

It was signed *"Vic Calvat."* And it included an address at *La Celle St.Cloud*, as well as a telephone number.

Scribbled in the corner of the letter was the following: (*ex Capitaine Dubois*). Now I knew who Vic Calvat was. He was my old friend, the one who, during the war, took good care of me, the one who in 1944 protected me during the few months I was in occupied France.

Finally, after all these years, Captain Dubois was the one who finally attempted a reunion between the American representing the Allied Forces in his sector and his small band of determined guerrilla fighters. Clearly I had finally succeeded in the initial steps of the search I began three years earlier. Now that I had one firm contact I was confident it would lead to others.

Ce 15 Avril 88

Je suis toujours à 145 de NICE où le courrier me suit
Tel. 93 58 01 96

Incroyable !!!

Je te croyais mort au Vietnam puisque je n'ai jamais reçu la boîte de chocolat qui devait m'assurer de ta survie.

Confirme moi vite ta résurrection et l'adresse qu'on vient de me communiquer.

Ton souvenir est resté vivace parmi nous tous, mais il n'en reste plus beaucoup. Hâte toi de me répondre avec bien des questions sans doute.

Bien fraternellement

(ex Capitaine Dubois)

Vic CALVAT - 14 Allée Jules Verne 78170 LA CELLE ST CLOUD
France
Tel. 16 1 39 69 74 62

Letter from Vic Calvat

2

Forty Years Later

First return to Europe

I had left France in 1939, and except for two brief unofficial visits, I did not return to my country of birth until 1984. Up to that time I took very seriously the warning I had received in China, and in India in 1945. The French, extremely unhappy about my activities on behalf of the United States, threatened to eliminate me permanently. They considered my new allegiance as illegitimate, and my behavior toward France detestable. Thus, to justify their position, they adjudged me a traitor to France. This turn of events did not worry nor overly concern me. I was a citizen of the United States and what French officials thought of me was of little importance. Yet I knew from experience that if the French wanted to, they could carry out their threat, but not as long as I remained in the United States. Thus for forty years I did not officially set foot on French soil.

For many years Dr. Carl W. Edds, my brother-in-law, had wished to take his wife Jeanne on a European vacation. Eventually he made up his mind and he suggested that my wife Ginny and I accompany them. We accepted and on the 5th of September, 1984 we left Chicago on our way to Amsterdam on the first leg of the trip. After a short layover in Holland we went by train to Paris for a few days, then to Orleans to meet one of my customers. For me it was a business trip. As it was, it placed us very close to the area where I had been during WWII.

I wanted to return to Cosne-sur-Loire, the town liberated by my resistance group in October, 1944. Rather than following the Loire River to our destination, from Orleans we decided to cross the Sologne, one of the poorest regions of France. When we reached the vineyards of the Cher we knew that we were close to Sancerre where some of the best wines of France are produced. At St.Satur, we drove over the bridge that had replaced the one I had blown up in 1944 and crossed the Loire River. I did not see the damage I had caused and hardly recognized the structure that we had partially demolished. We had to travel north to reach Cosne-sur-Loire, but not before stopping at Pouilly for a two-hour luncheon and visiting the castle and the caves where in 1944 I had met several local resistance chiefs. The castle was still there, but the damp cave carved in the side of a hill no longer held wooden barrels. These had been replaced by huge square stainless steel vats each holding a different brand of wine. The young man in charge had heard of the resistance, and he was so impressed by the visitors from another continent that he offered us a taste of each of his wines, and a tour of the winery.

When we reached Cosne-sur-Loire, despite a forty years absence, without help I found the   street and went directly to the building where our group had established their final base. The street was exactly as we had left it in October 1944. Standing on the sidewalk and looking across the street at the house where Simone and I had such great times was a very stirring experience. Her father, learning that we had spent the night together, to save her reputation insisted that marry his daughter. The garden where he grew beautiful roses had not changed. Forty years might have passed since I had seen these buildings and the small park separating them, but then it seems as if it were yesterday. Closer examination revealed that nothing had changed.

Standing under the windows of the room where our group often gathered, I instinctively looked down at the sidewalk expecting to see the half-consumed cigarette butts that we flipped outside from the second floor. I remembered the local people, deprived of tobacco, carefully picking them and using the unburned tobacco to roll their own cigarettes. I stopped a neighbor and asked about Simone's parents. She told me that Simone's father had passed away, and that she and her mother had moved away a few years back, but she did not know where.

The names of all those who were with me long ago had been forgotten. Real names were seldom used in those days, only nicknames or "noms de guerre" (code names) were used and known only to those involved with our activities. The only real names I knew were of those who had a real function

Secret Headquarters of Operation Licensee

in the community but who were not part of our group such as Simone's father who was a local banker. These included the members of the city council identified on a document presented to me by the people of Cosne-sur-Loire after its liberation.

The document stated that, on the 24th of September 1944 after the deliverance of the town, the Committee of Liberation had conferred on me the title of "Citizen of the town of Cosne-sur-Loire." All these years I had carefully kept the only proof that I had been there. It had never left my control - I thought - and it had yellowed with time, but was still very readable.

Thus, with the aged document, and accompanied by the members of our group, I proceeded to the "Hotel de Ville" (town hall) to see the mayor. The stone steps of the "Mairie" leading to an old oak door were still the same, but the door had been replaced by a modern all glass entryway. If the rest of the town had not changed much, the town hall most certainly had.

The mayor was not available, but his assistant, a glacial lady in her late 50s, received me and sternly inquired as to what was the purpose of my visit to the town's government center. Presenting her my delicate certificate, I asked her about the benefits accorded to an honorary citizen of her fair city. Surprised by the document and shocked by my request she stared at the paper, then at me, then again at the paper, and turning toward her   secretary sitting behind a desk next to hers, she asked: "Nadine, have you ever seen such a document before?" Leaving her chair, holding the document, and examining it carefully, Nadine replied: "I recognize some of the names, but most are dead, some have moved away. As for the others, I have no idea."

I inquired: "Are any former members of the resistance left in the area?"

Nadine replied: "It has been such a long time, people have forgotten." She continued: "However, I know a colonel who may well remember. I shall call him." She went to her telephone and dialed a number. It rang a couple times and from where I stood I could hear a strong voice.

"Allo."

"Colonel? This is Nadine at the Mayor's office. An American who was here during the war is in our office. He is looking for members of the resi__"
The voice interrupted her.

"Is he tall, blond, and does he wear a mustache?"

" Well! Yes colonel."

"Tell him not to move. I will be right over ."

The vice mayor who was attentively listening began to relax, happy that someone was taking over and she did not have to make a decision. She offered me a chair which I declined, preferring to join the rest of my group standing in the lobby of the Town Hall.

It wasn't long before a short individual in his mid-fifties crashed through the main entrance. Seeing the four of us standing in the center of the hall, he approached and grabbing me he gave me an accolade normally reserved to real heroes. I was as surprised as were the rest of our group. I wondered what those few local people standing in the hall thought when they witnessed this effusiveness.

I did not recognized the "Colonel" yet he seemed to know who I was. By the way he greeted me I felt that perhaps he was one of the men with whom I had shared unforgettable tribulations. He identified himself as Colonel Testard, a member of the resistance, but not a part of my group. He had heard about me from my former associates and he was certain that they would be happy to know I had come to Cosne to renew my association. As we had to return to Orleans that day, I gave him my card and told him to pass it on to any member of my resistance group so that they might communicate with me. He promised to keep in touch and after another cheek-to-cheek encounter we parted company.

Second Trip To Europe

Forty years after the liberation of Holland

The following year Ginny and I were invited by the American-Netherlands Foundation to attend the 50th anniversary of the liberation of Holland. While in Europe, having not heard from my former resistance fighters, we did not go to the Nièvre region. Instead we attended the reunion of the famed Rhin/Danube Association held at Besançon, in the French Jura close to my home town. It gave us the opportunity to visit several of my relatives, and to gain a few kilos.

Although I did not participate in the liberation of Holland, nevertheless Ginny and I were invited to the celebration of the 40th anniversary of its liberation from German occupation. This was the most memorable trip we had so far undertaken, not only because of its historical significance, but because it was free. The American-Netherlands Foundation was footing the bill. Former members of the 75th Division composed the group with whom we traveled by van from Switzerland to Belgium. It included a double amputee. It was his first return to where he had lost both legs at the very start of the Battle of the Bulge.

It was late April 1985, and from the day of our arrival in Europe the weather had been agreeable, even warm. From Mannheim Germany, after crossing the Mosel, and approaching Belgium, it began to snow. Although at first gently, by the time we reached Vielsalm in the Ardennes, the visibility was less than a quarter of a mile, the flakes were as large as quarters, and there was close to a foot of snow on the ground.

The temperature dipped down to 20° F and the countryside assumed a 1944 semblance, shocking our veterans of the Bulge. On the outskirts of Vielsalm we checked in the Chalet Val-de-Salm, a small inn next to a bubbling spring called the Salm.

When we entered into our assigned bedroom we discovered that there was no heat, and that there was a one inch space under the French doors leading to an outdoor balcony. We quickly retreated to the downstairs bar where the one and only fireplace kept us warm for a while. After several welcoming drinks, and we felt brave enough to face the freezing temperature in our bedroom, we went upstairs and discovered that, beside the traditional eiderdown, there was only one blanket! After stuffing it under the French doors, we slid between the sheets, each one hoping that the other would be warmer. We survived this uncomfortable night and in the morning, looking forward to a hot shower first, we ran the water in the sink and waited, and waited. Ginny took a washcloth under the faucet and when she looked at it,

Le Chalet of Wal-de-Salm

it had turned blue! We had no idea why, but we gave up on the shower, and rushed to the bar and its roaring fire place.

It was the 29th of April 1985, my birthday. This was duly noted and when the omelet I had ordered arrived it had a lighted candle stuck on top. How thoughtful were these Belgian hosts.

It was a Sunday and I volunteered to drive with one of our group to mass. The church was as cold as our room. I guessed   that these people did not believe in personal comfort, or they wanted us to remember 1944. When the priest appeared I noticed that he was wearing his overcoat under his chasuble. His breath and that of the altar boys was clearly seen from the pews, and so were the breaths of the parishioners.

Later that day we drove to Bastogne and made our way to Jauffalize the spot where our double amputee had lost his legs. It was a painful experience for all of us, but a particularly emotional time for him. His unit had been bivouacking in a wooded hill above the village. They were told that the village was free of Germans. When they came out in the clearing all hell broke loose. It seems that the entire German army was waiting for them. He did not know what hit him, but unlike many of his friends, he survived.

We heard many stories about the famous Battle of the Bulge not only from the veterans who were with us, but from the local people. We were listening to some survivors' accounts in a local inn, when someone quoted General McAuliff's famous reply to the Germans. A little local girl who

Bastogne memorial to the Bulge

spoke excellent English took the floor and said: "No monsieur, the general did not say nuts, he said sheet." That broke up the party.

From Vielsalm we crossed Luxembourg and made our way to Holland, stopping at the American cemetery of Maastrich where the brother of one of our group was buried. He found his brother's grave among the thousands of crosses aligned in a well manicured cemetery.

We spent our first night in Amsterdam and had a second birthday party at the famous Darien restaurant.

German tank at Jauffalize, Belgium

Graves at Margrabe American cemetery at Maastrich Netherlands

The forty American veterans, including General Kinnard and the families reached their destination the following day where they were treated royally by the people of Holland. We were lucky enough to meet Princess Margrit who spoke English with an American accent.

Hand shake with Princess Margrit

The highlight of our visit was a reception at the Town Hall of the Hague where we started a snake dance with the Lord Mayor, his last as he was not reelected.

But only four of us who had been designated to make a presentation on the grave of an American witnessed the most amazing ceremony held annually on the anniversary of the liberation of Holland.

A young American airman had survived a crash in the center of Holland. He was rescued by a resistance group and participated in their activities. Unfortunately, he and two young men of the group were killed by the Germans and buried next to the church of Zaetermeer. Every year on the anniversary of the liberation of Holland the entire town parades from the church to a park a quarter of a mile away where a semicircular memorial wall bearing the inscription "1939-1945" was erected. Under a cold drizzle we four assembled under the church tower with the Lord Mayor and the church's minister. When time came to move out, drummers   preceded us beating on their muffled drums. When we reached the memorial wall, a military band began playing martial music until the park was filled with standing people. After the last note as if it were understood, there was a dead silence. Not even a cough was heard when a single bell in the church tower slowly began to peal. I counted forty times. Then, as the band began playing a mournful tune, one at a time people approached and placed flowers in front of the wall. Some had bouquets; others, mostly children held a single flower. Soon the flowers reached the top of the wall.

The silence was deafening. There were no speeches and no one stood up to explain, but I noted very few dry eyes including my own. The band stopped playing and everyone quietly started to leave the park. Obviously these people did not need a speaker to remind them of the past.

We returned to the church to lay a wreath on the tomb of the lone airman and his two companions. His father had decided to let him lie with his friends instead of moving his body home, or to an American cemetery. It seemed as though the entire village was watching us.

For taking such good care of our hero, one of our group said a few words of thanks to the assembled people. Then we joined other local veterans at a neighborhood pub where a retired dentist, who had been the head of the local resistance group, greeted us and provided us with details of their past activities in perfect English which he translated later for the benefit of the local people.

Before returning to Amsterdam, we visited the local War Museum where there were parts of the aircraft which had crashed near the town. This was the most emotional time of my visit to Holland. Unfortunately, only four of us witnessed this simple but very meaningful ceremony

Four American veterans honoring an American airman buried next to the Church of Zaetermeer, Holland.

We flew back to the United States shortly thereafter. The year passed without a single word from my friends of the French resistance.

Third Trip To Europe

By April 1986, my sister Marcelle who up to that time had shown no interest in returning to her birth place, decided with her husband to go to Europe, but only if Ginny and I came along. We agreed, and after joining them in New Jersey, we flew first to Zurich, Switzerland. Then after a couple of days at Lausanne on the 1st of May we drove to Délémont in the Jura mountains. Later that morning we descended the Rangiers and reached Cornol shortly before noon. Marcelle did not know that I had arranged a birthday party for her at the Auberge of the Cheval Blanc where we had spent many years in our youth. She was happy to see familiar surroundings, including the orchard and garden, but was shocked when she entered the inn and found many of our cousins waiting for her, the relatives I had invited whom she had not seen for forty five years.

We remained in the area visiting our cousins who for   some reasons did not make the party, renewing our relationship, then drove to Paris. On our way back to Switzerland we decided to stop at Cosne-Sur-Loire to show my sister where I had fought the war.

I had not heard from Colonel Testard, and no one had contacted me from the area. I located the Colonel's house, but was told by the neighbors that the man residing there was so old that he probably did not hear the bell. This was strange, because Colonel Testard was not so old! We were about to leave when the door opened a crack, and a small obese lady of advanced age cautiously stuck her head out.

"Yes, what do you want?" she said abruptly.

"We are looking for Colonel Testard,"

"The Colonel is my son, but he is traveling. He will be gone for a few days," she said, keeping the door open just a crack.

I was explaining to her why I wanted to see the Colonel, when she opened the door wide and said:

"I know who you are, you are Daniel, the American officer who was here during the war! Come in, come in."

The door was part of a larger gateway blocking the entrance of a coach house full of artifacts such as arrow heads, fossils, old dishes and a multitude of objects which would have made an antique dealer envious.

She explained that the "very old man" was her husband, Dr. Testard, Colonel Testard's father, and that during the war she was the code clerk handling our communication with London. This was news to me. I always believed that Léon, or his assistant radio operator, were the ones who communicated with London. She apparently knew more about me than I cared to remember and started to tell us about incidents that had occurred during the war. My sister and I had a hard job translating to our companions these accounts spoken at great speed by an unbelievable memory bank. Other than Colonel Testard, her son, she had no contact with former members of the local resistance. However, she believed that a local man, Pierre Bon, who had been a member of another resistance group might know the whereabouts of those who have survived.

Following her instructions we located the house of Pierre Bon on the road that borders the Loire River. He was not at home, but his wife invited us in and immediately offered us a drink. We were sitting in the living room sipping a strong homemade liquor when Pierre Bon came in.

I explained to him that I had been in Cosne in 1984 because I wanted to locate former members of the resistance based in Cosne. Two years earlier I had met Colonel Testard, but not having heard from him I felt that he had failed to locate anyone connected with my group. After I mentioned my war name, excitedly Bon said:

"I know who you are. You are Daniel, the young French/American officer who helped the resistance and who blew up the bridge of St. Satur."

He had heard about "Daniel" but had not been part of my group. Although his own association of former resistance fighters met periodically, they were from another area in the region of Yonne. However, in the area there were former maquisards who had been with my group. He would search for them and let them know that I wanted to establish contact with my old friends.

Then he took us to his garage and after rummaging through boxes he came down a ladder with a Sten gun, the old standby of the resistance, and a red cargo parachute, a left-over from the drops made by our Air Corps. What was he doing with all that stuff? He must have had enough military equipment to stand a siege for a few months!

After exchanging addresses we parted company. I was certain then that, by the time I returned home, I would have a letter from one or perhaps several members of my group of maquisards. When we left Cosne-sur-Loire I was quite disappointed by my failure to meet any of the brave men who were with me during those trying times. I was also surprised that when talking to some of the local people, they appeared to have forgotten that only a few years back a war had been fought in their town. Most younger people had no notion of their parents' struggle for survival during the German occupation. In America, except understandably by the veterans, WWII had also been forgotten by many.

Surprise!

The year 1987 passed without a single communication from my former comrades. Perhaps all were gone! After all, at 23 I was perhaps the youngest of the group. Most were in their thirties and some were even older. By 1988 again I thought of returning and spending more time looking, even if it meant looking for tombstones. Ginny and I decided to be brave, and to travel to Europe via space available with the U.S. Air Force. We planned to leave in June and take advantage of the springtime in Paris.

Then in early May 1988, I received an unusual envelope from the U.S. Army Finance Center of Indianapolis, Indiana.

The letter included an address at La Celle St.Cloud near Paris and two telephone numbers: one in Paris, the other near Nice on the Riviera.

Another smaller page with more details stated the following:

May 10, 1988

René J. Défourneaux Major US (Ret.)

(ex-Lieutenant Daniel at Cosne in 1944)

Dear Julien:

I believed that you had died in Vietnam in 1945. Imagine my joy when by luck a few days ago I learned about your short visit at Cosne in 1984. The two individuals that you met (N. Marty and Mr. Testard) took no proper initiatives to locate those who have known you.

The letter that I immediately sent to you was returned, as your Indianapolis address had lapsed as well as the telephone numbers of René, Alain and Gisèle which I called in vain at that city.

I tried to send you this message through several routes. As soon as you receive one of these, quickly give me your new address so that I may send you news of the few survivors of this epic, those who have maintained a very good souvenir of your stay here.

I hope that you are in as good shape as you appeared to be in 1984.

I reside near Paris

    Vic Calvat
14 Allée Jules Verne
78170 La Celle St. Cloud, France
PS: I often reside on the Riviera near Nice where the mail follows me to:
Les Mimosas Residence du Parc
06140 Vence France
Impatiently I await your reply.
Most fraternally
S/ ex-Capitaine Dubois
Commanding the FFI Maquis of the Cosne Sector.

Finally I was in contact with Capt. Dubois, the head of the resistance group to which I had been assigned by SOE. This was better than expected because I knew that Capt. Dubois was a man of his word, and that he would know where every member of his group still alive was located. I also realized that our company clerk at Kunming OSS HQ. had succeeded in making believe my demise. When Simone received the news she told Capt. Dubois and his group that I was no longer of this world.

I could not possibly relate my forty four years of silence in a couple of pages. Thus I wrote to Vic Calvat, alias Captain Dubois, that I was planing a trip to Europe, and that I would bring him up to date when we met him. His reply read as follow:

Translation

My dear René (Since René it is...... and I must get used to it)

After three weeks of waiting each day, becoming more impatient and at times more anxious I finally received your letter announcing your anticipated visit. It's fantastic!!

I cannot understand why Testart and Bon did not tell me about your passing through Cosne. The mail pickup does not permit me to compose the long account I was planning to write to you. You will get it viva voce.

I wanted this to reach you before your arrival. So that you will know that only ten of those you knew well are still alive. For all you have left an interesting souvenir and at each get-together your name was evoked.

My spouse, (The Captain) died 13 years ago following open heart surgery. My daughter Nicole, who was three in 1944, spoke of you often as if you were an old acquaintance. She invoke your name when serving liquor in "Julien's service" (you had given us when you left, in fact it is still in my possession).

You see; because we thought you were dead you belonged to our Dear Departed.

Forgive the poor handwriting, I am in a hurry and not gifted.

Sunday June 5th I will be at Cosne for a display of the souvenirs of the resistance. On the 6 or 7 of June I will reach La Celle St, Cloud where I had planned to remain until the 6th of July to attend the baptism of the grandson of Jacqueline who shares my life for the past 12 years. If you do not have a specific program for your stay at Nice, I will return to Vence to show you the local points of interest ignored by tourist agencies

16

Thus I only have a daughter Nicole, married with three children:

Marie Ambre, 23 "Public relations" recently married threatens to make me a great grandpa in 1985. She spent one year in Iowa for language training. She would have been happy to visit you.

Marc 22 Student at a dental school

Adeline 21 Art student

They reside at Chatou near la Celle St.Cloud and have a summer home at St. Thibault 50 meters from the bridge you blew up (On the Cher side.)

Quickly a few words about the known individuals. Dead are Jean and Eugenie Guillot the farmers of Annay whose farm had become our logistical base, as well as capitaine Bauchet to whom I had given the responsibility of the defense of Pouilly while both of us went to briar to ask the help of Colonel Bourgoin's (Le manchot) paratroops. It is his son, Guy Bauchet, a retired colonel who is organizing the souvenir display.

Deceased 15 years ago Mr. Gadoin, became senator and great friend of Mitterrand our present president. I have lost contact with Madame Gadoin who must be close to 100 years old, and her Daughter Simone who married an architect, had one boy, then divorced and allegedly remarried a senator.

Norac after becoming a monk again has pursued his career at Rome.

I would be pleased to meet Ginny and to welcome you. I await your itinerary and a telephone call as soon as you land in the old continent.

Best wishes

S/ Vic Calvat

Fourth Trip To Europe and More Surprises

On the 17th of June 1988, we left our home on our way to Europe. For several years we toyed with the idea of traveling "space available," that is, care of the U.S. Air Force. We decided to try our luck and headed for Dover, Delaware. At Dover there were no immediate flights to Europe. They suggested that we try McGuire Air Force Base near Fort Dix, New Jersey, which we did. After spending a couple of nights at Fort Dix, at 5:30 PM on the 20th of June, we were finally loaded aboard a C-151, Galaxy, Ginny sitting in one of the few VIP seats, I as in the old days, on a "bucket seat." On our way to Europe aboard a Galaxy was like traveling inside a warehouse. Less than half the plane was occupied by cargo, the rest by travelers half in seats facing the tail of the plane, the others on bucket seats along the bulkhead. We eventually reached England, but not before refueling in the middle of the Atlantic, and a long stopover at the Azores.

We landed at Lakenheath, an RAF base, and were bussed to Mildenhall, a U.S. Air Force base. From there by taxi to a "bed and breakfast" at Cambridge where we stayed for a few days. With a rented car we visited old England including Chester, Manchester, the Lake District, and Stratford-on-Avon. We stopped in London, for a first-time visit of the Special Forces Club, a club I had joined several years earlier. There we met Sir Douglas Dodds-Parker who wrote *Setting Europe Ablaze*. He was on Sir Winston's staff and was very familiar with SOE and OSS.

We managed to abandon our rental car at Dover and after crossing the Channel aboard a ferry, we landed in Calais where a brand new Peugeot was waiting for us at the pier. We were a few miles from Calais when we realized that the gas tank was empty. They could have told us when we picked up the car. Apparently in France this is not part of the business deal! Nothing comes with batteries, and apparently cars do not come with gas! At the pump we realized why. A gallon of gas was over three dollars.

Our first stop was Dieppe, the site of the ill-fated attempt to invade the continent two years before D-Day. Standing on the beach where the landing occurred, Ginny and I could not imagine a worse place selected for a landing. The other beaches where the D-day landing happened were not much better. For the Germans it must have been like shooting ducks in a gallery.

After visiting the battlefields of Normandy, as well as the spectacular museum at Caen, we waved at Lt. John Steel still dangling from the belfry as we passed by the church at St.Mère Eglise. After a tortuous climb up Isle St. Michel with a million tourists we decided that we should continue to our destination, the capital of France. On the 30th of June we made our way toward Paris.

When we reached the suburbs of Paris, not knowing where La Celle St.Cloud actually was, we decided to try St. Cloud which must be close to it. After we reached the St. Cloud railroad station at 3:30 pm, I called Vic Calvat who took only fifteen minutes to reach the parking lot where Ginny and I were waiting.

I recognized him immediately. Heavier, he was just as handsome as when I knew him many years ago. He presented Ginny with a red rose, gave her a kiss and he and I hugged for a minute or so. For both it was like finding a lost brother, a brother neither of us had. He drove ahead and I

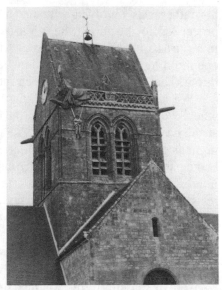

Effigy of Lt. John Steel hanging from the steeple of the Church of Sainte-Mère-Eglise.

followed him with our car. First to his home at Rue Jules Verne, then to his granddaughter's apartment where we would stay while in Paris. It appeared that Marie-Ambre had placed her apartment at our disposal while she and her husband Olivier were staying at his nearby parents' residence. Both were so giving. Marie told us that she had heard so much about "Julien" that she felt that he was a departed member of her family, and it was very natural for her to give up her comfort for a "resuscitated" relative.

Vic had not changed at all and still has a very sheltering and caring attitude toward me. Our exchange of stories and the reminiscing produced reactions from laughter to tears, provoking thoughts of sadness for those we can no longer touch.

At 3 pm on the 4th of July we finally got away in the direction of Orleans where I was to meet a client. The following day we decided to go to St.Benoit where Father Norac (Caron was his real name) was supposed to be in retirement. When we reached the monastery we learn to our sorrow that Father Caron had passed away a couple of years earlier. This was most unfortunate, because he was such a wonderful individual.

We remained in Orleans a couple of days and on the 6th of July we headed south along the Loire River, first to Bourges, then to Sancerre for a bite to eat. We were to meet Vic and Jacqueline at the Auberge of Annay. The small restaurant is owned by Armand Guillot, the son of Jean and Eugenie Guillot - both deceased. Armand did remember me because he was seven at the time his father was involved with the resistance. After a sumptuous meal we proceeded to the farm where Vic and I spent time with the Guillots, my favorite Maquisards. The barn was still there. The barn where I was awakened one morning by his wife Eugenie who had the sharp tip of a pitchfork on my throat. That was before I had been introduced!

We made the round of the places we had been hiding, the drop zones where we had received supplies, the bridges we had destroyed. We stopped at the castle of Entrains where Vic and I, after a grueling day, had spent a night as guests of the Duke of Montemart. Despite having only one arm, the Duke participated in all the dangerous tasks of the Maquis. We explained our interest to the gatekeeper who, after we   told him that we were former resistance fighters, let us in. For both of us, sleeping in a real bed had been quite a treat, and the breakfast with the entire family left an indelible impression on Vic and me. We wondered if the children of the Duke had the same recollection! As we were walking casually through the estate reminiscing, a car pulled up to us. A lady in her forties wanted to know why we were trespassing! We explained the nature of our interest in her castle and immediately we were invited in. Unfortunately we had to decline because we had to go to another noteworthy spot to visit.

When we tried to find Pierre Brisset we found that he was living as a recluse, and was not very friendly with his neighbors. That was not the way I remembered him. After knocking at his door for several minutes he opened it. Once he realized who we were, we were invited to a tour of his house and studio. Both were full of pictures, paintings, and sculptures. He presented each of us with one of his masterpieces.

Then Vic took us to a goat farm to pay a visit to the owner who wanted to meet me, and question me about the past. In her late forties she was a

The Castle of The Duke of Montemart

20

pleasant woman, but could not have been a member of the resistance. The noticeable scars on her face suggested that something serious must have happened to her. Vic reminded me of an incident that had occurred in late August or early September 1944. Neuvy, a small town within our territory, had been completely destroyed by our own Air Force. In a matter of seconds over four hundred villagers were killed and only a couple of houses remained standing. I had to do some fast talking that day. The local

Artist Pierre Brisset and the sketch of one of his paintings

survivors were very upset. They accused the Allies, specifically the American Air Force, of having deliberately bombed the small town for no apparent reason as there were no enemy installations or concentrations in the area. I believed I had smoothed the situation, and that the villagers had accepted my explanation. The great height of the planes and shifting winds had been responsible for this deplorable accident. This unfortunately was not the case.

At that time, unbeknownst to me, in the town of Neuvy was a small factory making rubber washers. The owner and his family were in the plant when it was leveled by our Air Force. Three days later, as people were searching for victims among the wrecked buildings, they heard the cry of a baby. They found a little girl buried under tons of concrete. Because she was terribly mutilated and disfigured, she was not expected to survive, but she did.

Following an official complaint to the Allied command, the U.S. Air Force accepted full responsibility for the bombing of Neuvy and offered to compensate the locality for the damages. It included payment for the facial reconstruction - 26 operations of the little girl - the sole surviving member of the family who owned the small factory making rubber washers. One would think that this was the end of the story, but it was not.

The bombing of Neuvy, although declared a mistake by the U.S. Air Force, was not accepted as such by many local people. They accused the little girl's family of having collaborated with the Germans and claimed, without real proof, that the plant was supplying the enemy with material for their war efforts. They based their theory on the belief that it was inconceivable for the U.S. Air Force to have made such a mistake and they had bombed the town because it was considered a military target, even if they did not want to admit it. Why did they agree to pay for damages? This was the only logical answer for the bombing of Neuvy.

From the end of the war until the present, as a result of this idiotic idea, she was reminded, at time not subtly, that her parents were collaborators, traitors, and enemies of France.

She begged me to help her dispel this notion and tell the local people that her folks had not collaborated with the Germans, and they were good people. She had a stack of documents from the U.S. Air Force - unfortunately all in English - but these did not convince the local people who still believed that her family's factory was the cause for the bombing of Neuvy.

It was difficult for me to understand that, after forty years, French people would be so cruel as to blame a woman, who as a little girl had been lucky enough to survive a tragedy. I told her that I would try to help, but this incident occurred so long ago I doubt if I would find additional information regarding the incident.

After petting her goats, and tasting some of her delicious cheese, we left her farm and continued on our tour visiting several former members of our group, many of them too old or too ill to attend the grand reunion of former resistance fighters which was to be held the following day at the Town Hall.

At 6:30 pm on the 8th of July, with Vic and Jacqueline, we proceeded to the town hall of Cosne-sur-Loire. Standing in the center of the lobby, through the glass doors, I could see people coming in. Some ignored me, but a few came directly to me and shaking my hand profusely told me that they were so happy to see "McCormick!" after all these years. Initially I did not recognize many of them, However, after listening to their tales, I was able to connect them with specific incidents many of which I had forgotten. But why did they called me "McCormick?" They must have taken me for someone else.

Close to one hundred persons, mostly old-timers of all description, gathered in a large room on the second floor of the Town Hall. Dr. des Etages, the mayor, opened the meeting praising the survivors of the last great war and offering me the medal of the city while Vic offered me a corkscrew, a symbol of the region where I traded my taste for milk and steak with that of Crottin-Pouilly and Sancerre nectars. Then Vic took the floor praising me and calling me "an angel" from the sky. This was quite embarrassing because I did not expect this kind of eulogy as I was still alive. Didn't they realized that by playing dead I had fooled them? To top it all I was supposed to reply to his comments. I was unprepared but said something funny to liven up the gathering.

Then the mayor gave a bouquet of flowers to each of our spouses. After which the "amuse gueule" (snacks) were served and the wine flowed while the tales of remembrance continued until it was time for dinner. I asked Vic why so many people had attended this meeting; I doubted if some were even

The Mayor and City Council of Cosne-Cours-sur-Loire honoring author and the resistance fighters of Operation Licensee, July 1988.

in the resistance. Vic replied that free wine attracts even the most anti-war among us! Then I asked him:

"What about "McCormick?" Why did some of these fellows called me McCormick?"

"That is a long story. Someday I will tell you."

Pierre Bon and his spouse with another couple, Mr. and Mrs. Tartrat, invited us four to dinner and for additional war stories. I discovered then that Roger Tartrat, better known as "Kiki," was a great story teller, and that eventually he would play an important part in my quest. I wished that I had a tape recorder to capture some of these unbelievable war anecdotes. Vic, incapable of containing himself, gave an account of his unit as it involved the "angel" he had just introduced. I felt that he gave me too much credit for the little I had done.

His recollection was most interesting and worth recording if only to compare it with mine. It took me years to convince him to record his version of the war. But he finally did and sent it to me.

Captain Dubois Recollection

The following is a translation of Captain Dubois' account of the activities of Licensee operation:

If a chicken finds a knife!

As a Maquisard standing before the pile of modern arms delivered by parachute by the British I felt completely helpless! We were anxious to exchange our rifles and rusted cartridges for newer weapons. Léon, the agent/radio operator sent to help us, transmitted my request by radio to London. The legendary Diane (Virginia Hall), the head of the net, instructed him to see about our needs. She decided to enlarge my Nièvre sector with the area assigned to the Mission Licensee responsible for the support of the resistance in Central France.

The first parachute drop was an unforgettable event! We were looking forward to it for so long. Also great was the excitement when the BBC announced "Le singe et la giraffe emboitent le pas": It was the coded message we were waiting for. It meant that the delivery will be tonight. We can hardly believe it. On the prepared field the waiting is long. The sun will soon rise. We fear the worse. Did we stamp our feet all this time for nothing?_it was too good to be true.

Finally. Yes, these are for us, these large airplanes heading for our lights quickly turned on. Then a miracle occurred. In the dark night, right above the small field where we were waiting, containers were released. We could hear the rustling of the silk as the parachutes opened.

It was too late for us to check their content before daybreak. We have only the time to bury them in prepared hiding places. Frustrated as children kept away from their presents on Christmas morning, we must wait a few more hours before discovering our "toys."

A small team composed of my most trusted men must conduct an inventory. They cannot wait. Despite a sleepless night they are on the job way ahead schedule. With feverish and awkward movements they fall upon the sheet metal cylinders, these strange packages.

Jean, is the first who managed to open his: Solidly wedged Jerry cans full of gas did not lose a drop. He is disappointed, but our "traction" (front wheel drive vehicle) liberated of its "Gazo"(Charcoal burner) will fly.

From another container Siamo (the one with slanting eyes) uncovers a complete grocery store including sugar, flour, chocolate, coffee.. real coffee! and cigarettes same as ours! Our brothers in arms are spoiling us.

Johndeux (he looked American) triumphantly brandishes what we have been waiting for, carbines, pistols-real Colts! Soon our veterans are demonstrating their working to the young volunteers, those who have joined us before doing their military service.

The search continues as if the booty had been acquired after a fierce battle. An unusual perfume escapes from these containers. We inhale it deeply as if it permeates the air from a free country. Perplexed before these strange discoveries we all stop. What do we do with these powerful magnets? What about this tube open at both ends and as long as our old rifles? In turn each handles it, weighs it, and looks at it from one end to the other. The tag indicates that it is called "Bazooka," this famous anti-tank weapon we had heard about. How is it used?

A recess long enough to ponder and to taste some "K-ration," this complete meal for the GI in battle. While we chew the compressed biscuit, and other curious food stuff Dédé, a butcher by profession, attacks a meat patty. Then professionally he decides to try a bite. Stupefied, he makes a face and spits all of it with disgust crying, "Ah the jerks, they made a mistake, they have put in sugar instead of salt!" Thinking of offering us a treat our good "Amerloques" even have included their indispensable toothpicks.

This was not our only surprise. One of the inquisitors questioningly shows us a well-sealed package full of strange metallic pencils. These remind us of medical thermometers used in our behinds since our early youth. Be careful, perhaps these are detonators, as these were not in the same package with the blocks of putty, assuredly "plastic," this fantastic explosive. I handle it myself with care under the sudden anxious and silent gaze of the others.

Here is something else: It looks like a champagne cork with a shoelace rolled around. It has a miniature skirt that may be tightened at the base by means of a real hem and a lace running through it. Concentrating Paul examines this type of doll. Staring at it he scratches his head with his left hand while with the other he turns and returns the object and hefts it. He wrinkles his nose one way then the other so as to capture his inspiration: " What is this gadget?"

We are contented but somewhat disappointed. I must divide this material among twenty groups. How can they use it? The instructions are many, but all are written in English. No one to translate them correctly. A poor interpretation may result in a serious accident. A bilingual instructor is imperative. In response to my request the London Headquarters of our Buckmaster Net agrees to send us one as soon as available.

A Coveted Guest

By nightfall on the 8th of August we are gathered on the prearranged field to receive him. It is the first time that we will see a man under a parachute instead of a container. We are all very excited. The small reception committee is composed of the key reliable individuals of our group. There were Léon, the liaison officer of the net, Dubois (myself) commander of the Maquis, and Jean Guillot, illustrious chief of the Annay-Neuvy sector. Jean controls "Anguille," the code name for the field where our instructor will land. The waiting begins.

What does he look like this new comrade? We did not select him from a set of photos. We imagine the anxiety of the poor fellow they will toss out in the dark in a unknown country peppered with enemies. We are ready to reassure him. As soon as he hits the ground, accolades, and vigorous slaps on the back will relieve the shock. In addition, Jean will offer him a generous ham sandwich he prepared himself as well as a slice of cream cake, a specialty of his spouse Eugenie. To conclude this welcome, a shot of marc (home-made brandy), a proven tonic. He does not know his good fortune, the lucky fellow!

Luckily the weather is mild tonight and the waiting continues. Taking advantage of the spare time we comment on the "Les Français parlent aux Français"(the French speak to the French) a Radio-London daily broadcast. It does maintain our morale high. Under the bombings of England it must also swell theirs. We discuss a story we heard about these cowardly gendarmes (French policeman) and their mercenary deeds; these zealous individuals with cushy jobs, who find it too dangerous to tease the Boches, but who prefer shaking down returning Parisians on the platform of the railroad stations, stripping these poor famished of the food they had acquired with much pain in the distant country farms.

For three hours we dawdle, our ears open, ready to light the markers as soon as we hear the drone of a large aircraft. Suddenly, a noise brings forth uneasiness: it is the put-put of a German spy plane. Flying low in their tiny craft the Germans occasionally make the round over the area. Instinctively everyone covers the red glow of his cigarette. Ha! What a relief when the danger drifts away. The operation could have failed.

Still nothing for us, but let us be patient. The last parachute drop had occurred early morning near the end of the night. But something in the air almost impossible to define announces the arrival of the sun. Everyone tries to hide from the others an increasing feeling of pessimism. The situation becomes uncomfortable. We have exhausted our supply of cigarettes, including that for the next three days. Prudently I gather my cigarette butts, scarcity obliges savings. The cold makes us shiver. A round of "goutte" (alcohol) is welcome. The one who is the coldest empties the jug. Toward the east a rosy glimmer announces the arrival of the sun. Evidently it is useless to wait any longer. Our guest will not show up. The setback affects the most optimistic. We must accept the fact that we were stood up.

Quickly the material is gathered. Sleepy, frustrated by our disappointment, quietly each goes his own way. The last straw hits when I noticed that the sentries that were to assure our security laid unconscious near their posts. Outraged I kick them to reality from a wine-induced sleep. I had entrusted Ponsard and his team for this most important job. He thought that a glass of red wine would keep them awake during the long hours of loneliness. For sure his idea was good, but the quantity was much too generous.

When it doesn't work, nothing works

What could have happened? Was the plane shot down? Was the passenger unable to leave at the last moment? In clandestine operations a failed rendezvous causes increased vigilance. Obsessed and with a sick feeling impatiently I wait for London's explanation. Near noon, Léon leaves for the hidden site where he maintains his radio. When he returned with a sorry smile caused by uncertainty and anxiety, he says: "Our instructor has apparently left England, and the pilot who flew him to his destination claims that he dropped him at the right spot." The fact remains we were expecting him at the right field. His escort must have made a mistake, an excusable error, because we are always surprised when they would find us, a small dot in an immense territory and in the dark to boot, a condition imposed by the occupation.

Where is the one we were expecting? Did he jump headfirst and drown in the Loire? If he fell in the hands of the Gestapo for us it will be worse. We easily imagine the torture he is enduring right now. What does he know about us? What information will they extract from him to cause us harm? Panic replaces my anxiety. Immediately I place all our groups under red alert even if it will disrupt our entire organization. I recommend a more covert behavior, and an alertness greater than ever before. I order the detailed search of the region with special attention to witnesses. In our rural district everything is known. I would be surprised that no one had seen anything. Feverishly I await for any useful indication.

It's Hell On Earth

"Where did he drop me?" wonders the bewildered parachutist. "Where are the Maquisards who are supposed to greet me? The bastard! He dropped me blind as a bag of garbage!" Angry as hell he chokes with apprehension. Yet, the pilot had assured him that it was the right place. He gropes and rolls his parachute to bury it. Around him complete silence. His eyes began to get used to darkness. He is on a flat field, but is it possible? A quantity of posts their sharp ends pointing toward the sky (The Germans had thus neutralized the terrain). Miraculously he did not impale himself on one of these. The thought of the possibility brought a shiver up and down his spine. Then unconsciously this gift of fate reassures him - his time hasn't come yet - and with less apprehension he follows his lucky star. Above all he must not be captured by the Boches. Prudently he moves away from his position. But before he could react out of the darkness four men as felines appear and surround him, their flashlights blinding him. His lucky star did not protect him long. His escort to the plane was right "Those who leave as you never do return!"

As disconcerted as their captive the slant-eyed aggressors in a strange language discuss his fate. By then nothing surprises their prisoner. "The bastard, he dropped me in China." But it is in French they ask: "A while ago was it you that came down from the plane flying so low?" He cannot deny it. "We belong to the maquis; we shall hide you." His heart had not yet recovered his rhythm when they took him to a sleepy village. They left him in a miserable room to spend the rest of the night. So much excitement in such a short time would have distraught anyone. Thankful for his fortune which so far helped, he decides to have a few hours of refreshing shut-eye in the safety of the four walls. Stretched on his back in the dark his breathing having returned to normal, slowly falling asleep reviewing the frantic hours he had just been through. He had his fill; for him it was enough.

Then a rumbling of motors drawing near awakens him. Did they tell him that this was safe house where they had taken him? Now he is fully awake. Soon a convoy of trucks enters the street. His stomach suddenly tense when through a slit in the shutter he sees German uniforms passing below his window. Despite the dim light of the blackout headlight he has no doubt as to what he was seeing. Thus he did not wait long before finding the enemy he was to battle. Will they stop and search the village, find him defenseless, and shoot him as a rat? So far his mission has been a series of distress. Again he escapes the danger, but his shirt is soaked with sweat and he remains alert until sunrise. Finally a friendly villager releases him from his trap. By trails through the fields he takes him in a wooded area where the maquis was entrenched. There he delivers him to a lookout who escorts him to his chief, a captain in uniform,　who was waiting for him. Strange for an undercover individual.This area must be quite secured. Finally our parachutist will be able to relax. The reception is friendly. They offer to help him reach his destination and find his contact which was our Léon whose only characteristic known to him is a small scar on his lip! No wonder that, after one week of searching, we were not able to locate him because he was stuck with this group. It is the habitual visit of a doctor which brings this situation to an end.

He cares for the resistant fighters in the vicinity of Entrain. He knows how to locate Léon because he is also our doctor. I believe that our comrade having parachuted so near our position could have joined us rapidly. I suspect that his host who knew us but whose group was not recognized as legitimate held this agent from London hoping to obtain his valuable cooperation.

As for me, I fear that after ten days of searching the mysterious disappearance of our paratrooper was final. To ensure the strict adherence of measures of security that I had ordered I proceed to the Maquis of Entrains. But what is this Gazo operated vehicle (the only one authorized) approaching our group? How did it pass the guard protecting our camp? He must have been known to the lookout. At the wheel I recognize a member of the nearby resistance group. Smiling he leaves his car and shaking my hand warmly he is visibly relieved to find me there. "Are you the one waiting for a team mate from the firmament?" How did he know that? "He parachuted near our position approximately forty kilometers away. Because he knew so little about his destination it took ten days to detect it. I am delivering him".

I don't believe what I am hearing, and when I see this tall blond fellow extricating himself from the rear seat of the car, I forget all my anxiety. He has the contented smile of a marathon runner reaching the finish line in good shape. Profusely I thank his escort who regretfully leaves him with us.

Sympathizing, our parachutist is immediately at ease. Very young (no doubt this is his first mission to France), his thin reddish mustache gives him a British look. He speaks our language well with a tone different from the local people. He tells me his tribulations and shares my relief to see the end of his odyssey. He tells me that he is an American. His build is tall and slender which seems to me to confirm that that he is "ricain" (slang for American). Subsequently I learned that stereotyping distorts the truth. At that moment as warmly as I could make our first contact I allow him a glimpse of the enthusiastic reception he will receive from the rest of the group. I take him to Léon, his prearranged "contact" who no doubt would assure him as I did that he had reached the end of his worries. But the subsequent hard blow that hit him was unexpected. Addressing Léon:

"Finally here is the one we were waiting for. He dropped far away. Friends picked him up and after a long search brought him to us. He is a "ricain" and for us his name is Julien."

In contrast to my own introduction and to my great confusion an aloof Léon eyed him suspiciously from head to foot, and without grace enjoined him to follow. Then started the prescribed procedure for positive identification. It must not be a simple formality. I am very surprised when his replies did not satisfy Léon. Despite his protestation and a sack of documents he had safeguarded by sheer force our parachutist had become a suspect. We must be certain of his identity, and he must remain out of sight.

Unfortunately only a pigsty freed of its tenants is available to hold him up. That is the price one pays when late, it is the rule of covert operations. Yet it is hell for our guest.

Welcome Julien

"It is unreal! For two days I've wallowed in this pig's droppings. All they have to do is ask London if I am really Julien Daniel."

The distressed captive blames everyone. This abnormal delay begins to torment him. "They will think I am a traitor and execute me." The cage where he is stuck stinks, and there is not enough space for his long legs. His mystified jailers treat him with reserve. The injustice and humiliation to which he was subjected is the most difficult for him to ignore. Thus when his identity is finally recognized, and Léon liberates him, he vigorously objects to the treatment imposed upon him. Julien feels the humiliation caused by this hazing was justified by the excessive suspicions of Léon.

In the evening I took charge of our new team mate. In secrecy I took him to the hayloft of "Patis'" barn to spend the night. Had his trust returned ? Was it the shot of "gnole" (alcohol) Jean Guillot had given him before leaving him to his dream land ? As it were, this young man, still deep in sleep, feels something sharp poking his throat. He awakens and is stunned when he sees a woman with menacing eyes ready to stab him with her pitchfork. "Who are you, and what are you doing here?" she says. His colt is gone and he must explain himself, in the embarrassment of the situation he does not know what to say.

" Well?" she said.

"Then this breakfast is for you." Laughing she reveals what turned out to be the best breakfast he had since leaving London. This is not the best way to greet a stranger who has just been subjected to such rude ordeals. This joke planned by Jean amuses his entire team who is itching with curiosity. Who is this fellow coming from the heavens? He comes to help us to chase the "Boches." But is he aware of the dangers, and the constraints imposed upon underground fighters? His cover name is Julien, but who hides behind it? Will we gain a friend, or be subjected to a conceited helper? Will he agree to be one of us? It will not be easy to be accepted by a group that had existed for such a long time. Will we like his behavior?

This outrageous awakening for us is the first test to pass judgment over him. Well, our young "Amerloque" recovers very quickly and finds the joke amusing. This is a worthy reaction, placing him on the side of the teasers and making his hosts well disposed toward him. The proof is that for them he has become Julien, period. Already he has moved one step closer to them.

These incidents have delayed the program of instruction. Our expert will have to get in gear. I do my best to get him in good shape. Léon's mistrust still causes a lump in his throat. His painful detention was humiliating. To erase his bitterness I fuss over him. Nothing better than a full stomach to raise the morale. I know this personally. Without hesitation I ask him for his culinary preferences. "I prefer a good steak and some milk". No problem we are at the Charolais cattle heaven.

I had known that on the other side of the Atlantic they are obsessed with the rigid problems of hygiene. Thus I assured him that his shirts would be washed regularly despite the shortage of soap. "Well" he said "you are still washing shirts? At home when it is dirty we throw it away and wear a new one." Here is a display of a well-to-do individual. Wanting to show off is typically American. Fortunately because of his unusual generosity he is forgiven. It took a while for me to realize that he was pulling my leg. His familiarity, energy, and optimism are welcome. Perhaps too much I believe. Doesn't he pretend that his training will enable him to frustrate the traps of a Gestapo interrogator? This audacity of a neophyte worries me. I must watch over him to prevent him from this type of experience; to us he is too precious. Thus I decide to keep him close to me, and place him under my protection. My vigilance will avoid unfortunate encounters, yet his mission will be full of unexpected events.

Viva Bacchus

The heat was unbearable late that morning when we reached the outskirts of Pouilly. Because of delays we have been pedaling hard for two hours. Julien's face had assumed the shade of raw steak. Sweat streamed down his temples, his short mustache can no longer hold the drops of perspiration it retains. I cannot judge my own condition, but internally I feel the same, very dry. Our only chance of survival suddenly appears. It is a small rustic bar next to a deserted cross road. Visited only by field workers, the Germans are probably not aware of its existence. The chance of meeting them here is nil.

We rushed in before I could warn my companion that here they do not serve milk, only white wine. At this stage of his condition he is ready to drink anything. At that point I would have drunk Coca-Cola! The first glass of cool Pouilly-Fumé went down without difficulty. Two more disappeared quickly, the others relaxed us completely. I admire how easily he adapts himself to circumstances. Regretfully we leave the cool penumbra of the bistro without having had the time to sit down. Revived we climbed on our saddles. A moment later Julien stops, he looks back stupefied at the steep hill we had just climbed. Scratching his head he mumbles: "How did I manage to climb that without realizing it?" Dogmatically I assured him: "It is because of the wine. As a stimulant it is far more effective than milk. The same occurs when one replaces Gazo with gasoline in a car." He does not object, but I am not certain that I have scored a point. However, I must have succeeded because from that time on he has never asked for milk with his steak.

He was closely watched, but he never knew that the story had spread throughout the unit, and his prestige has increased with his companions. For them to drink at the same bottle (a la fillette, as we say here) is as if one becomes a foster brother. This was an important step towards his integration.

This is not speaking French !

In one of the containers there was a device whose utilization was unknown to us. Julien tells us that it is a radio which allows communication with the pilot making delivery. Thus the pilot will know if he has reached the correct drop zone (there were cases of wild drops) and his drop will be more precise because he may be guided from the ground. Our instructor, loaded with knowledge, is anxious to demonstrate. He does not have to wait long.

Tonight is the night. Punctual, our Julien is on the job, his chest sandwiched between elements of the device, the earphone in place and the microphone in hand. In the penumbra the onlookers gather close to him. They don't want to miss a thing. Silent, and attentive, their eyes do not leave the wearer of this impressive paraphernalia. The waiting puts them on edge even more than before. "Will this plane show up?" As the fly attracts the fish, the "Eureka" beacon placed in the middle of the field will guide the navigator toward it. We have a strike, a distant drone of an aircraft seems to approach our position. Yes, it must be for us. Instantly as a star surrounded by his fans, Julien enters into action. Calm, powerful, he broadcasts his code signal: "This is carrot, this is carrot, over." This is really professional! No reply. He continues in the same tone of voice. Nothing yet. His correspondent is not very far, he should reply. Surprised, Julien realizes that the aircraft does not receive his signal. He speaks louder, a wasted effort, they hear him no better. The plane is almost upon us; we must act quickly. A final desperate attempt, he hollers, "This is carrot" until hoarse, but in vain. Furious, our comrade normally so courteous loses his cool and cries: "Ah shit! This jerk does not have his switch on to hear me," he protests. To whoever will listen he chastises.

The stupidity of the crew is responsible for the failure of Julien's demonstration. And he is more vexed by the fact that the drop was successful without his intervention.

Hi McCormick

The Crowning

This failure observed by all those he wanted to impress upsets him very much. Nevertheless, despite his views to the contrary, he did not loose face. Those who witnessed the incident remember only the spontaneous invective, a true cri-de-coeur directed at the incompetent pilot. That is real French! He is truly one of us, and they are touched threefold.

A few people can express to others the sympathy they inspire (the contrary seems easier). Either they say nothing or they express it with an awkward gesture. However in France we have our way: When someone earns our friendship or our admiration we cloak him with a nickname. Even if it lacks respect it is given as a pledge of consideration. Often it is a passport to our heart. A sense of decency must be attributed to this means of revealing its feeling a roundabout way.

As always after an operation this early in the morning, we end up in the cellar of Jean Guillot, our master of ceremonies on particularly solemn occasions. Facing Julien and raising high his glass "Tonight the toast is in honor of McCormick." (Well known American farming equipment manufacturer.) Far from joking it is a true christening, a consecration, a promotion in the order of friendship. Julien acquires his nickname naturally and forever. This mark of brotherly affection between him and his French comrades will affirm itself on many occasions. It is in suffering that we find real friends. Thus, during this dramatic episode, we are not too numerous to sustain the shock.

(This is incorrect. I did not participate at this ritual. I only found out about this nickname 44 years later when I was greeted at the Cosne Town Hall. This was done behind my back because Jean Guillot wanted to pull something on me. They called me by other names, but I did not know "McCormick.")

Adieu Marcel

It occurred this afternoon. Accompanied by my inseparable protégé we are checking the camouflage of the containers received the evening before. In the forest of Annay, green branches hide the containers well for a short period. Suddenly close-by there was a burst of submachine gun fire. Taken aback, looking at each other, we move in unison directly toward the firing. We only have our colts, no time to extract the carbines from the containers. By the time we arrive on the site the shooting has stopped. Now a strange silence reigns over the area.

Near the road a witness bends over a body which lies in the grass. He watched the entire incident: a German convoy, unexpected on this small road, encountered one of our patrols. Its leader facing the enemy opened fire to

Memorial to Sgt. Marcel Suppliciau
Killed Here for his country, August 17, 1944

cover the escape of his men. A direct hit to his heart killed him. He is Marcel Suppliciau who was one of the key men of our team. The first casualty among us.

An emotional wake secretly conducted in an abandoned hay barn was followed by a concealed burial in a provisory grave witnessed by a few dismayed friends. With us an overwhelmed McCormick bows before our fallen comrade and shares our grief. Jean Guillot had judged him well. He is one of us. With his nickname he seems to fit in even more.

No panic

Comforted by the feeling of solidarity our instructor, with an unruffled sense of humor, accepts all the uncertainty of his mission. This precious virtue is only accorded to beings overloaded with intelligence.

A rebel

We decide to cut the road where Marcel was killed. It runs too close to our hideout. The destruction of a small bridge would prevent its use. After a quick examination our specialist assures us that it will be a cinch. He did not come from London for nothing. The load of plastic in place, the detonators programmed, in the sleepy countryside we hear a huge boom!

Bravo, mission accomplished, and we can relax quietly the rest of the night.

Before daybreak I send a message by my dispatch rider. As soon as he leaves on his motorcycle I discover that he was to use the road that we had cut and he had not been warned. I curse myself, and the thought of him crashing in the open pit, he who drives so fast without light in the night, brings fear into my heart. But to my great comfort, I see him return unharmed. "How did you manage to pass through the crater on road?" He looked surprised. "What crater? I saw nothing."

Returning to the bridge, where it should have been a huge hole, not the smallest crack could be seen. However on either side of the bridge the force of the explosion had blown all the leaves of the trees to a distance of twenty meters. McCormick is amused by the unexpected results and graciously accepts his failure. I am pleased that my messenger is sound and safe. This type of bridge, vaulted and squat, is unknown in America. Our saboteur did not learn to destroy such a bridge. But it did not take long for him to find out the correct technique, and the second attempt resulted in a crowning success.

A good remedy

Another surprise gave him additional concern. Before an attentive group he praises Plastic, explaining the extraordinary possibilities of this explosive. To suit the action to the word he demonstrates that it is possible to knead it with the hands, and that a small amount may be lighted as solid alcohol to warm up his coffee. The men half convinced maintain a cautious distance. It happens that the manipulation of plastic provokes a severe headache. One of the group feels the effect. "You come here" Julien said encouraging him. "Look, you fellows. To get over a headache all you have to do is to chew on a bit of plastic the size of a small nut." Tense, the guinea pig dares not refuse this unusual treatment. As soon as he closed his mouth his jaws tensed. He began to drool, his entire body tensed in violent convulsions. Startled, the instructor is shocked and only the relative calm of the bystanders overshadows his anxiety. They are aware that the subject had one of his customary epileptic attacks. They should have warned him. McCormick will remember this for a long time.

The one that would not fall

A drop was expected at the field of Entrains. That night McCormick was supposed to join me on the prearranged field because according to his mission he must be involved in all of our activities. Perhaps he will come early enough to establish radio contact with the pilots. Prevented by an inspection I entrusted him to the mobile team a group of tough guys outfitted with a car. They are able to intervene rapidly where and whenever the condition demands it. They do bring him as planned. However, judging by the looks of their passenger, I see that something must have occurred on their way over. Duplessis, the driver wanted to show to the Amerloque what a "Traction" (front wheel drive) can do.

At full speed on the straight road they approach Entrains. Labeuth, the advance guard at the edge of the town, a daring Maquisard with his sub-machine gun at the ready, jumps out of his hiding place and believing that there were Germans, he aims his weapon. Surprised, the driver in full speed swerves to the shoulder. There stood a wooden pole deprived of telephone lines. The shock shears it at the base. But instead of falling, wedged by the front bumper, it remains straight as a candle until the vehicle and its stupefied passengers were back on the road. Tired of his immobility, the pole could not hope for a better adventure.

Our "ricain" was able to confirm that our "traction avant" is a road champ, and that the sentry was able to maintain his cool. This type of unusual incident will have a place in his memory as great as the glorious exploits of his career.

An agreeable parethesis

Thanks to the intervention of our American specialist, the anticipated drop was successfully conducted. The Duke of Montemart was part of the reception party. Despite the fact that a while back he had lost an arm in a hunting accident, he wanted to be involved in all our activities. As we were leaving the area to spend the night in some hay barn, he discretely offers us the hospitality of his castle. This is an imposition as the local "Boches" are watchful. What a great occasion to be sheltered with the descendants of the Marquise de Montespan who gave six illegitimate children to Louis XIV, flattering herself in public by claiming her nobility was superior to his!

We are so tired, especially McCormick who had enough excitement that evening, that we do not waste time admiring the elegance of the decor of our room. We were looking forward to a breakfast sheltered from the inquisitiveness of the other occupants. No such luck. Our host decided to display his unusual guests to his large family. We are placed at the honored seats of a long table where the Duchess and five or six children of various ages are waiting for us! An unanticipated situation for two secret agents. Instantly in this refined familial environment we feel transported into a new planet where sweet life is without danger. Thank you dear comrade for these hours of illusion.

Also we shall never forget the modest refuge provided one night by two young teachers. Only one narrow bed was available in their guest room where they hid us. There on that scanty couch so close to each other we were able to rest if not sleep. In their village where news travel fast, this gesture could cost their lives. They will be in our thoughts forever behind the cloud of a stupid traffic accident involving both.

Useful lessons

Thanks to contacts finally correctly established with the supplying planes, arms and ammunition arrive in adequate quantity. Because of security reasons it is impossible to train with live ammunition. McCormick intensifies the theoretical training and can flatter himself on the brilliant results. One day the Pompel squad is in position at the edge of the village of Entrains on the road to Bouy when an alert sentry, signaled the approach of an enemy convoy lead by a light armored vehicle. It is an opportunity for the one with a bazooka to show how good he was as a student. For a long time he had hoped for such an opportunity, yet stage fright hits him. He does not show it to his buddies who are watching him. All are aware that this weapon has never been used and that he has only one rocket with him. The result of the encounter will depend entirely on his accuracy. They hold their breath. By sheer luck the convoy stops a short distance from their position. Well aimed he hits the bull eye, the vehicle explodes. The frantic passengers run away, then surrender. The shooter must have had a good instructor!

The gasps of the end

The great day's run

At Cosne early this morning we hear explosions, The bridge over the Loire River is cut, and a portion of the barracks is destroyed. The Germans are getting ready to leave town. For a few days we noticed their preparations. I am told that protected by hostages to cover their flight they are withdrawing south toward Nevers. I am not eager to needlessly sacrifice my men to hurry them on. They seem willing to leave, as we had hoped they would, so be it.

As a result of their departure a good portion of our zone becomes a part of Free France. The Maquisards leave the discomfort of the underbrush. The resistance fighters proudly reveal themselves to their sheepish fellow citizens. I set up my command post in a large building. Although the new security frees him of my protection, I assign to McCormick a room close to mine. With satisfaction he exchanges his clandestine clothing for his uniform as an American Lieutenant. Imagine the girls! He is now a target. To succeed, the most skillful girls together have created a flag with the stars, a real feat. We fix it on the rear of our car. When seen it unleashes applause along the road for the benefit of our sympathetic ally. He better take advantage of this because his own people may not praise him so kindly.

Sour encounter

Returning to town we observed a helmeted giant standing next to a Jeep. He was an American captain. A crowd of enthusiastic curious people surrounds him. No doubt he comes to collect information on our sector. We arrive just in time to help. He smiles at the sight of a compatriot approaching him. I stay close to Julien, hoping to use him as interpreter. The giant at great length exposes his business to the attentive ears of my young colleague. When he is finished I asked: "What did he say?" Lightly he replies: "I did not understand. He must be Texan. He has a terrible accent." The colossus does not take him lightly. Upset by the indifference of his interlocutor he assumes the aspect of a predator before his prey. Extracting his colt 45, he grabs our poor Julien by his shirt accusing him of being an impostor and a German spy. Which is understood by the entire assembly. I can only add gestures of denial to the protestations of the accused who uselessly defends himself in an English the other does not appear to understand. How to get out of this dispute? As often happens, the unexpected shows up in time. It is the apparition of Léon. Who would have guessed? He, a Frenchman wearing the uniform of a British Army captain. With his approximate English he immediately gains the confidence of the Texan who recognizes his mistake but still looks at his compatriot with contempt and suspicion. It is not the first time that our hero, while famed by the Cosne population, is confronted by one of his own.

Another occasion occurs. German units abandoning their bases on the Atlantic may want to cross the Loire River at the bridge of St.Thibault in our sector. My own forces could not contain the push of their columns. I decided to mine one of the spans and to blow it if the enemy attempts a crossing. This is Julien's job; this type of bridge cannot resist his technique. In no time that morning the explosive charges are fixed to the girders of the deck. Under the vigilance of the watchful eyes of a group the bridge is ready to be blown if and when the enemy's advance party reaches it. That afternoon we check the installation carefully. Everything is O.K., the Boches will not pass here.

At that time a Jeep came to a screeching halt near us. An American captain is looking for the people responsible for the area. He came at the right place and at the right time. In an English now understood by my interpreter he explains to us that General Patton wants our bridge destroyed immediately. I point to him that that it is the last bridge from the mouth of the Loire, that we are fully capable to prevent the crossing, and that we are determined to maintain it intact except in case of ultimate danger. I refused to comply with the order of his chief. "In this case we shall destroy it with aerial bombing with the usual casualties to the neighborhood," the American captain said.

Faced with this cynicism and scorn for our reasoning, I choke with anger and indignation. Thus I am no master of my own house. I cannot express my feelings in his tongue. Then Julien, exceeding his role as interpreter, takes our side, cause, and interest and enters in a violent argument with his compatriot who retorts to becoming increasingly abrupt and overbearing. It appears that their confrontation will end with a pistol duel western style. I intervene and continue the discussion in another more casual tone. Wasted time, Patton's envoy came to give us an order, not to debate. To appease me, he assures me that, the danger passed, the U.S. Corps of Engineers will repair the damaged bridge. At that time I gambled and accepted this lie.

Immediately we ask the inhabitants of the surroundings to leave their windows open to prevent injuries from flying glass. Then with his heart full of misgivings, our master artificer, certain of the results, resolutely pushes the electric plunger. The power of the explosion proves that all the charges have exploded at the same time. One section of the bridge completely collapsed. It was a beautiful bridge, solid, recently constructed. It could not resist the plastic and the casual way of this operation. Although satisfied with his work, but having done this stupid thing against his better judgment, McCormick is upset. He, usually so levelheaded, lost his temper against one of his own to defend this small architectural work of our country. No doubt in him hides one of our brothers.

Reconstructed bridge at St. Satur.

For a long time we have dreamed

It is noon, about 15 of us are in the large dining room of the house where I have set up my command post. Credibly all are busy with their forks. It has been so for a few days since Louisette has restored the standard of our table. It goes without saying as she is from Burgundy. Up to now, Norac, her assistant, had been in charge of the management of the mess. His only reference was that, as a monk, he was responsible for the administration of the La Pierre Qui Vire monastery. From there, for the duration, he had been assigned by the Archabbot as a military chaplain to our Maquis. Wanting us to benefit from his past experience, he reduced the group to the disciplined regimen of his former community. It was most certainly an economical diet, proper to discourage the most fanatic candidate to monastic life. Moriset, our finance officer is the only one with a guilty conscience. However after Norac withstanding abuses we are ready for any sacrifices. Viva our Louisette! How was Marcel, our driver, a white-hair adventurer, able to get her? I notice that since she is in charge of the kitchen my team leaders more and more bring their report at feeding time. One cannot ignore the importance of the mess for the moral support of fighting men. In fact we needed that support as the situation eventually developed. Yes, the Germans have left, but if they return in force are we incapable of protecting the town? Unaware of this danger the population indulges in excessive abuses including the persecution of alleged Nazi collaborators. It takes very little proof to provoke terrible reprisals as often seen elsewhere. Even the traditional after dinner drinks cannot stimulate our optimism. We do not have the means to prevent this potential tragedy.

Drowsy by the digestive process, each probing for a proper solution, when the door suddenly bursts open as if under the push of a tornado. A small joyous individual, leaps into the room. Dressed in the uniform of British paratroopers he rushes into our arms and vigorously embraces each one. It seems that he had waited much longer than we for this memorable reunion. During all the years of clandestine struggle we had imagined such an encounter. Finally here comes a happy and friendly soul. One could easily imagine that these brothers-in-arms were old companions meeting again. This time Julien's English is so well understood by the newcomer that he endured several additional taps on the back. One would believe that the sole purpose of this Captain Davis and his excited "rough riders" was to join us. These exuberant congratulations contrasted with the arrogant attitude of the emissaries of Patton. McCormick feels it as we do.

But Davis' mission is not to reinforce us. He is only passing through on his way to cover the right flank of the Allied Army. Nonetheless he wants to be helpful. He and his men, as excitable as kids, made such a ruckus before the enemy's positions that so impressed the Germans that they decided, for a while, not to move towards us. Thank you Captain Davis, you are a true brother in arms.

A useful uniform

This did not last long. A few days later the "Chleus" (local name for German soldiers) risk a strong reconnaissance toward Cosne. A determined Ponsard and his flying squad push them back. This first true combat will be forever remembered. Some of our people, no doubt collaborators, told the enemy the disposition of our advanced posts comprising the firing line protecting the town. At night the Germans shower them with bursts of machine gunfire.

That same evening supper was not yet finished when an excited liaison officer rushes into the room. "The Boches are hitting us with artillery." Bauchet, an experienced officer confirms it. He believes that an enemy assault is imminent. Are we close to a possible catastrophe? Let us deal with this as if it will be. We must have reinforcement. Who will want to help us? The paratroopers of Bourgoin are at Briare (40 km), let us alert them. Meanwhile faced with a superior aggressor force I gave the order to withdraw by successive leaps.

Right then I leave to seek the help of the airborne unit. I fear a rejection because generally speaking their relation with the Maquis is not the warmest. For this reason I ask Julien to accompany me. Wearing his American officer uniform he may have a better chance of success negotiating the affair.

Dragged out of his bed at the Grand Cerf Hotel at 2300 hours the famous one-arm colonel decides to send us help immediately.

Three light armored vehicles loaded with ferocious warriors followed us on our return trip. Without slowing down they furiously charged the aggressors and unquestionably stopped them. Unfortunately their officer in charge returns to our position mortally wounded. Those who surrounded him will never forget that day. Despite the care of our doctor he passed away humming the Marseillaise. It is at that moment that in the chest of McCormick beats a heavy French heart.

The hunter becomes the prey

What a relief. The strong enemy columns threatened by Patton's army move south away from our sector. They search for a route across the massif of Morvan in this zone favoring the partisans who are ready to harass them. Evidence of reprisals follows their route. In isolated cases enemy soldiers take a chance and on their own try to return to their country. Often spotted by the local people they are captured and turned over to our patrols combing the countryside. Occasionally these prisoners provide us with useful information. Julien, trained for that purpose, transmits by radio to our London Headquarters every thing that appears useful. When retained by us as prisoners, they escape the savage retaliation of the people which occasionally was fatal.

An unexpected process

Julien and I were in my office sorting the results of our investigations when a furious woman knocked over the guard and hollering, rushed toward us! She finally agrees to sit down. Hoping to calm her I ask her to identify herself. " What's this! don't you know me?" she replied indignantly before our dubious stare. "I am Irene de Trébert" Why should an American newly landed know that before him stood a national star, our own Rita Hayworth? By a gallant reflex made in France, McCormick justified our blindness caused by the arrival of this unexpected dazzling apparition among us. Taken aback for a second, she continues her raging accusation. "Why have you arrested Raymond?" "Who?" For her there is only one: Raymond Legrand, our own well-known Glen Miller. She is his companion and she obviously bears his offspring. We find him in jail. The Milice of the Committee of Liberation is proud to have captured an incontestable collaborator. Before us Le Grand caustically defends himself. It is true he was in the limelight of occupied Paris. I love his music too much not to have faith in his patriotism. At my suggestion Julien, using the authority of his uniform, had him freed and does not refuse the kisses of the grateful Irene.

This incident attracts our attention to the people crammed into the prison cells. We inquire about the motives of their incarceration. This one had been trafficking with the Germans. These others had slept with them even though the doctor had declared them virgins! Gossips, accusations more or less justified, we obtain the release of a few bewildered by a salvation they did dare hope. None were accused of treason which seems to keep them off the danger list for a while. Here we are led to the role of administrator of premature prosecution. Prosecutor, judge, and attorney, none are our profession. We cannot become involved with things other than our military assignment which is our only function. Others believe that they are better qualified to settle the fate of their compatriots.

C'est la vie

We close shop

The overall situation has changed drastically. The Germans have left our area. Their fleeing units no longer represent a danger to the population. The regular French army fights their way eastward, but without our help which value they probably ignored. The volunteers who had joined the resistance to "do something to get the Boches out of chez nous" return to their homes and their usual activities. The professional soldiers among us who have returned to their respective service hope to continue their careers and retain the stripes they were so generously given. Clandestine activity no longer exists, but in the town a quantity of "alleged" resistants shamelessly display their assumed titles. Now one may be photographed, and the stores selling film are doing a booming business.

We drink to that

Every evening after supper, a "cheer for Louisette" was heard. Aware of her talents, without modesty she accepts it. Then, it is the circle of the late-to-bed gathering around a tray full of spirits, gifts of the grateful population. Hunters and bridge players are not the only ones who remember their exploits. We have our own tales such as the sabotage of the telephone cable with an enema syringe! And Marcel who found himself unharmed in a field when his car crashed into a tree. The funniest stories are told by Pierre the undertaker. As far as Norac is concerned he is the star. Former student at the medical school he has some spicy ones. Becoming an authentic Benedictine monk, he is on leave of absence from his monastic mortification. Near the end of his tour of duty, with the resistance group he commanded, he enjoys his last drinking days. Only his stomach can stock such copious reserves of white rum. What a bottomless pit! But very strict. He downs the ultimate last drop a second before midnight as he must fast for the six o-clock mass. Yet, what a leader, what a great relationship with his men! One of them an anticlerical militant giving him a goodbye embrace said to him: "Captain, it is time for us to part. Three more months I would become a priest and you a militant communist." Soon he will obediently bend with humility to the strict rules of his order. The least regular to these evening gatherings was our American. The prestige of his uniform and his mischievous mustache work havoc among his admirers who demand his attention. He must face them all.

If his winning charm is part of his mission every one agrees that his success will result in a prompt promotion. Who at Cosne had not met this young sympathetic allied officer so congenial? Each pretends to know him better than the next. "I know for sure that he is a Canadian." Fashionable parlors snatch him, he has girls to beguile. The end of hostilities is near. Why should he not settle here? In a short time he has become a familiar sight in the city; he is now part of the landscape. To justify the distinction, he was named honorary citizen of the town of Cosne, Applause !

It is not au revoir

The operation LICENSEE is over. The ill-assorted group gathered by the events will scatter. Each one going to his destiny with identical memories which will unite them forever. One of those we shall never see again is our friendly paratrooper. As member of a secret service none of his tribulations will be revealed. He is so deeply integrated within our group that we have trouble accepting his departure. A farewell banquet brought us together. Sad at heart we cannot accept the inevitable as we leave him without spurious expressions as if we would see him again tomorrow.

Strange is the passing through of this young man: He came to us as an American with a French name, and he leaves our group as a Frenchman with an American name.

In memorial

Thirty years later

We are not the three musketeers however. This Sunday, Paul Fougerat, and Jean Guillot are at my table. Friendship had brought us into the arms of the Resistance. With the help of our spouses the clandestine struggle had created a quasi-familial link among us. Since the end of the war we did meet regularly so that time has passed without undue notice. Thus it is surprising when we hear kids calling us "grandpa." Are they mean-spirited or pitiless?

It is true that today our faces do not reflect a juvenile happiness. This reunion is morose as some of us have lost our spouse. Our sorrow is too recent to invoke the circumstances. We have enough trouble controlling our sadness. Thus we try to think about something else:

"Secene fell off his roof, he is now paralyzed."

"The Grand Louis was buried last week, we must admit that cirrhosis did him in!"

"Henri and his truck fell in the canal. They found him in the cab drowned like a rat."

We are not the only ones with misfortune.

Our appetite satisfied, we switch to more constructive subjects such as our children. There is good news for some and difficulties for others, but hope for all. Then we are almost ready for an after dinner drink. Paul tells me:

"Say! Do you still have the service Julien gave you as a souvenir? It is said that he fell in Indochina."

"That is the information given by his embassy," and I add what he told me before leaving:

"If after the war you receive a box of chocolates without the name of the sender, it is because I came out of it alive. As an agent I may not reveal my true name. So far I have received nothing."

"Poor McCormick," said Jean,

" He was a good fellow, it was I who christened him with that name. Ah! He was not proud when Eugenie woke him up pretending to make a kebab out of him with her pitchfork. He is probably still laughing at the joke." "And the scolding he gave the pilot who could not hear him with his radio," said Paul roaring with laughter. Then it is my turn:

"Do you remember his face when he discovered that the charge which was to destroy the bridge only blew off all the tree leaves on either side of the road? So not to hurt his feelings all of us laughed up our sleeve. We liked him, he left us with some good souvenirs."

When it is time I bring the special issue of Historia where in the jungle of Indochina between Ho Chi Minh and Giap stands Julien, he who, when he was with us, wanted nothing to do with the communists!

He asked me to join him in this operation. I am glad to have refused. Never would I have shared his sad destiny."

Ah! If he could have been the fourth at our table! With Paul and Jean his memory brings back an instant of serenity.

Have you noticed that, after the disappearance of one dear to you, at first he cannot be remembered without the return of a feeling of grief? Moist eyes seem to look inside. More discreet is the trembling of the chin contracting the lower lip. Then later when he is seen again in good times you smile.

"He was really funny that day."

Time has allowed our neuron to refine the reasons which attenuate insupportable grief. An auto-defense against the negative refusal of destiny. That is why I wish so much to recount the strange or amusing anecdotes which recall our dear departed comrade. For this reason when we have invited guests his story is mentioned over and over. Since that time some must have heard it more than once

The good opportunity

Today for example I wait for the proper moment, the after dinner drink. After a hearty meal I respect the tradition and offer a stiff alcohol drink to which digestive virtues are attributed as a good excuse. To me it has the inverse effect, especially sweet liqueurs heavily perfumed. I must not be the only one, yet at each occasion, I never fail to respect this ritual. It incites the prolonging of the sitting position and of the conversation. Good manners require that it is followed by approving clicking of the tongue and the religious sniffing of the vapors drifting from the heady solution carefully warmed between the hands.

We all have a collection of these small jiggers for that purpose either inherited or obtained by an impulsive purchase. Because of a personal motive I use always the same set. It is heavy crystal indestructible as the memories related to it. Without imposition I announce: "You are drinking from glasses which I care for very much (subtle precaution). These were given to me by a war comrade who unfortunately was killed in Indochina." Attentively they listen and I continue. "For us his name was Julien, but this French name is only a war pseudonym. In fact he was a young American officer parachuted in our area to show us how to use the material we received at the maquis. They could have sent us an impatient instructor anxious to complete his mission to return to the comfort of his base in England. On the contrary Julien quickly became one of us sharing all the dangers and the constraints of the clandestine struggle taking at heart his function with us. He made us forget that he was a stranger. His competence and conviviality, his relaxed manner when meeting difficulties, have created around him a confident and fraternal atmosphere."

All goes away

Now forty years have passed since McCormick had left on the short road to his destiny. Paul and Jean, my two accomplices, have also departed. No doubt they were hoping that I would take care of their funeral orations. I have lost my taste for the evocation of this period when we lived together. I have closed the curtain on this period which seems so far away this day. No old friends left to talk. To maintain these precious memories they must be locked behind the fence of the past. Happily life has other plans.

It's impossible!

An information accessory

It began with a letter to bring me back to reality. Guy Bauchet of Cosne, a retired colonel, asked to meet me. What a jolt! What the devil does he want? Already retired, he was only ten years old at the liberation. I, who do not admit to being older, how will I stand with him? At times we are driven out of our league. However this depressing situation was about to be compensated by an incredible surprise. It occurred at the end of my visit with the colonel after we had covered many unimportant subjects between us. I almost left before he mentioned the actual reason for our meeting. Then to satisfy my curiosity he casually said:

"No doubt you must have known an American officer who worked with the maquis in the area. He passed through here a while ago."

"I only know of one who was parachuted to our maquis. He was killed in Indochina. Perhaps it was one of Patton's army who made a short visit soon after the liberation of Cosne."

I concluded that it must have been one of these customary U.S. veterans making a tour

"He seemed to know the area quite well and he was looking for comrades of those days. He failed to find any but he left his address at the Town Hall hoping that he would renew his contacts."

At that point I hear the most bewildering information which shook me up.

"He said that his name was Daniel."

"It's impossible! Julien is still alive?"

On the trail

Is it really he? Miss Marty, the secretary at the Town Hall is positive. "There is no mistake, he looks exactly like the picture that we had of him."

My doubt returns. Julien never wanted his picture taken. And on a document related to the liberation she points to a photo. Surrounded by a crowd of people I recognize the giant, the tall Texan who gave Julien such a hard time. What a short-lived happiness! It is the confusion I feared, this Daniel could not be our McCormick. I ventured:

"Did he leave his name and address?"

She is very efficient. From the same file she extracted what she should have shown me earlier. Yes, I am not dreaming. It is written: René Défourneaux at Indianapolis. But for the first name (he used so many) Historia stated that it was his name. Miss Marty had not looked carefully enough at her visitor who because of his short visit was not able to locate the people he knew. Why did our friend Bon, who had the records of all the local

Maquis, not put him on my track? Now I can follow his trail. With a light heart I immediately start the search. My air mail letter is entrusted to the nearest Post Office. In it I tell him how happy I am to know that he is still alive. Soon I shall hear from him!

The mail carrier places letters in my mail box. I rush. It is too early to have a reply from Indianapolis, but we never know. I am on pins and needles. Perhaps tomorrow. Yes, but it is my own letter which is returned! Julien has moved a while ago and his correspondence no longer reaches him. What to do?

Certainly he must have a telephone. Only the central Post Office has all the telephone books of the United States. I check with them. No René Défourneaux, only a Gisèle Défourneaux. She must be family and with such a first name she must speak French. But no! She does not understand my stuttering, and no doubt taking me for a nuisance, she hung up on me.

I cannot leave Paris and abandon my search. Could he still be under cover? It doesn't seem possible that the American Embassy cannot locate Major Défourneaux. At the Embassy, as soon as I enter the door protected by a marine is full dress uniform, two charming secretaries greet me. However it is with a ravishing smile that the one who hears my inquiry refuses without appeal to reveal the location of a compatriot, especially an officer. I insist. "I must locate this war comrade who expects me." Then she proposes a solution. Write three letters that we shall give the various military organizations. Perhaps one will recognize him as one of their members and will pass on your letter. "Unfortunately I do not write English." With good graces she translates my message. All I have to do is sign it. How thoughtful! Without listening to my thanks she left wishing me prompt success in my enterprise.

Positively, the quarry I am tracking is not easily located. This time, as a castaway waiting for his salvation from a bottle thrown into the ocean, I stiffen my patience. I did all I could and with a clear conscience I leave this task to others. Two weeks, three weeks pass, nothing. In their offices as in our country nothing moves very fast.

This morning as I was to accept my daily disappointment my dear Jacqueline triumphantly cries: "It came." Happy to contribute to my joy her arm raised high she hold the envelope she had extracted from our mail box. As usual I check the origin and the sender's name. Then feverishly, but delicately, I open the envelope. No doubt it is the picture of our McCormick! The small mustache, the same smile, he hasn't changed, and next to him his pleasing Ginny seems to send us a friendly smile. We shall see them soon; they are coming to France in a few weeks. Time enough to organize a memorable reunion.

As a sleight of hand

I am ready to experience an extraordinary event. To find without his mask Lieutenant Julien resuscitated as René, Major of the C.I.A.! The ring of the telephone make me jump out of my chair where I attempt to fool my impatience. As planned he calls.

"Hello, is it you old boy? Pick us up, I am parked in front of the Saint-Cloud station. Don't make us wait too long."

With his word carefully spoken the particular quality of tone of his voice intrigued me in the past. No wonder, he a native of the Jura, almost a Swiss. I had promised to be calm. But all of a sudden I find myself plunged into the unreal. I have trouble measuring my gestures.

" Do as if you were going to do something ordinary." Repeats my own wisdom, but in vain. I cannot forget that I must be facing an exceptional emotional moment. My look has changed so much he will not recognize me. I must draw his attention:

"You will see a guy with a rose in his hand. That's me."

It is also a French way to greet Ginny with a first gallant gesture.

Perhaps not too reassured, but as impatient as I am, they are sitting quietly in their vehicle no doubt wondering if I will find them. I recognize Julien immediately. His embarrassed smile is of one who has played a dirty trick on someone and who is not certain to be forgiven. "See, I disappear forever_ Peek-a-boo here I am again." He has fooled us with his magical trick. I have the impression that he only left us yesterday. The accolade is no less memorable. We break it up with laughter. We shall prolong it in a more appropriate location. With a rose and a kiss for Ginny with my dear Jacqueline we greet them as members of our family.

Then we feel the need to set foot on the ground where we first met. Alerted, the Mayor of Cosne organizes a reception for this prestigious visitor who by the way is an honorary citizen of the city. Red-faced, forty former members of the Maquis surround him emotionally. They do not see a resuscitated body every day! A solemn moment: Major Défourneaux receives the medal of the city, one more tie to the crowd waiting for him.

In the family

From this apotheosis we multiply the occasions of alternate visits one to the other. To these we include long sightseeing circuits each hoping to amaze the other with the wealth of his own country. Superlatives often are necessary to ensure its prestige. Evidently it is something other than trite, even warm, reunion of good war comrades. Why, after residing poles apart for a half century, this simple return has revealed in us this profound and unpredictable tie? Yet, in the past, hazard had brought us together for a very short period. The harmony of our relations is sealed by the active complicity of our spouses.

Each one fills the second phase of our life. Both of us seem to have found in the other a brother he has never had. How was this profound affinity born? An affection which ties old traveling companions more than a solid friendship. We cultivate the same moral values, the same political analysis. We regularly share the joys and worries of our family life; our health and our children provide abundant material.

When we ride together on the road, he next to me, watchful for our planned itinerary, I forget these fifty years of interval. I find myself at the time when we roamed the countryside, infested with Germans, trying to protect him. Since Julien's reappearance I again take pleasure at recalling these eventful adventures. This renewed interest for me is a fountain of youth and optimism. His example is a solid help. Unconsciously, as he does, I profit from the leniency of the years.

Towards a mea culpa?

I fear that for a moment his conscience will crumble under the weight of repentance. After all, after giving me a liqueur service he played dead for almost half a century. He thought that I would have a good excuse to multiply the occasions to render homage to his memory. I could have, as exemplified by the Sioux of his country, developed a taste for firewater. To reassure him, I do not lean toward alcoholism.

Of course if he had offered me Coca-Cola, I would have greater merit in searching for adequate circumstances to recall his sad destiny.

I imagine the obese condition I would find myself if he had decided on a sweet box, I who cannot resist chocolate!

"No false modesty, McCormick, you do not have to smile when you learn how many time we have "raised the elbow" in mentioning your name. I even sympathize with you for the privations this unfortunate scenario imposed upon you. How many years have you dreamed of these toasts with Pouilly-Fumé? This divine beverage, which once upon a time after hours of pedaling, had comforted and plunged us in a restored beatitude. Today we raise very high our glasses, happy to be able to salute your resurrection.

Follow up ideas

Since this story is not a fable, it is useless to try to discover in it a moral lesson. But how precious the lessons that may be learned from it! Only foolish people scorn the lessons of experience. René has quickly proved that he wasn't. So efficient was the liqueur serving set for him to be remembered by his friends that he could not ignore its value. How to prolong this convivial practice? Would he allow the virtues of his gift to disappearance with me? Will the new generation forget the peregrinations of McCormick? As always, René found a logical and simple solution: "I observed," he told me "that you are extremely fond of your granddaughter Marie-Ambre. To make sure that your wishes are respected, and in anticipation of your demise let her have the liqueur serving set now." How can I refuse? How appeasing the thought one's memory will survive in one's heirs! "Be reassured dear René. Your fragile small glasses will be handled as a precious relic, and the rite of the "Pousse-café" is not about to die with us."

———————————————————————————————Đ

It was early the next morning when we returned to our hotel. The following day we kissed our new friends goodbye and headed for my home town of Delle and all the cousins waiting for us.

By way of Lakenheath RAF air base we returned to the United States aboard a Galaxy, but not to the base from which we had left. Instead we landed at the Charleston International Airport, quite a distance from our parked car.

Before the end of the year I received a large envelope from Vic. It was a copy of the report Léon had provided to the FFI on or about the 7 October, 1944.

Léon's Report

Translation of Léon's report to the French Military Command

FRENCH FORCES OF THE INTERIOR (FFI)
MILITARY COMMAND OF THE NIEVRE
9thBATTALION, COSNE

GENERAL REPORT
OF THE OPERATIONS CONDUCTED BY THE FFI IN THE
SECTOR of COSNE-sur-LOIRE

I.- PRIOR TO D-DAY.

Period of assembly of the various resistance elements under the unified F.F.I. Command, and of organization of a progressive mobilization of FFI units for the purpose of a future general action.

Creation of two Maquis (Donzy and Entrains) by resistance fighters known and sought by the Gestapo. These Maquis are to be the rallying points for D-day. Their mission is to stock food, material and weapons. So as to not reveal their presence and their location, their operations against the enemy will be limited to accidental encounter, small raids to obtain arms, and sabotage of railways.

GRANDJEAN MAQUIS January 1944
Leaders: PETTI, Jean, and BELLOT, André.
At CIEZ: Skirmish, one German dead, Resistance: no casualty.
Max DESSONS chased a German Military Police vehicle: 2 Dead, Interpreter: wounded, Resistance: no casualty.
Maquis chiefs Jean PETTI and Geo arrested.
Leader: VILNAT.

May 15, 1944: At CORVEL L'ORGUEILLEUX an attack of a vehicle of the Special Police: 3 dead, Resistance: No casualty R. Brisset.

June 8, 1944: At PRESSURE one Lt. Colonel and three Germans killed. Resistance: One killed, one wounded. R. Brisset

June 8, 1944: At VARSY. Two German motorcyclists killed. Resistance: No casualty. R. Brisset

June 26, 1944: Annihilation of the Maquis of CHAPPE. Nine Germans presumably dead. Resistance: 2 executed, 4 KIA. German attacked the GRAND BOIS: 9 KIA including VILNAT the leader.

II.- AFTER THE LANDING OF THE ALLIES

A) Before the reception of arms (June 6th to 24th July 1944).

Goal: Cut off Cosne from all rail and telephonic communications. Operations conducted by local sabotage teams.

RAILROAD LINES:
Cosne-Paris Line:

June 8, 1944: Derailment at La Celle-sur-Loire, 3 days interruption.

June 30, 1944: Destruction of the Pelus bridge at Neuvy-sur-Loire. 8 days interruption.

June 10 1944: Lines of communication between Cosne & Pouilly severed at Pouilly.

June 27, 1944: Lines of communication between Cosne and Clamecy interrupted for 10 days by the destruction of the bridge at St. Laurent.

TELEPHONE LINES:
Between Cosne and Pouilly:
22 June 1944: The cutting of the overhead lines   interrupted communication for 12 days. The cutting of underground lines interrupted communication for 5 days.

Between Cosne and Neuvy:
27 June 1944: The cutting of the underground lines interrupted communication 5 days.

5 July 1944: The cutting of the same lines resulted in 8 days of interruption.

Between Cosne and Nevers via Clamecy:
22 June 1944: The cutting of overhead lines at Varsy resulted in a 12 day interruption.

27 June 1944: The cutting of the overhead lines at Saint Laurent caused a 5 day interruption.

3 July 1944: The cutting of the overhead lines at Donzy caused a 5 day interruption.

Note: The lack of arms and the enemy protective defense oblige the spacing of perilous sabotage operations.
The reception of arms conducted for the most part at close proximity to the enemy without incident. See annex Parachute Drops.

The creation of two maquis (Arquian and Entrains) in support of the local sabotage teams. Because of the open and flat terrain no more than 400 men were voluntarily involved in action in the sector.

COMMAND PLANS

- Isolation of Cosne

- Channeling the retreating enemy toward the east toward
    possible ambushes.
        Northern portion, towards the Bonny-Auxerre road
        Southern portion, towards the Nevers-Dijon road and
        Charité-Clamecy road.

Toward this goal the following operations were conducted:
Note among the ambushes and daily patrols.

- Railroad isolation of Cosne
    Sabotage of the railroad lines.
    Cosne-Clamecy: Derailing at Perrey, 5 days interruption.
        at Donzy complete interruption.

    Cosne-Nevers: 10 August 1944, destruction of the railroad
        bridge at Bois-Gibault, resulting in a 3-days interruption.

A simultaneous operation conducted at La Charité allowed the
capture of a train containing 327 cattle destined to the enemy.

On the 17 August 1944, a cutting of the rail at Tracy delayed
the withdrawal of German railroad men from Cosne toward
Nevers allowing the attack of the convoy a few kilometers
farther.

- Channeling of the enemy convoys and ambushes.
    Sabotage for the interdiction of the roads.

18 August 1944: Destruction of the bridge on the La
    Celle-Annay road.

18 August 1944: From that date on interdiction of the Bridge at
    St. Thibault, then destruction of the bridge 1 September 1944.

- Battalion strength operations-Ambushes and Patrols

    14 August: St. Amand-Myennes. Enemy losses: I KIA. 3
    Wounded. 1 vehicle damaged. Friendly losses: None

16 August: St. Amand-Myennes. Enemy loses: 3KIA, 8 Serious
    wounded

17 August: Road of La Celle-Annay. Enemy loses
undetermined, friendly losses: 1 KIA.

22 August: Road of Clamecy: Enemy losses 1 KIA, 4 prisoners,
    Friendly losses: None

23 August: At Crat de la Pourron Route No 7 St. Thibault.
    Enemy loses: None, Friendly Losses: None

24 August: Road of Bouhy: Enemy losses: 2 KIA, 7 Prisoners, 7
    vehicles out of action. Friendly losses: None.

27 August: At Entrains: Enemy losses: 7 prisoners, Friendly losses: None.

3 September: Porte de Charenton: Enemy losses; 2 KIA Friendly Losses: None.

4 September: Porte de Charenton: Enemy losses: I Renault truck, Friendly losses: I wounded.

4 September: At Charenton: Enemy losses: I probable KIA, Friendly losses: None

4 September: Night attack at Charenton-Pouilly: Enemy losses: Ignored FFI losses:1 Wounded.

4 September: Ambush at Pouilly: Enemy losses: 2 KIA, FFI losses: None.

5 September: At Pouilly. Artillery bombing of the FFI positions, losses: None

21 September: Ambush at the Bannay bridge: Enemy loses: 3 KIA, FFI loses: 1 Wounded.

20 September to 5 October: Cleanup operation: 12 Enemy prisoners. Creation and utilization of an military information gathering service over a 50 km radius with daily missions used by the allied armies from the 24th of August to the 25th of September 1944.

S/Captain Dupré Alias Léon of W.O.

SUMMARY Of THE ACTIVITIES OF THE "LICENSEE" (LÉON) NETWORK IN THE COSNE (NIEVRE) REGION

ARRIVAL OF CAPTAIN LÉON:

Parachuted in the vicinity of Léré (Cher) early July 1944.

RECEPTION OF WEAPONS:

Following the request of Léon and with the aid of Captain DUBOIS (Calvat) chief of the maquis responsible for the protection of the region of Cosne the net received 12 parachute drops on the drop zones of "Rouget" at Entrains, "Anguille" at Annay, and "Barbillon" at Arquian. Despite the close proximity of the enemy these operations were conducted from the 20th of July to the 5th of September 1944 without incident.

ORGANIZATION OF THE NETWORK:

From the first weapon drop the net was composed of two (2) maquis at Arquian and Entrain each composed of 250 men, and five local sabotage teams each composed of 10 men.

OPERATIONS CONDUCTED BY THE NETWORK:

SABOTAGE:

From the 25th of July repeated sabotage operations effectively caused the permanent isolation of Cosne a regional hub of all telephonic railroad communication. Specifically the destruction of the underground telephonic cable Paris-Marseille and at Tracy the capture of an enemy train with 320 head of cattle.

COMBAT OPERATIONS:

From the 5th of August the goal of the network was the protection of the right flank of Patton's army and to channel the retreating enemy columns coming from the southwest toward the Morvan by:

The occupation and interdiction of the bridge of St. Thibault on the Loire River, the only remaining bridge above Nevers, and on the 1st of September, faced with a sizable enemy force, the mining and destruction of the bridge. The unit lost 2 officers and three men in the defense of the bridge.

Attacking the retreating enemy columns with many ambushes, specifically the spraying of several convoys of enemy vehicles with automatic fire resulting in an undermined number of casualties, then on the 24th of August the complete destruction of an enemy convoy including an armored vehicle and the capture of 20 prisoners. Losses to the unit included: One NCO and a vehicle.

Preventing enemy columns from crossing the Loire River at Nevers and moving north by creating a plug at Pouilly. From the 1st to the 4th of September an enemy column of about 3000 men, supported by artillery and mortar fire, conducted day and night attacks against units of the net composed of 600 men spread over a 5 km front. Because of the incomparable guts of the men and the clever maneuver of the command, the enemy exaggerating the importance of the force facing them, decided to take to road toward the Morvan where terrain permitted other maquis to attack them.

In these operations the enemy lost 30 KIA and 3 vehicles destroyed. The maquis had 3 KIA, 5 wounded, and two vehicles destroyed.

Clean up operations in the area: Up to October 1, 1944 (end of the mission of the net) the enemy suffered 7 KIA and among small enemy groups escaping or in sabotage mission 11 were taken prisoners.

Intelligence activities: In addition to information related to the general situation in the area transmitted daily to London, between August 24th, and September 25th 1944 a special team reported on an hourly basis enemy troop movement within a radius of 50 km around Cosne. Counterintelligence activities allowed the discovery and the arrest of several Gestapo agents preventing several operations by the local enemy forces.

Note: The net was reinforced on the August 10 (*) with the arrival of Lt. Julien who had been requested by Léon.

* Not correct, it took me eight days to locate Léon and Dubois.

The report was a typical military report, vague without any details as to what individual members of the group did. The facts that I was missing for a while, and that Léon had doubts concerning my identity were completely ignored.

The fact that telephone cables were cut, rail lines sabotaged, and bridges blown was indicated, but how and by whom and some very interesting actions were not described. None of Kiki's stories I had heard during our visit at Cosne were mentioned.

Buckmaster

In June 1989 L'Amicale Buckmaster (Buckmaster Society) of Paris sent an invitation to all WWII French members of SOE, F-section, to their annual reunion to be held early December at The Cercle Interallié at Paris.

Vic Calvat, the regional commander of SOE operation in the north of the Nièvre Department, suggested to Jean-Bernard Badaire, the president of the Federation Nationale Libre Resistance (Amicale des Réseaux Buckmaster), that an invitation be sent to me because, as a former SOE agent, I was part of his operation. As a result I did receive a formal invitation.

My decision to attend this function was primarily because the keynote speaker was Colonel Maurice Buckmaster, the wartime head of SOE, F-Section, the one who finalized my transfer from OSS to SOE. On November 30, 1989, a TransWorld Airline 1011 took me to my destination. At the Charles de Gaulle airport at Roissi near Paris Vic Calvat and his wife Jacqueline greeted me.

I was told that it was to be a formal affair, black tie etc. As a retired U.S. Army officer a dress blue uniform was for me a formal attire. We waited a few days at La Celle Saint Cloud at the home of Vic Calvat before the evening of the meeting. When we entered the Cercle Interallié it appeared that I was the only one wearing a uniform, until another individual arrived wearing a Norwegian military dress uniform.

I was fortunate to be sitting next to Odile Boulot de Vomécourt the widow of the late Baron Philippe de Vomécourt, a hero of the French resistance. She was the guest of Badaire who had been the second in command of the Antoine group. The group was led by her husband the Baron, who helped Virginia Hall in the Cher region prior to my joining Léon and Captain Dubois.

A few years prior to the reunion I had been contacted by Lt. Colonel Pierre Fayol a retired French officer who, as a French resistance leader, had been associated with Virginia Hall. Doing research prior to writing a book about her, he was contacting all those who knew her. Through VOSS, he contacted me which resulted in a correspondence between us, even though we had never met. We were both very pleased when we finally came face-to-face at the reunion.

Colonel Fayol's first book entitled *Le Chambon-sur-Lignon sous l'Occupation* (Le Chambon-sur-Lignon under the Occupation) was eventually published in 1990. He was kind enough to send me a signed complimentary copy. His book is about French villagers who at great risks hid Jewish children from the uninvited Gestapo and the dreaded Vichy police. It includes the activities of the French Resistance in the upper Loire region

Lt. Colonel Pierre Fayol, author and Vic Calvat.

of France, and a great deal about Virginia Hall's war activities, but very little about her subsequent assignments with CIA. The book also covers the activities of some SOE/OSS operations including observations on the agents some of whom I knew well. When I inquired about my friend Michel Block he told me that Michel was his cousin, and that he had not returned to the United States, but had remained in France changing his name to "Bloit."

As usual with French reunions the food served was excellent, the wines superb, and the service princely. SOE was represented by active and retired British intelligence personnel, and the first speeches were in English for the benefit of the guests who did not speak French, that is until Colonel Buckmaster took the podium. In perfect French he spoke for approximately twenty minutes. His statesmanlike speech at first startled his audience, and inspired, everyone stood up to cheer him.

He looked much older and not as trim as when I met him in 1944 but he was just as mentally sharp. I had a few words with him and his daughter not realizing that I would not have another opportunity as he passed away a few months later.

It was also the first and last time I spoke to Colonel Fayol. Subsequently I returned to France on business and tried to see him, but he was too ill to see anyone.

Vic Calvat, who resided close to the Colonel, upon learning that his book was about Diane (Virginia Hall), went to him to purchase a copy. At that time Fayol was very weak and spoke hesitantly. Calvat recalls the following:

"He told me once that he did not get along with Virginia. Why did he write her biography? At the liberation he was backed up by the cocos

61

Col. Maurice Buckmaster with his daughter and unknown.

(communists) in actions conducted against him. Why? This explains a certain embarrassment, a certain distance he cannot dominate entirely vis-à-vis our net. Perhaps that is only our impression."

The fact that Fayol did not get along with Virginia was surprising not only to Vic, but also to me. Up to that time I believed that Fayol was a close friend of Virginia Hall. Of course if Fayol had been supported by the communists, and if he knew what they did to Vic it is understandable why he was reluctant to speak. This war created some strange relationships. Until I read Marcel Ruby's book *F SECTION, SOE*, I was not aware of the problems existing among the British, the French and the Americans in the direction and control of the French covert operations. Ruby writes:

SOE's problems were compounded by other affairs related to the progress of the war. The BCRA, commanded and comprising only French nationals, always took offense at British agents' activities on French soil. Politics, too, often cast its shadow on SOE's relations with other organizations. At the beginning Churchill has categorically stated that "de Gaulle and his handful of followers could not claim to be an effective alternative French government," and he continued relations with the Vichy government right up until May 1943. Roosevelt, for his part, never acknowledged de Gaulle as the true leader of France.

Before his death in 1994, Col. Fayol wrote another book entitled *Les Deux France (The Two Frances)*. It is about the German and French strategy concerning the Jewish population following France's capitulation. As per his father's wishes, after the funerals his son Serge sent me a copy of his last book. After reading it I realized that even though I was born a Frenchman I never really knew France. I was raised in a predominantly Catholic community with a few Jewish families. If there were problems or persecution of our Jewish neighbors I never saw them. I was often invited to Jewish homes and their children were welcome in ours.

When in 1939 my family settled in New Jersey, in a predominantly Catholic community, I was shocked by the attitude of some of my friends who referred to Jewish people as "kikes" or in other more descriptive terms. Up to that time anti-Semitism was unknown to me.

When after the war I learned that only one of my Jewish friends in France had survived and that all the others had been exterminated in Nazi concentration camps, I was sad. Subsequently, when I discovered that it was the French police who did the Nazis' dirty works, and had collected my Jewish friends and neighbors to send them to Germany I was really upset. I did not return to France for forty years.

Could anyone have prevented this collaboration? I know of only one. He was not a Frenchman; he was a Swiss national who resided in France, on a small farm close to the Swiss border. When the Jewish mayor of Belfort came to him with the French police and the Gestapo hot on his tail, the farmer dressed him as a field hand and handed him a rake. When the search party reached them working in the field, they did not recognize the mayor. Later on the mayor slipped across the border and escaped to Switzerland. That farmer who risked his life and that of his family to save one man was my uncle Lucien, the brother of my mother. He, his brother Achille, his wife Marcelle and their three children all were part of an escape and evasion network. Lucienne, the youngest of the three, in reply to my questions concerning her war activity wrote the following:

"What shall I say about the American and British airmen passing through our farm? I have general recollection, but many of the details have escaped my memory. Only the great fear is still distressing to me. All of us had responsibilities. We the children, my parents, Achille (my uncle), were constantly on the lookout for the Germans. We also help hiding net leaders, resistance fighters, a variety of weapons and the passing of secret messages. All these represented a very dangerous activity. What saved us was our discretion. Even our close relatives were not aware of our activities or of those who directed us.

We knew the smallest detail of the farm area. The most insignificant change was suspected, and surveillance increased. Each crossing was carefully planned so that it was without the slightest risk to the escapee. Day and night we were on the quivive. I will never forget the truckload of German soldiers searching our house. We were terrorized wondering who was next to be taken away.

Do you realize that at my age I cannot see films about the resistance! Talking about the past brings back unpleasant souvenirs. We shall talk about it at your next visit."

Every member of her family received an individual citation from General Eisenhower, the Supreme Commander of the Allied Forces. Subsequently, on several occasions, I asked her about her war experiences, but she always said "tomorrow."

Fifth Trip To Europe

In May 1990 we decided again to try our luck on space-A travel. We drove to Scott Air Force Base, stayed there overnight, and traveled by bus to Lambert Field at St. Louis for a flight to Frankfort, Germany. On the 19th of May, we landed in Rhein Maine Air Force base near Frankfort. There we waited a couple of days for a flight to Italy were we were to meet our friends Vic and Jacqueline at Genoa.

There was no flight to Italy on Sunday so we had to wait until the following day to sign in and get on the manifest. We reported at 5 am at the terminal and at 7:30 am with three other retired military couples we boarded a C-9 Nightingale Med-Evac aircraft hopefully bound for Italy to pick up military patients and delivering others to their stations. Our first stop was to be Verona then on to Pisa.

Aboard with the retired couples were a general's aide and her driver. At Verona there was a delay due to a change of orders. "We might not go to Pisa" said the nurse in charge, " but to Heidelberg instead." While waiting on the tarmac for a decision by the upper echelon, we began talking about our past experiences in the military, exchanging war stories. One of the experienced space-A travelers, Marie-Jane and Harold Oberg after hearing my story as an OSS agent who parachuted into occupied France during the war, said that they knew a pilot who had flown a black B-24, dropping agents and supplies behind the German lines to help the resistance. Harold also said that the activities of the Air Force groups conducting these operations had been recently declassified and that the veterans of these two groups had formed an organization called The Carpetbaggers! This was news to me, very good news indeed. Finally, after all these years, I may be able to find the crew who dropped me in the wrong place.

Two hours later, the nurse in charge of the Med-Evac came back to the plane and announced that we were going to Pisa, which was a relief for all of us. I am sure that the general's aide who was arranging an R & R trip for him at Camp Darby had much to do with the decision. So on to the Leaning Tower of Pisa! After a day touring the area, we took the train to Genoa where we met our friends and together we went to their residence at Vence for a great vacation on the French Riviera.

A couple of weeks later we drove back to Frankfort, dropped our rental car at Rhein Main, then failing to get on a space-A flight we returned to the States on a commercial flight.

Space-A Party at Salinas

We were home a couple of months when we received a strange invitation from the Obergs. It was customary for them, once a year, to have a party to which they invited those they met in their space-A travels. We had made their list and were invited to attend their annual get-together at their home at Salinas, California. Their invitation stated that members of the Carpetbaggers would also be attending. This piqued my interest because after learning of the existence of this organization I felt certain that I would be able identify the crew who had dropped me in the wrong place and hopefully locate its members.

On the 4th of February, 1991, we drove to Scott Field, Illinois, hopped a bus to Lambert Field and had no trouble getting aboard a Federal Express 747 chartered by the Department of Defense to fly military personnel to overseas destinations. They deposited us at Los Angeles International airport where we spent the night at a motel. The next morning we rented a car and went directly toward San Diego and stayed at the Pendleton Marine base. After spending some time with our niece Debby, following the scenic highway 101 we drove to Monterey, stopped at Fort Ord to check in their Guest House, then the following day we proceeded to Salinas where we found the Obergs with their house full of guests.

Harold had prepared a great Italian spread fit for space-A habitués. The guests were all retirees from the military services. I had brought a Video tape of our European trip when we had met the Obergs. At one point Harold described our trip to Pisa and when he learned that during WWII I had been a passenger aboard a black B-24, and that I had been dropped behind the German lines, unfortunately in the wrong place. He had invited us to the space-A party because among the guests were Wm. and Mary Bartholomew (Bart) and Henry Gilpin a former B-24 pilot. Both had been on several missions behind the German lines during WWII.

Bart was a navigator, but after discussing our involvement we decided that he was not the one responsible for the error. I did not recognized Gilpin as the pilot who flew me to my destination even though he displayed a small metal flask identical to the one I had received from my escort officer before boarding and which I gave the dispatcher who directed it to the cockpit. He teased me for a while telling us that a "Joe" had given it to him. After he claimed that he did not return to the United States on the Queen Mary at the time of the Bulge I knew that he was not the pilot who took me to my destination, but I did not realize at that time how close I was to the crew I was looking for.

Gilpin suggested that, from now on, I should attend all the reunions of the Carpetbaggers. By chance I will recognize members of the crew who dropped me, or perhaps one of the crew will recognize me, which will be very unlikely.

The next day all those who were billeted at Fort Ord met at the Officers Club for lunch. Bart, an accomplished bagpipe player, serenaded us in front of the Officers Club. The members of these two groups were the friendliest bunch of people we had ever met (of course not all were retired) but there was a common bond which united them; they were all veterans of WWII. After promising to meet again we left these great people and continued on our vacation to the wine region of Napa.

Beginning Of Earnest Searches

The next Carpetbaggers reunion was in September 1991 at Houston, Texas. We took this opportunity of visiting our son Alain and his family at New Orleans and from there we drove to Houston hoping to see our son Paul. The reunion was interesting, but I was not able to identify the crew I was looking for, nor did we meet our son. We returned home via New Orleans looking forward to the next reunion which was to be held in Virginia.

The historical town of Williamsburg was selected by the Carpetbaggers for their reunion. After stopping in Washington DC we reached our destination on the 19th of September 1992. It was great to meet my old friend Bill Colby who was to be the keynote speaker of the reunion. Ben Cohen, a stamp dealer, was among the members present, but he and many of the others were not part of the crew that I was looking for. We became very close to Jim Heddleson, a Carpetbagger who had spent some time in France hiding from the Germans. His plane had crashed on the hill of Haute Loire and only he and two others had survived. He was in contact with those who had rescued him, but had trouble communicating with them. So I helped him with the translations of his letters and their responses from his French friends. I interrogated the Carpetbaggers attending the reunion for the first time, those I had not yet met, but not a single member of the crew I was looking for surfaced at that time.

The next reunion was to be in Europe in two different locations, one in England where the groups had been based, and another in Paris where the French would try to outdo the British and perhaps themselves.

When in early 1993 I was diagnosed with two cancers, the surgeon who was a French wine expert assured me that I would be able to attend the next reunion of the Carpetbaggers. I decided to skip the French celebration and to attend only the British reunion. He was right! Not only was I able to go, but both cancers had been licked without radiation or chemotherapy. With my new internal bladder it was not easy for me to travel. I had to empty every four or five hours with the help of a catheter. It was quite a trick when doing it in an aircraft lavatory! Somehow I managed.

England - Harrington -Scotland

My life style was drastically changed but not enough to prevent a trip overseas, so Ginny and I made it aboard a Northwest 747. Not only were we able to attend the reunion and meet new members of the association, but with all the others we were treated royally by our host Carl Bartram, owner of the land where the Harrington Air Base was located. A few structures including the operations building and a couple of Quonset huts were still standing as a museum to the past. After a memorial ceremony at the marker dedicated to those who had lost their life in the pursuit of freedom, we gathered at the Kettering Park Hotel for a great banquet. The keynote speaker was Squadron Leader Verity who in WWII specialized in picking up people behind the German lines with his Lysender. None of those attending the reunion were part of the crew of the B-24 who missed the target and deposited me in the wrong spot. Many local people, too young to have been involved in the war, attended the banquet as guests. Clive Bassett, a very interesting young man, sat at our table with his wife. He was a collector of memorabilia related to the Carpetbaggers and the war in general.

Memorial to the crews of operation Carpetbagger at former WWII Harrington Air Base. (The aircraft on the marker is number 211 which took the author to his destination.)

I was not discouraged, because I knew that there would be other reunions and eventually I would find a member of the crew. While the rest of the group went to France, we decided to remain in England and to go to Scotland where I had trained with the British Commandos.

Through my membership in the Special Forces Club of London, I was able to find out the name and the location of the SOE training site in Scotland. We drove through the Lake District, to the Highlands and settled in a B&B at Fort William. From there we went to Mallaig to see if I could locate the Traigh House, an old fortified farm house which was our training base.

We missed it on our way to Mallaig which had remained pretty much the same as when I was there during the war. It is still a fishing village and the end of a rail line where, as saboteur trainees, we had to familiarize ourselves with the important parts of a coal-burning locomotive.

We were told by the local gentry approximately where the Traigh House was but to make certain, we stopped at a store offering woolens to tourists. It turned out that the owner of the store was also the owner of the Traigh House, but he was on a trip to a nearby island.

We finally located the building that had been my home for a while. Nothing had changed much aside from new doors, and new windows, but the roosters and the chicken with pure black combs, probably descendants of those we knew in 1944, unconcerned by our presence were still scratching and picking here and there! The woman who opened the door told us that the owner was away, but as I was one of those who had stayed at Traigh House

The Traigh House, Mallaig, Scotland.

during the war, he would have been happy to talk to me. As he was not expected soon, we did not linger long. But before leaving Traigh, while Ginny waited in the car, I went across the road to the beach, and picked up a small rock as a souvenir, something I could not have done during the war. Then looking back on the road to Mallaig I remembered the many mornings I and our group double timed for 100 yards and did quick steps for another 100 yards, followed by a few pushups to sharpen our appetite for breakfast!

Then via the low road to Loch Lomon we returned to Glasgow for our flight back to the United States.

San Diego was to be where the next get-together of the Carpetbaggers would be held in conjunction with the reunion of the of the 8th Air Force. The Carpetbaggers had accepted the leadership of a symposium. Bill Colby was designated as the one to represent the "Joes," or the agents that were dropped in occupied territory with containers and packages. He was the best choice because he had had experience in both France and Norway. A month or so before the reunion, Col. Robert W. Fish, the CO of one of the groups, called me. Apparently Bill Colby could not attend the symposium, and perhaps I would consent to take his place, to which I agreed. Ginny and I flew to San Diego and met our old friends, whom we have known now for a few years. All are aware of the reason why I joined the Carpetbaggers. So there is no doubt as to my relationship within the group; on their membership listing I am identified as "a Joe."

By then all Carpetbaggers realized that I was not discouraged, but I felt that my chance of finding members of the crew alive was rather slim. Again I contacted the Special Forces Club of London and asked about documents or reports related to my mission called *Licensee*. I was told that all documentation involving members of OSS had been transferred to the United States and there was nothing in the UK. CIA, which was supposed to be the keeper of the records, had nothing to offer. It was difficult for me to accept that a critical incident such as the loss of an agent would not be recorded somewhere. I began to assume that there was a deliberate attempt to squash the incident so as not to embarrass either the Army Air Corps, or perhaps SOE who did not provide those responsible for my transportation the correct information.

I decided that if I by-passed SOE and contacted the SAS in order to locate a captain Davis who was in my area in France, I might be able to penetrate the system and find out about my mission. The SAS association did locate Captain Davis, but not in England. He had emigrated to South Africa, and that is where I lost his trail.

At San Diego, we met the old usual gang, including Richard and Bernice Sizemore, Mary and Bart, Col. Fish, plus a new crop of Carpetbaggers. Also present were members of AFEES (Air Force Escape and Evasion Society), those airmen who either were never captured such as Jimmy Heddleson, and those who were captured but somehow escaped. The French people called "Helpers," who risked their own lives to help escapees were honored. I tried to find out if they knew about my uncles who ran an escape route to Switzerland, but they did not.

At the speakers' table of the symposium moderated by Roger Freeman, foremost historian of the 8th AF, I sat patiently through the glorification of the two Air Force Bombardment Groups. Colonel Fish the Commanding Officer of the group from August to September 1944, was followed by Bestow Rudolph, the Group Training Officer, and Colonel Robert Sullivan the Group Operations officer. Then tearful James Heddleson gave the usual emotional version of his life in occupied France while hiding in the comfortable home of Louise Boyer. Finally it was my turn. I described the part that I played as a passenger, or as a "Joe" - the term the Carpetbaggers used to refer to us agents. The audience was listening quietly up to the time I left the aircraft through the "Joe Hole." But when I told them that on the ground there was no one to greet me and offer me a glass of wine with a piece of cheese, and that two Orientals appeared while I was folding my parachute, that I firmly believed that they had dropped me in the wrong continent, there was pandemonium in the hall.

So, the Carpetbaggers never made a mistake, eh? Every one of their missions were accomplished flawlessly? No kidding! We had just heard how efficient they were in the field! How do they account for this? Of course they could not, and they assured me none of those present would have done such a dreadful thing. If they were present they were not about to admit it! At least I had unloaded in public what had been in my mind for many years, and even if I never found the crew of the black bird which took me to France that night it was a matter of record that I had been a "Joe," a lost Joe!

To cool matters somewhat with the Carpetbaggers I decided to skip the 1995 reunion which was to be on a cruise ship from Florida. But the following year we could not resist the temptation of Colorado and flew to Colorado Springs. Again we met our old friends, plus new ones, and enjoyed their company in that ideally selected location. I was expecting a quiet reunion without much hope of discovering the crew I was seeking. However, Lt. Col. Bradbury, "Brad" to his friends, a Carpetbagger who has a close relationship at the Air Force Academy, convinced me that speaking to a French class would be great for the cadets. Thus I accepted his offer. Before addressing the class Brad introduced me to the instructor, lovely Captain Mary O'Connor, then we all went to the class room where a dozen or so cadets were waiting. My talk was well received by some incredulous cadets, but also by another instructor who had the next French class. She imposed on my good nature and suggested that I talk to her students, which I did. It turned out that

I spoke to three French classes and missed much of that day's program with the Carpetbaggers. But it was worth it especially after learning from Brad that one of the female cadets had described me to her friend as a "Cool Dood". A complimentary remark I was told.

This was no doubt the best Carpetbagger reunion we had attended, not only because of the surroundings, the close proximity of the Academy, but it seems that we have become members of a big family. I no longer felt as a "Joe" but as a Carpetbagger. I heard so many stories about their dangerous activities that I felt that my role as a Joe was really insignificant. While the trip was dangerous on the way over, once on the ground I was relatively safe while the crew had to face the same dangers on the return to their base. Even after a successful drop, some were shot down on their way back to England.

We certainly did not intend to miss the 1997 reunion which was at New Orleans because that is where our son Alain resides with his wife and two children. There we met a few members who had never attended reunions including other Joes who discovered that Carpetbaggers reunions are great. Clive Bassett the collector of memorabilia we had met at the England reunion, and a faithful friend of the Carpetbaggers, was there with his spouse.

Getting Warm

At that meeting I learned something new, something that I did not know existed. Apparently upon returning to their base each crew had to complete a form which indicated the date, the time, and the destination of each flight. No one up to that time including Brad had mentioned this to me. I had seen some of the information in Parnel's book, *CARPETBAGGERS*, but it was incomplete, and too vague to be of value. For example, there was no flight listed on the night of 8/9 of August, 1944. I was told that Igor Petrenko (Pete) knew where these forms known as Mission Reports (MR) were. Additional information about the activities of the Carpetbaggers were in file at Maxwell Air Base in Alabama, and that Pete, Brad, and Charles Fairbanks may possibly go there to check it out.

Shortly after returning home. I received a letter from Jimmy Heddleson. He included a copy of a typical mission report. It was exactly what I was looking for, but this particular one was not about my own mission. Shortly after I heard from Brad who gave me the name of an individual, the son of a late Carpetbagger, who was doing research on the two groups responsible for the support of the resistance in Europe. His name was Tom Ensminger and he resides at Fairborn close to Wright Paterson Air Force Base, only a couple of hours from Indianapolis. Tom was collecting information about two Army Air Force Groups of the 8th AF, the 801st and 492nd Bombardment Groups, and about OSS and SOE operations, the two organizations they supported under the code designation "Carpetbaggers." This information was included in his extensive and impressive web site.

Without much hope I asked Tom about the whereabouts of the missions reports, but he referred me back to Pete and Brad telling me that these two could obtain the information I wanted from NARA (National Archives Records and Administration). Tom had been trying to obtain copies of MR, from his NARA contact, Dave Giordano, but so far had been unsuccessful. Because Tom had a few mission reports I gave him the coordinates of the drops zones where I was supposed to have been dropped. I had obtained these from Roger Tartrat (Kiki), a Frenchman doing research on the support the Air Force gave to the BCRA, the official French resistance. Unfortunately as of July 1944 these mission reports no longer indicated the coordinates of the drop zones. After that date there was no way of knowing the exact destinations to which the planes were directed.

About that time I received a call from John Taylor of NARA. He had discovered some OSS pictures related to the Deer Team, the South East Asia operation to which I was assigned in 1945. I needed these for the book I was about to publish. Without wasting time Ginny and I headed for Leesburg to check with our dear friends Elizabeth and Fred McIntosh. The following day with Betty we drove to College Park and went into the attractive office building of NARA. There we met John Taylor with whom I had had several previous communications including telephone conversations. We settled in his office, identified the "boxes" where the pictures were stored and were told that it would take a while for these to be located and made available for inspection.

Tom Ensminger had asked me to check with David Giordano, the individual responsible for the Air Force or Army Air Corps past records including that of the Carpetbaggers. He happened to be in the same area as John Taylor. Tom Ensminger had asked him to copy over 4000 mission reports as several of us had agreed to share the cost of his service. In poor health, David was unable to complete this formidable task; however he agreed to locate the mission reports dated from July 15th to of August 15th 1944. Among those I hoped to find the ones in support of the Licensee Mission, the one that I needed. He located the boxes containing these MRs and would make them available that afternoon.

The three of us waited until we were told that the boxes were there, ready for our examination. First I checked the pictures of the Deer Team. They were there all right, but these were not as numerous as I had expected. Only two were worthwhile and were copied.

However, when we asked for the mission reports, we were told that the boxes containing these were being used by someone else! I felt that we were getting the runaround and that we would never get the opportunity to see them. We returned to Dave Giordano who could not understand why these boxes he had just seen were no longer there; fortunately he found them in the storage area. The documents at NARA are tightly controlled to prevent their disappearance.

I signed and received four boxes, each containing several hundred fragile documents yellowed with age. I began a systematic search examining them carefully, checking the dates, the number of "Joes" aboard, the comments made by the crew members, etc. When I reached one of the MR dated 8/9 August 1944, there was no Joe aboard listed even though the mission was scheduled for Operation LICENSEE! When I pulled the next MR with the same date to the same operation, with a load of 12 containers and 10 packages, there was a Joe!

Eureka! That was my operation! The name of the crew was clearly listed, but nothing abnormal was indicated on the report. I looked further, but only two other MRs were listed for LICENSEE because the dates in the documents in the box stopped at August 15th. I knew that we had received many more planes after that date.

I was elated. After all these years I had the identity of the crew that dropped me into occupied France on the night of 8/9 of August 1944. I did not know their full names. However, I felt that it was a good beginning and that Tom Ensminger, who was far more knowledgeable than I with the Carpetbaggers, would know. It was too late to dig further, so we decided to quit and if necessary I would return later. I had what I had been searching for over fifty years. It was with great satisfaction that we left College Park for Leesburg where we celebrated at Betty and Fred's farm.

On the way back to Indianapolis, we stopped at Wright-Paterson Air Force Base. After checking in at the base guest house, we went to look for Tom. Without much trouble we found him at the nearby town of Fairborn. When I showed him the three mission reports he was pleased to see that these were part of the four thousand MRs he was expecting from NARA. The mission report listing a Joe indicated only the last names of the crew. Amazingly Tom was able to give me not only their full names, but their rank and their serial numbers as well.

My greatest surprise was when he identified the aircraft as being that of the B-24 number 51211 called "Miss Fitts" a very appropriate name for that mission. It was the same aircraft depicted on the marker erected in England where the Harrington air base was located, and on the cover of the Directory of the Association! This was indeed a famous plane, and many Carpetbaggers claimed that they flew it. What is even more inexplicable is the fact that among all the pictures of B-24 I was given, I had selected that one for my book! Finally, after all the years spent searching for the plane and the crew who dropped me in France I had found them all. I had no idea who the crew members were except one whose name seemed familiar. I had heard the name Roy Korrot before, but where and when I could not recall. Perhaps he was one of the Carpetbaggers I had met over the years.

Satisfied with the results of my trip to NARA, and happy to have met Tom, an unusually gifted and dedicated individual, we drove back home. Only then when I checked the names against the Directory of the Carpetbaggers did I find one name listed: Eugene Ruh, the engineer who was aboard the "Miss Fitts" on that fateful night. It seemed strange that he had never mentioned this to me because he knew what I was looking for. When I called him he realized immediately who I was because he had been attending the reunions of the Carpetbaggers regularly. Unfortunately, when I asked him about the night of 8/9 August 1944, he recalled very little. Only after he saw a copy of the Mission Report did he remember flying only once with a pilot named Seccafico who was the group's Operations Officer. On that day or night he believed that the flight he was on was a practice flight. After landing he was surprised to learn that he had been to France. Upon returning to the base the pilot did not want the landing lights turned on. As a result the plane hit one of the runway lights, and for that he was reprimanded. But more surprises were to follow.

With his reply Gene enclosed a photo of the crew of the Miss Fitts which was the crew of Captain Gilpin, the first Carpetbagger pilot I had met at the Obergs in 1993! The only reason he did not know that it was his plane that dropped me in the wrong place was because he was not flying it that day.

Gene also indicated that Roy Korrot could have been the dispatcher, a replacement for the regular dispatcher who a few days earlier had accidentally fallen through the Joe hole over the English channel.

I kept thinking about Roy Korrot, still wondering where I had seen that name when I decided to check my little black book, the one I used during WWII which included the names of friends and acquaintances. Many of the names were no longer familiar to me. When I occasionally thumbed through it and I reached the "K" and saw "Roy Korrot" with an address in Philadelphia it did not ring a bell even though in small letters "d.i.s.p." was written above the name. In addition it was not in my hand writing!

This time however, when I look though the little black book I realized then that "d.i.s.p." meant "dispatcher."

Shortly after leaving Glasgow in December 1944, as I was walking alone on the promenade deck of the Queen Mary, a young sergeant approached me and said; "Are you the fellow we dropped in France a few months ago?" He looked familiar, but it took a while for me to realize that he was the individual with whom I had spent some time in the dim tail section of a B-24. He was the one who pushed the packages through the hole and made sure that my parachute was on properly before tapping me on the shoulder, the signal to jump.

Then I did recall when and how his name was entered in my little address book and why. Upon learning that he lived in Philadelphia, close to my home town in New Jersey, we had exchanged addresses expecting to meet later.

This was an old address probably no longer valid. On my computer I decided to try my luck with the white pages of Yahoo. On the first try, two addresses listed for Roy Korrot appeared. One at Atlantic City, New Jersey, the other at St. Petersburg, Forida. First I tried Atlantic City, but the telephone had been temporarily disconnected. When I called the Florida number a woman answered.

"May I speak to Roy?" I asked.

"Who is this" she replied.

"I am a friend of Roy" I said without thinking.

I heard her saying; "Roy, there is a fellow on the phone who speaks with an accent."

Roy got on the phone, " Hello." Then I said,"Roy, you better sit down. You probably do not remember me, but we met many years ago". Roy mentioned a name that I did not recognize. "No, it is not he," I replied. Then Roy said: "Then it's René!"

"How the hell did you know it was I?" It was my turn to sit down

"I have been thinking about you all these years wondering what you were doing. How are you?"

"I am fine. I have been looking for the crew who dropped me in France during the war. I have been attending the Carpetbaggers reunions for the last five years hoping to meet a member of the crew. But until now no luck."

"Who are the Carpetbaggers?" Roy asked.

Roy did not know about the Carpetbaggers. I told him as much as I knew about that organization, and why I had joined them.

I explained to Roy how I discovered the identity of the crew members and the name of the plane. I mentioned Gene Ruh from Wisconsin and the others, but he did not know their whereabouts. I could tell that he was excited and when I told him about the next October reunion of the Carpetbaggers at Savannah GA he assured me that he would be there. It seems strange to me that he was not aware of the existence of the association of former member of the 801st/492nd Bombardment Groups called the Carpetbaggers. However he assured me that he would never dream of missing the next reunion, so as to be reacquainted with his former buddies. I wondered how many members of these two groups were still alive but not aware of the existence of the association.

Now I had located two of the crew of the Miss Fitts. I was making progress, but to find the other members I needed help from the knowledgeable people of the association and of course from Tom Ensminger who had a better handle on the wartime activities of the Carpetbaggers than most former members.

I was able to obtain a telephone number for Harold Wersell, the tail gunner of the Miss Fitts. His widow answered the phone. She told me that Harold had passed away in 1966, but when I told her that I was one of the Joes that were dropped behind the German lines she became very interested. She was not aware of the Carpetbaggers, but her husband had been in contact with some of his war buddies until he passed away. She recalled that he had told her about dropping agents and supplies in occupied France. He also stated that on one occasion a Joe had been dropped in the wrong place! I made her repeat what she had told me. Then, when I told her that I was the Joe who had been misplaced for a while, she became doubly interested and wanted to know more about the Carpetbaggers. She wanted to hear from those who had known her husband. I promised that I would pass on her request to the group when I meet them at the next October reunion.

Now three of the eight-man crew were positively identified. Unfortunately, one had gone to his reward, the one who from the tail end of the plane had test-fired the only twin 50 Cal machine gun aboard, scaring the hell out of me.

The two individuals I wanted to face more than anyone else were Seccafico, the pilot and Miller, the navigator. Upon learning that I was looking for Capt. Seccafico, Sizemore, the Secretary of the Association, warned me that I may have a problem locating him because he had changed his name to James Roberts. Jokingly Si added, "Probably he learned that you were looking for him!" Of course you must understand that Si is a great kidder and what he says has to be taken with a grain of salt!

Saccafico had lived with or had been adopted by an individual named Roberts. He had changed his name in esteem to his adopted parents. Roberts had been a member of the Carpetbaggers up to 1993. He was listed on their directory as residing in Fort Lauderdale, Florida. His address was a Post Office Box 4034 and his telephone was (305) 524-0902 but it has been temporarily disconnected. Subsequently I obtained another address 741 Culpepper Terrace also in Fort Lauderdale with a different telephone number (954) 452-9738. Still no response at this number either. I am still searching for James Roberts and I have contacted several veterans, and military organizations which have included my inquiry in their magazines.

The navigator was named Miller, a common name. Amazingly, there were several officers with the name of Miller in the two groups, and even more confusing all were navigators. I called Frederick W. Miller and George F. Miller, but neither were on my flight on that particular day. George Miller suggested that the Miller I was looking for was A.B. Miller the "A" standing for Armand. No one knew where A.B. was. Obituaries listed several A.B. Millers having passed away. Perhaps one of these was the one I was looking for.

Batting zero with the navigator and the pilot and failing to locate the copilot, I wondered if I would ever locate the entire crew, those who were still alive. Thanks to Andy J. Wilkinson, an Englishman doing research on Air Force units, I located Charles D. Pou the bombardier who resides in Atlanta, Georgia. He and his wife sounded as if they were in poor health. His memory was not the best. He could not recall the specific mission of the Miss Fitts, but he has written an article about his landing in Occupied France aboard a C-47 piloted by Col. Heflin. As a reporter, he returned to France in 1966 to locate some of the folks he had met during the war. He sent me a copy of his article together with a picture of his crew including some of the French people, the descendants of those he had met in 1944.

The copilot was Russell Lauzon. Lauzon is not a very common name. On the Internet, Yahoo and Bigfoot listed several Lauzon, one Russell in Oregon, the other Russell in California. After dialing the California number several times during the day without response, one evening before retiring I dialed the Oregon telephone number of Russell J. Lauzon. A lady answered the ring.

"Is this the Lauzon residence? Russell Lauzon?"

"Yes."

"Was he a pilot during the War?"

"Yes."

"May I speak to Russell?"

" He is not here, he is at our other house in California."

I explained to her who I was, and why I wanted to talk to her husband who had been the copilot on the plane that dropped me behind the German lines in Occupied France. She said that Russell will be so happy to talk to me because recently, after seeing a B-24 at a museum, he had mentioned his past military activities and was wondering where all his war friends were. She said:

"You must call him right away at our California home."

"I did call there but there was no reply."

"You probably had the wrong exchange number. It is now 949 instead of 714."

Shortly after hanging up, I called the new number and Russell answered. At first I did not tell him who I was. Only that I was an old friend and that I remember him as a handsome fellow. He laughed, and joked about getting old. Then I told him that I was a passenger on the plane he flew as a copilot with James Seccafico as the pilot and Miller was the navigator. He did remember Seccafico but not Miller, who was not the regular navigator. He stated that he remembered that flight very well, that it was the worst flight he ever had, and that the crew which was not the regular crew was incompetent. During the flight, seeing a red light the pilot took evasive action to avoid a non-existing threat. When I told him that I was dropped at the wrong spot he did not appear surprised. He remembered Ruh the engineer; the rest of the crew was unfamiliar to him. He knew that a portion of the crew was Gilpin's because he was a member of his crew, and that Seccafico was the operations officer, who needed flying time to keep his flight pay.

That night once the aircraft reached land, lights were seen ahead. Thinking that these were German night fighters, the pilot took evasive actions which according to Russell were not needed. Lauzon was not impressed by either the pilot or the navigator. He stated that the best pilot of his squadron was Captain Henry Gilpin, and he wished he could see him again having lost track of him years ago. He was quite surprised when I told him that Gilpin was the first Carpetbagger pilot I had met, and that he resided in Monterey, California. So it appears that I had flown in Gilpin's plane but with only a portion of his crew!

It was a matter of a few days when I received the following letter from Russell:

13 May 98

René,

You have awakened some long dormant memories through our phone conversation and the photo you sent, which I thank you for (p.p. English!!.) Would you believe I heard from Gilpin the next morning (7th)! Thanks again! Hank tells me that Ruh, he and I are the only ones alive from his original crew. My wife Barbara and I trek between OR and CA twice a year and intend to see the Gilpins on our way south next Oct. On Ruh's crew photo, I believe Eubank's first name should be spelled FORBIS and that La Pointe's was Joseph. Unidentified Dispatcher is Michalak.

Barb and I head north to OR next week and will stop in Sacramento to visit my son and his wife. If my old records are still there I'll secure team and do a little checking. I was pretty close to Fred Sager, copilot from Wren, Miss. And Mike Mirola, navigator from NYC during our Italian stint. Would like to contact them. I do not remember any names from the crew I took over. "My memory shrinks, my hearing stinks. The golden years are here at last, the golden years can kiss my ass!"

Two questions: Were you with OSS? And what organization is AFEES?

Thanks again René, Will keep in touch

Best regards

S/Russ Lauzon

PS: Guys went blind drinking Calvados in Italy !!!

Member of the Carpetbaggers, Lt. Russell Lauzon, who wrote the letter above was the copilot of the B-24 Bomber called the Miss Fitts, which took the author to the wrong destination on the night of 8/9 August 1944. He was the copilot of the original crew of the B-24 Bomber No. 251211 assigned to Captain Henry Gilpin who did not fly that night.

Mision Reports Discovery

I was invited to attend the AFEES reunion at Falls Church by Richard Rendall and his father Bill, both friends of Jimmy Heddleson -also known as Jimmy le Chat. Taking advantage of this opportunity we all went to NARA to continue my search of the MRs related to the flights in support of operation Licensee. I had asked Dave Giordano to isolate the Carpetbaggers MRs from August to September 1944, because I wanted to know how many drops had been credited to Licensee during that period. I found 29 missions listed as completed, and a few listed as incomplete. I copied all and returned to the Still Photos Division, but found nothing related to the *Deer Mission*.

The 29 mission reports listed the last name of the members of the crew as well as their function. The following is the condensation of the information on these reports. A few of the names of the crew members listed are known members of the Carpetbaggers Association, but others are not. If the reader recognizes one or several of these gallant airmen, they should contact Tom Ensminger, the historian of the group.

The following is a list of the brave crew members of the B-24s who dropped this agent and supplies in support of Operation LICENSEE.

Information extracted from MISSION REPORTS of the squadrons assigned to the 801st/492nd BG by Thomas Ensminger, son of a Carpetbagger.

Crew members identified as members of the 801st/492nd Bombardment Group Association (CARPETBAGGERS) are indicated by an *.

Date: 30/31 July 1944   Report No. 1339

Squadron: 788   Aircraft: 231

Crew members
Pilot: Richard C. Robins   Copilot: Fred L. Deutsche
Navigator: Charles C. Park   Bombardier: Edward Nicholas
Dispatcher: William B. Bellah   Radio Oper: Francis W. Hanlon
Engineer: John C. Di Bella   Gunner: James E. O'Brien

Date: 30/31 July 1944   Report No. 1341

Squadron: 788   Aircraft: 262

Crew members:
Pilot: Kenneth L. Driscoll*Copilot: Edward.D. Halpin*
Navigator: Robert R. Ricketts*   Bombardier: Joseph E. Fox *
Dispatcher: Carl E. Bradshaw   Radio Opr.: Robert Brink
Engineer:James. H. Wright   Gunner: Blair G. Henry

Date: 30/31 July 19   Report No. 1342

Squadron: 850   Aircraft: 259

Crew members:
Pilot: Runyon P. Coleman   Copilot: Edwin C. Lloyd
Navigator: Robert C. Bray   Bombardier: Kenneth R. Beno
Dispatcher:Raymond S. Jablecki   Radio Opr.:Beryl F. Bryant
Engineer: Stanley B. Swain   Gunner: Martin L. Talley*

Date: 2/3 August 1944   Report No. 1404

Squadron: 788   Aircraft: 231

Crew members:
Pilot: Richard C .Robins   Copilot: Fred L. Deutsche
Navigator: Charles C. Park   Bombadier: Edward Nicholas
Dispatcher: James E. O'Brien   Radio Opr.: Francis W. Hanlon
Engineer: John C. Di Bella   Gunner: William B. Bella

Date: 6/7 August 1944   Report No. 1471

Squadron: 406   Aircraft: 975

Crew members:
Pilot: Clinton H.Rabbitt*   Copilot: Ernest G. Asbury
Navigator: Floyd M. Olson   Bomb.: Donald E.Leinhauser*
Dispatcher: Nicholas Rasnak*   Radio Opr.: Steve C. Sianis
Engineer:Arthur Bogusz*   Gunner:Meyer Tauger
Passenger: Floyd E. Cross

Date: 6/7 August 1944   Report No. 1472

Squadron: 36th   Aircraft: 960

Crew members:
Pilot: Robert W. Fish* Copilot: Oliver C. Carscaddon
Navigator: Edward C. Tresemer   Bombardier: Charles R. Teer
Dispatcher: Leroy H. Suther   Radio Opr.: Everett L. Weidner
Engineer: Wyman L. Stedman   Gunner: Verne R. Jacobs
Passenger: David E. Deutsch

Date: 8/9 August 1944

Report No. 1512

Squadron: 788

Aircraft: 211

Crew members:
Pilot: James A. Seccafico
Navigator: Armand. B. Miller
Dispatcher: Roy L. Korrot*
Engineer: Eugene A. Ruh
Passenger: One Joe (Julien)

Co-Pilot: Russell J. Lauzon*
Bombardier: Charles D. Pou
Radio Opr.: Albert Dahlke
Gunner: Harold J. Wersell

Date: 8/9 August 1944

Report No. 1513

Squadron: 36th

Aircraft: 618

Crew members:
Pilot: Richard R. Norton
Navigator: Lloyd L. Anderson
Dispatcher: William M.Lynch
Engineer: James H. Husbands

Copilot: Connnie O.Walker
Bombardier: Benjamin Rosen
Radio Opr.: William H.Noncy
Gunner:John W. Gillikin*

Date: 10/11 August 1944

Report No. 1552

Squadron: 406

Aircraft: 960

Crew members:
Pilot: Robert S. Hendrickson
Navigator: Malcom W. Stiles Jr.
Dispatcher: Tharon F. Heuston
Engineer: Thomas L. Wills

Copilot: Thomas E. Newton Jr
Bombardier: William A. Boyd*
Radio Opr.: Clarence E. Craver
Gunner:Clarence O. Theriault Jr.*

Date: 10/11 August 1944

Report No. 1553

Squadron: 850

Aircraft: 290

Crew members:
Pilot: William F. Reagan
Navigator: Allen P. Morains
Dispatcher: Chester R. Damas
Engineer: Glen J, Echtenkamp*
Passenger: Jack R. Sayers*

Copilot: Peter C. Fulrang
Bomb: Jerome M. Petersen
Radio Opr.: Peter J. Villari
Gunner: Kenneth B.Gregg

Date: 11/12 August 1944

Report No. 1575

Squadron: 406

Aircraft:801

Crew members:
Pilot: Rivers
Navigator: Bethart
Dispatcher: William Price Jr.
Engineer: Donald F. Menser

Copilot: I'Lone L.Norman
Bombardier: Loftus
Radio Opr.: Culyer D. Leach
Gunner: Joe A. Escalada

Date: 11/12 August 1944   Report No. 1576

Squadron: 788   Aircraft: 382

Crew members:
Pilot: Keith O. Martin   Copilot: Edward R. Kregor
Navigator: Frederick W. Miller*   Bombardier: Gains M. Newton*
Dispatcher: George W. Meador   Radio Opr.: Joseph W. Meek*
Engineer:Alonzo G. Dixon   Gunner: Melvin Masut

Date: 16/17 August 1944   Report No. 1688

Squadron: 856   Aircraft: 768

Crew members:

Pilot: Maurice E. Jacobson*   Copilot: Norman K. Russell
Navigator: James C. McKenna   Bomb: Davenport Cleveland*
Dispatcher: Joel K. Carter Jr   Radio Opr.: Mitchel T. Hart
Engineer: Robert B. Marriett   Gunner: Seymour B. Chinich

Date: 16/17 August 1944   Report No. 1689

Squadron: 859   Aircraft: 003

Crew members:
Pilot: Wm. F. Dillon*   Copilot: Ralph Morrow Jr.*
Navigator:Robert G.Bullock   Bombardier: Michael A. Baldino*
Dispatcher: Max D.Rufner   Radio Opr.: Russell K. Bond*
Engineer: Kenneth. Tompson   Gunner:Claud T. Stinson

Date: 25/26 August 1944   Report No. 1750

Squadron: 858   Aircraft: 871

Crew members:
Pilot: Robert S. Hendrickson   Copilot: Thomas E. Newton
Navigator: Malcolm W. Stiles Jr.   Bombardier: Wm. A. Boyd*
Dispatcher: Tharon F. Heuston   Radio Opr: Clarence E. Craver
Engineer: Thomas L.Wills   Gunner: Clarence C.Theriault*
Passenger: Richard E. Bellgardt*

Date: 24/25 August 1944   Report No. 1751

Squadron: 859   Aircraft: 054

Crew members:

Pilot: Leonard M. McManus   Copilot: Gerald T. Flaherty
Navigator: Levi O.Rust   Bombardier: Sam A.Cox
Dispatcher: Joseph Moravich   Radio Opr.: Francis O. Pluhar
Engineer:Robert L. Van Buren   Gunner:B. E. Williams

Date: 25/26 August 1944

Squadron: 857

Report No. 1752

Aircraft: 695

Crew members:
Pilot Wm. L. Bales*
Navigator: Milton Silverstein
Dispatcher: William H. Fox
Engineer: J. P. Bowden
Passenger:Earl D. Cartmill

Copilot:James J.Doyle
Bombardier: Arthur J.Simcik
Radio Opr.: William M.Lynch
Gunner: Douglas R.Chandler*

Date: 25/26 August 1944

Squadron: 858

Report No. 1754

Aircraft: 859

Crew members:
Pilot: George J. Stinchcomb*
Navigator: William B. Firman
Dispatcher: William H. Spencer
Engineer: Edgar Rollins
Passenger: George F. Bradbury

Copilot: Robert S. Rohrkaste
Bombardier: James S. George
Radio Opr.: Bradley J. Taylor
Gunner:Clyde C. Coke*

Date: 25/26 August 1944

Squadron: 856

Report No. 1755

Aircraft: 618

Crew members:
Pilot: Robert J. Swarts Jr.
Navigator: Grayson Cocharo
Dispatcher: Ralph L. Schiller
Engineer:Bernard J. Beverly*

Copilot: Vonderau !!
Bombardier: Donald L. Barrett
Radio Opr.: Charles T. Butler
Gunner: Raymond L. Croteau

Date: 5/6 September

Squadron: 858

Report No. 1946

Aircraft: 801

Crew members:
Pilot: Richard A. Luttrell
Navigator: Robert A. Wright
Dispatcher: Ervin L. Brown
Engineer:Arnold V. Noland

Copilot: Leonard M. Brock
Bombardier: Keith L. Green
Radio Opr.: John A. Wright
Gunner:Jack W. Horton*

Date: 5/6 September

Squadron: 857

Report No. 1947

Aircraft: 131

Crew members:
Pilot: Charles C. Deano*
Navigator: Charles J. Brejcha Jr.*
Dispatcher: Ernest J. Cabral*
Engineer:Wilbert A. Silva

Copilot: Robert W. Collett*
Bombardier: Adam M. Wojack
Radio Opr.: Francis G. Wylong
Gunner: Eugene O. Marion

Date: 5/6 September 1944

Report No. 1949

Squadron: 856

Aircraft: 786

Crew members:
Pilot: Roy L. Zink
Navigator: Robert K. Bender*
Dispatcher: James W. Wilson
Engineer: Ray W. Martin

Copilot: Wm. R. Corrin*
Bombardier: Nicholas V. Libeg
Radio Opr.: Worden F. Day
Gunner: Corvin L. Lanning

Date: 5/6 September 1944

Report No.1950

Squadron: 856

Aircraft: 682

Crew members:
Pilot: Abe M. Thompson
Navigator: Wm. K. Clarke
Dispatcher: Nelson L. Covey
Engineer: Harold E. Parvi*

Copilot: Donald A. St.Martin
Bombardier: David C. Groff
Radio Opr.: Lewis W. Meyer
Gunner: Garrett Parnell

Date: 5/6 September 1944

Report N_1951

Squadron: 857

Aircraft: 663

Crew members:
Pilot: Thomas S. Curran Jr.
Navigator: Warren E. Campbell
Dispatcher: Harold R. Johnson
Engineer: Arthur J. Robinson

Copilot: Thomas I. Colkett Jr.*
Bombardier: Alvah N. Winfield
Radio Opr.: Robert M. Campbell
Gunner: Stanley J. Janik.

Date: 5/6 September 1944

Report N_1953

Squadron: 858

Aircraft:

Crew members:
Pilot: Thomas O. McCarthy
Navigator: Robert E. Beach
Dispatcher: Charles S. Jones
Engineer: James B. Tate

Copilot: Rosslyn C. Anderson
Bombardier: Armando Carlino
Radio Opr.: Mack H. Dias
Gunner: Robert J.. Webber

Date: 5/6 September 1944

Report N_1954

Squadron: 856

Aircraft: 506

Crew members:
Pilot: Stanley A. Seger*
Navigator: Ralph Mack
Dispatcher: Joseph P. Johnson
Engineer: Robert F. Marvel

Copilot: Joel K. Carter*
Bombardier: Henry D. Colyer
Radio Opr: Ralph P. Beaman*
Gunner· Jack A. Hammond*

Date 5/6 September 1944   Report N_1955

Squadron: 857   Aircraft: 695

Crew members:

Pilot: William L. Bales*   Copilot: James J. Doyle
Navigator: Milton Silverstein   Bombardier: Arthur J. Simcik
Dispatcher: William H. Fox   Radio Opr.: William C. Jungbluth
Engineer: Bowden   Gunner: Douglas R. Chandler*

Date: 5/6 September 1944   Report N_1956

Squadron: 858   Aircraft: 300

Crew members:
Pilot: Rivers   Copilot:I'Lone Norman
Navigator: Bethart   Bombardier: Loftus
Dispatcher: Stanley E. Nickelson   Radio Opr.: Culyer D. Leach
Engineer:Presley W. Smith   Gunner: William Price Jr.

Date: 5/6 September 1944   Report N_1957

Squadron: 859   Aircraft: 152
Crew members:
Pilot: Roderick E. Ewart   Copilot: Walter L. Saline
Navigator: George M. Haber   Bombardier: George N. Boes
Dispatcher: Sidney D. Kagan   Radio Opr.: Kenneth E. Larsen
Engineer:Steve Korpash   Gunner: William A. McNeil

S E C R E T   Report _1512_

1. Squadron _788_ A/C # _311_   Date _8/9 Aug_

2. Name of Operation _LICENSEE 2_   Alt. _____
   Country _____ FRANCE _____

3. Crew: Pilot _SECCAFICO_   Disp. _KORROL_
       C.Pilot _LAUZON_   R.O. _DAHLKE_
       Nav. _MILLER_   Eng. _RUH_
       Bomb. _POU_   Gunner _WERSEL_
       Pass. _____   Pass. _FARMAN_

4.

	J	C	P	N	PH
Load Carried	1	12	10		
Load Dropped	1	12	10		

5. Result of Operation. _COMPLETE_

6. Time of Take Off _2229_   Landed _0325_

7. Was Exact Pinpoint Found? _YES_. How was point identified?
   "C" TYPE FLASHING "R"

8. Estimated Dropping Points _A LITTLE LEFT OF LIGHTS_
   ↑ THEN FEU
   TWO PACKAGES STUCK IN HATC ABOUT ½ MILE
   EAST OF TARGET ON 1ST RUN

9. Bombardier and Dispatchers Report. _TWO RUNS - ALL OUT_
   O.K. EXCEPT PACKAGES MENTIONED ABOVE

10. Target Area From _0101_ to _0118_. Time Dropped 1ST _0111_
       2ND _0118_
    Height above ground 1ST _650'_ Course 1ST _110°_ 1ST _193_
       2ND _400_   2ND _240°_   2ND _131_

11. Routes - Time, Altitude and Point of Crossing English and Enemy.
    Coasts _LITTLEHAMPTON-2311-9000 - ELETOT -2238-9000_
    - ELETOT-0236-8600 - LITTLEHAMPTON - 0303-7500'

12. Leaflets dropped _NONE CARRIED_

S E C R E T

Mission Report 1512

89

Report _1513_

1. Squadron ___36___ A/C # ___618___   Date ___8/9 Aug___

2. Name of Operation _LICENSEE 3_ Alt. _____
   Country _____FRANCE_____

3. Crew: Pilot   __Norton__ Richard R   Disp. __Lynch__ William W
         C-Pilot __Walker__ course a   R.O.   __Money__ willy H
         Nav.   __Anderson__ Lloyd L   Eng.   __Husbands__ James H
         Bomb.   __Rosen__ Bayann   Gunner __Gillikin__ John W
         Pass.   Pass.

4.

	J	C	P	N	PH
Load Carried	12	9			
Load Dropped	1✓	9			

5. Result of Operation. _Completed_

6. Time of Take Off _2147_   Landed _0450_.

7. Was Exact Pinpoint Found? _Yes_. How was point identified? _____
   C type lights flashing "R". terrain.

8. Estimated Dropping Points _60 feet from line of lights_

9. Bombardier and Dispatchers Report. _Everything out OK._

10. Target Area from _0121_ to _0125_. Time Dropped _0124_
    Height above ground _450_ Course _280_ MPH _130_.

11. Routes Time, Altitude and Point of Crossing English and Enemy
    Coasts _Start Pt-2257-8000'; Penikon-2329-8000_
    Penikon-0314-7500'; Start Pt-0341-7500

12. Leaflets dropped _____

Mission Report 1513

90

Based on the analysis of the two MRs related to the two B-24 flights in support of Licensee Operation on the night of 8/9 of August 1944, in one of which I was a passenger, I asked the following questions to Tom Ensminger:

René: In reply to the two MRs you sent me it seems to me that there is something really fishy. These two missions were to the same DZ "Licensee 3." Licensee 3 where I was expected was called "Anguille." Yet neither plane unloaded at that DZ because on the night of 8/9 August 1944 the reception party waited, and waited, but nobody and nothing was dropped to them that particular night.

Tom: Do/did they record their code letter for the night?

René: Note that Seccafico claimed ground haze on the target area and Norton stated that it was clear. It was clear where I dropped. Seccafico left the area at 0131 and Norton arrived at 0121. If they had been in the same area they surely would have seen, or bumped into each other, no?

Tom: Not necessarily - Have hundreds of reports where times overlap on multi-plane drops at the same DZ, a mention of another plane, and sometimes there were up to six in the area at the same time, is rare.... unless a close call happened... Apparently the camouflage paint job worked better than they ever expected...

René: Did anyone check these MRs at the time?

Tom: Only hung-over S-2 officers in dim light...

René: In the MR# 1512 why is there a difference of 250 feet altitude between the first and second drop? Normally the Joe was dropped last so that he would not get hit by a container. The lower the aircraft the least dispersion which is what we wanted with containers. Jumping higher, the Joe could guide his chute to a safe landing. I could not believe how low we were when I jumped!

Tom: Controversial subject. Usual recommend was to drop Joes and containers at 600 feet, together. This gave the Joes, theoretically, time to steer their parachutes away from trees or obstacles and was the preferred height for the containers. Packages, because they were lighter and would disperse farther, were to be dropped at lower altitudes. But things often got mixed up, hung up, or just plain fucked up.

René: Both Seccafico and Norton acknowledge a light flashing the Morse letter "R."

Tom. Read again - I do not see Seccafico saying he caught the letter "R", only that he saw a code letter.....

René: ...because they never assigned the same letter to different drops on the same day!

Seccafico had a fast ride: He left 2229 hr. and returned at 0355 hr. or 5:26 hr. flying time, whereas Norton left at 2147 hr. and returned at 0450 hr. or 7:03 hrs flying time, a difference of 2:17 hrs!!!! And yet Seccafico made two passes, whereas Norton made only one!

René: *Not unusual either, depending on what they did on the way back, what route they chose, what flak emplacements they had to skirt, what enemy aircraft they ran into, how much fuel they had, how much flight time they wanted to get in, whether they had a hot date when the next night, etc....*

René: *Do you mean that the Norton crew crashed?*

Tom: *Yes, in the middle of August, at Duerne, they were all killed except for Gillikin. It's in Parnell's book.*

René: *Anderson is a Carpetbagger!*

According to my records, Lloyd L. Anderson has been dead since August of 1944. Sorry...

The Drone

The following crew members are listed on the 1999 directory of the CARPETBAGGERS Association:

Baldino, Michael A.	Isle Lamote, VT	Bales, Wm. L.	Lampasas, TX
Beaman, Ralph P.	Plainfied, IL	Bellgardt, Richard E.	Itasca, IL
Bender, Robert K.	Cedar Rapids, IA	Beverly, Bernard J.	Niles, IL
Bogusz, Arthur	Warren, MI	Bond, Russell K. Sr,	Clabash, NC
Boyd, William A.	Joliet, IL	Bradbury, Julian W.	San Antonio, TX
Brejcha, Charles J.	Indian Head Park, IL	Carter, Joel K.	Big Spring, TX
Chandler, Douglas R.	Irving, TX	Cleveland, Davenport	Woodstock, VT
Coke, Clyde C.	Waco, TX	Collett, Robert W.	Pike Road, AL
Corrin, Wm.	Pleasanton, CA	Cox, Joseph P.	Binghamton, NY
Diano, Charles C.	Metairie, LA	Dillon, Wm. F.	Amarillo, TX
Driscoll, Kenneth L.	Derry, NH	Echtenkamp, Glen J.	Omaha, NE
Fish, Robert W.	San Antonio, TX	Fox, Joseph E.	Jamesport, NY
Gillikin, John W. Sr.	Moorhead City, NC	Halpin, Edward D,	Oklahoma City, OK
Hammond, Jack A.	New Castle, PA	Horton, J. W.	Bellview, TX
Jacobson, Maurice E.	Sedgwick, CO	Korrot, Roy L.	St.Petersburg, FL
Lauzon, Russell J.	Eugene, OR	Leinhauser, Donald E	Springfield, MA
Luttrell, R. A. Mrs.	Morehead, MN	Meek, Joseph W.	Westland, MI
Morrow, Ralph Jr.	Fort Lupton, CO	Newton, Gains M.	Alexandria, LA
Parvi, Harold E.	Vancouver, WA	Rabbitt, Clinton H.	Memphis, TN
Rasnak, Nicholas	South Bound Brook, NJ	Ricketts, Robert R	N. Eastham, MA
Ruh, Eugene A.	New Holstein, VI	Sayers, Jack R	Fort Mitchel, KY
Seger, Stanley A.	Rochester Hills, MI	Stinchcomb, George J.	Carmichael, CA
Talley, Martin L.	Houston, TX	Theriault, Clarence C.	Mountain Home, AR
Webber, Willard E.	Schuykill Haven, PA		

Notes:

Roger Tartrat's research and Léon's report indicated that Licensee operation had received only 19 drops whereas the records of the U.S. Army Air Force (Carpetbagger) indicate 29 completed drops. Who received the other 10? Why were these ten drops considered successful when these ended in the hands of people other than personnel assigned to operation Licensee?

The Sitting Duck Pub

Betty McIntosh, the spouse of one of my late commanding officers, wrote a book called *Sisterhood of Spies*. In her book she mentioned Virginia Hall, the agent who had organized Operation Licensee to which I was assigned in France in 1944.

I did not want to forego Betty McIntosh's book signing at the Sitting Duck Pub of the Evans Farm of Langley, Virginia. It was a splendid affair, a gathering of former secret agents who had seen better days. I felt pretty good. Considering my age I felt lucky to have survived in such a good shape.

The highlight of the day for me was meeting Rita Kramer, the author of *Flames in the Field,* with whom I had been in telephone, fax, and e-mail communication since 1990, but had never met. She is as remarkable as I expected her to be, and more so in many ways. The luncheon was too short for the things we had to discuss and ponder.

At the Sitting Duck Pub, a CBS television crew was filming Betty and the assembly which included my old OSS friend and comrade Major General John K. Singlaub. When the director of the CBS crew asked me if I minded being interviewed because I had known Virginia Hall (the subject of one of the chapters of Betty's book), I agreed. In subjecting myself to their attention I could take advantage of their production to promote my own book. The interview was to be aired during the Bryan Gumbel program on the second of August 1998. I wondered how they would handle his interview. (They never did, because the Bryan Gumbel show was canceled.)

The following Monday Betty and I returned to NARA to continue our search. Betty was helping Michelle the CBS director of the Brian Gumbel show. John Taylor had called me earlier about having seen my name in some documents related to SOE. The SOE F-Section was the designation of Buckmaster's operation in France. Were these documents the ones which had been transferred to OSS ? I was puzzled, but before checking the boxes which contained these documents, I wanted to check NARA's records to see if names of operations, of agents, or of missions were indexed. None of those were listed. John Taylor admitted that the indexing had been very poor, probably because it was accomplished by volunteers who may not have been expert in that activity. Thus it was pure luck that he noticed my name on a document and he knew me.

I obtained the boxes which did contain the documents, and began a close examination. Half-way through my search I noticed a document titled "LICENSEE ex-LOINCLOTH". Thus LOINCLOTH must have been the operation to which Léon had been sent, and not LICENSEE.

Examining the twenty-two-page document I noticed that I was the originator of a field report. It was strange because while in France I do not remember having written anything other than coded messages related to enemy activities. I recalled having been debriefed after my return to our London headquarters, but as I read the report I noticed that chronologically the report was completely off. And surprisingly, the fact that I had been dropped at the wrong place was barely suggested. Furthermore some of the names of individuals mentioned in the report were unknown to me. This document could not have been written by me.

The Official Report of Operation Licensee

In May 1944, Diane, who had a roving mission in France, reported that she had established contact with a resistance group at Cosne in the Department of the Nièvre. This group consisted of about 100 men based in a maquis near Cosne. Because Diane was busy with other engagements she was unable to devote herself exclusively to the development of this group. In view of the importance of the area, it was decided to send an organizer to take over the control function. As a result, Léon left for the field during the July moon period. Prior to his arrival Diane had organized several receptions of arms and material. Subsequently Léon received 100 containers. His group was reasonably well armed and although no details as to its actual strength were available, it was assumed that it had increased considerably after his arrival.

On the night of 8/9th August 1944, 2nd Lieutenant René J. Défourneaux, AUS (Daniel), was dispatched by air to serve as lieutenant and instructor to Léon, the organizer of this new circuit referred to as Licensee, in the zone of Cosne.

OPERATIONAL BRIEFING

Léon's operational instructions and target set forth his mission as follows:
Operation: Licensee
Field name: Léon
Name on papers: Louis Jean Duguet

INFORMATION

Your organizer, Diane, has made known to you that she is in constant contact with a group at the town of Cosne in the Department of the Nièvre. This group consists of approximately 100 men and is based in the vicinity of Cosne.

We have no information concerning the state of organization of this group or their armament, with the exception of 12 containers which were delivered to them under the control of Diane.

Diane is an experienced organizer who during two lengthy missions has worked successfully for us in France. We have the greatest confidence in her ability and judgment.

Furthermore, Cosne is a strategically important region, particularly from a point of view of railway communication. Therefore, we are anxious to develop a circuit in that region.

INTENTION

"You will be parachuted into France as soon as possible during the July moon period. You must be ready to leave by 5 July 1944.

"Your mission is to lead the Cosne group which is mentioned above, especially to instruct them how to contact and communicate with us, and advise them about our latest directives.

"It is of the greatest importance that this group be absolutely "Au Courant"(aware) of our methods to enable them to report the location of the drop zones they have selected for the delivery of material, and to learn our methods for the organization of the reception committee designated for receiving the material.

"We are well aware that your training has been limited for the most part to that of a radio operator, but we ask you to assume also the functions of an organizer, taking into account the experience that you have already gained while in France.

"During the next moon we intend to send you a lieutenant who will have received special technical training, which will permit you to complete your mission.

"You will go the circuit (Licensee) at Cosne as an officer to carry out the orders of General Koenig who is the head of all the resistance groups in France. You will explain to your group that the British organization which sent Diane into France is still directly responsible for the circuit and at the same time responsible to General Koenig. This organization is also responsible for all supplies of material which concerns the circuit.

"You will also make them properly comprehend that their relations with other elements of resistance in France should be clearly defined in as much as they are directly under the command of General Koenig.

The general policy to follow vis-à-vis other resistance movements in the region is that all are under the same command and that they must, therefore, try to establish a reasonable separation of responsibility which must be put into effect in the region.

We have learned by experience that, on D-Day the organization of resistance made itself known, and had ceased all clandestine activities without taking into consideration whether or not the state of their armaments permitted them to take such action. It has become necessary for General Koenig to order all forces of the resistance, under any circumstances, not to engage in open combat, and not to recruit volunteers to whom they could not provide weapons. To the groups that are already armed and organized, he asks the resistance to continue guerrilla activities and the attack against enemy communications. These directives must be maintained until counter orders are received. It is extremely important that special attention be given to the principle that, the recruiting of new elements must only be following the acquisition of material and of arms, and not prior to it.

It is equally important to take into account that all actions against special targets are to be undertaken by small groups. Utilizing this principle, and organized in a clandestine fashion, these small groups will be capable of living an ordinary life until such time when they will be called upon for action against their objectives.

It is always possible that the resistance will be forced by the enemy actions to abandon its clandestine work and to make itself known. It is therefore recommended that a sort of Maquis be developed at the same time as the clandestine groups.

Please note that the inevitable consequence of military operations will forcibly include the extremely concentrated and intense bombardment of the railway junctions, the triangular centers, the workshops, the depots etc.; therefore, this must be borne in mind when you choose your target points which you have been allotted. Evidently you must take into consideration the fact that the RAF will no doubt occupy itself with the junctions, depots, etc. in your region. You should, therefore, concentrate your efforts on the lines of communication situated far from RAF targets.

In connection with the bombardment, we bring to your attention the fact that the devastation will probably be severe and consequently you and those who depend upon you will do well to go far away when the alert is sounded.

It is of the greatest importance that you maintain a high degree of discipline of your circuit so that your group should not take action except upon receipt of specific orders to this effect.

We may ask you to be prepared to receive parachutists in small or large numbers. For the reception of a small team, a normal reception will suffice, but for the reception of a large team you must be prepared to hold and defend the ground for a period of 48 hours.

ADMINISTRATION

With the considerable number of airplanes at our disposal, we should have no difficulty in satisfying your needs. You should at all times, as previously indicated, control the number of recruits and also look very carefully at their security.

Your great advantage vis-à-vis you and your men is your technical knowhow, and your knowledge of our directives and our methods.

TARGETS:

The following are the specific targets which were assigned to this circuit:
"Railways: Cutting of the following lines
Cosne - Bonny
Cosne - Clamecy
Cosne - Veaugues
Cosne - Nevers

If you have groups extending west towards the Cher, you should concentrate on the lines which converge toward Bourges, i.e.:
Bourges - Argent
Bourges - Cosne
Bourges - Saincaize

Roads: The following are the principal roads in your region used by German troops with military intentions:
Route Nationale 77, Auxerre - Nevers
Route Nationale 65, Gien - Auxerre
Route Nationale 151, Bourges - Clamecy

"Telephone communications: All underground and overhead telephone cables converging on Cosne."

DEVELOPMENTS:

The following signals communications (coded radio messages) from the field during the quarter under review, and report of Daniel, American member of this circuit, conclude the activities thereof:

16 August: Léon reported that he was in contact with his lieutenant, Daniel, who was as heretofore stated, dispatched to the field on the night of 8 August.

20 August: Léon was prepared to begin guerrilla activities as soon as the necessary messages (authorizing him) were passed.

25 August: Since Cosne has been occupied by the FFI, Léon stated that he was going to carry out his activities south of the Cher, around Sancerre and Bourges. This region had become

quite active but lacked organization. Léon requested the new Sous-Prefet of Cosne to collaborate with him. (**)

27 August: A resistance group guarding the crossroads near Chatillon - Coligny was attacked by American aircraft for a quarter of an hour, in spite of recognition displayed. The result was three vehicles destroyed, two men killed and one man wounded. The same incident occurred six kilometers further north on the same day, 20 August between 1500 and 1600 hours.

26 August: Loincloth, W/T (radio) operator for Léon, reported that 200 German were guarding the bridge route (Road Bridge) over the Loire at La Charité. One thousand Germans coming from the Cher were due to pass over the bridge, but would be ambushed. The bakers of Bourges had received orders to bake 20,000 loaves of bread, and it was evident that about two German divisions would pass through the neighborhood.

29 August: F-Section advised Léon that a Battalion of French Paratroops would arrive shortly in the Cher area with mission of harassing German troops. Léon was instructed to give them all the help possible.

1 September: The bridge at St. Thibault, near Sancerre had been mined and was guarded by the FFI. The possibility of holding the bridges would depend upon the strength of the enemy attack. The road and bridges of Cosne and Charité were strongly held by Germans and an attack on these objectives was impossible without air or artillery support.

2 September: A bridge at Saint Thibault was blown up on 1 September and American reinforcements were awaited in order to attack the Bridge at Charité.

4 September: Two hundred road mines in the region were taken up by prisoners who had not been killed. Paratroops reinforcement was requested, due to the fact that there had been a serious engagement with the enemy at Charenton, between La Charité and Pouilly.

5 September: Léon requested assistance by the Americans in the form of artillery and armor, stating that there was a serious situation at Pouilly.

10 September: Léon's W/T(Radio) operator signaled that they were harassing a column of 5,000 German crossing the Loire at Decize.

14 September: It was confirmed that there were practically no German troops in the department.

This circuit was overrun by the American Army and therefore, the members were ordered to return to London. Daniel, upon his return to London on 4 October 1944, made the following report of his activities while in the field.

** The Sous-préfet must have been Mr. Gadoin the father of Simone.

ACTIVITY REPORT
OF
2nd Lieutenant René J. Défourneaux, AUS (Daniel)
REPORT OF ACTIVITIES:

The flight was uneventful. My landing was perfect, though on poor terrain, approximately ten kilometers from my pinpoint. (Note # 1) Realizing that the reception committee did not know how to use the Eureka properly, I took it upon myself to signal the three other planes that followed (Note # 2). Captain Mike, member of BOA, chief of the reception committee, assisted by his wife, managed all the "parachutages" (drops) in the Yonne region. (Note # 3)

Captain Mike took me to a safe house belonging to a farmer in Lainsecq where I left my money for safekeeping. (Note # 4)

The next day I contacted the chief of the FFI district (Note # 5)and briefly explained the situation to him as he appeared to be totally ignorant of the details of my arrival. Nevertheless he advised me to join Dédé's Maquis and promised to do everything possible to put me in touch with my sector.

Dédé took me to his sector in his car, 20 kilometers from Lainsecq. On our way we met a German patrol. It was a tense moment. After we passed by we breathed a sigh of relief. (Note # 6)

In the Maquis I assumed the role of a "political refugee" awaiting the results of a "political investigation" (Note # 7). I spent my time instructing the officers in the use of weapons that had been sent to them, and having a long conversation with the W/T(Note # 8). I witnessed the torture of a Gestapo woman "Rouquine" (red hair). Plastic was inserted between her toes and set on fire. A complete and hasty confession was the result. She remained silent for three days sitting under a tree, her wounds unattended and infected. Finally an adjutant gave her some blue methylene to ease her pain. The day before leaving the maquis, I dropped some pills unnoticed into her coffee to deaden her pain (Note # 9).

A liaison agent who had worked for the Germans had similar treatment. Another woman who had betrayed some Maquisards was dragged for a mile by the hair and then forced to dig a hole into which she was thrown and covered with earth after having been shot point-blank (Note # 10).

A German prisoner did our cooking; he led a solitary and relatively free life finding this preferable to returning to his unit.

Around 12 other women prisoners were brought to the Maquis. Two of them were intimate with the French officers (Note #11).

I thought very highly of this Maquis (Note # 12). It was a rugged life they led, sleeping in tents and under tarpaulins or rolled up in parachutes. The day's schedule was planned along military lines; reveille at six, then roll call; orderly assignment of guard and fatigue details; formation of armored patrols(Note # 13); retreat at sun-down in the woods.

Still without news from Deux Fouets, chief of the FFI, I decided to make an investigation throughout various sectors of the Nièvre (Note # 14). I made the acquaintance of a sergeant who had belonged to one of these sectors and who explained to me the organization of the district. He immediately sent a liaison agent to Laboué, one of the chiefs of the sector. That same afternoon I was picked up in a car. Laboué's assistant, Mr. Phillipe was in charge. There was a Gestapo agent in the same region named François, who strangely enough answered to my description. Had he not been arrested a few hours before, I would have been in a difficult position as he was to have followed our route.

Mr. Phillipe took me to what he thought to be the Maquis of B sector, the nearest point to Cosne, my rendezvous (Note # 15).

A few Maquisards directed us to the site of the new camp (they had to change location) and a young chap took us there (note # 16). There, a Captain Dubois, who had been anxiously awaiting my arrival, greeted me rather skeptically. Léon, the only one able to identify me, was not there. We arranged a rendezvous, but Léon did not appear. In the meantime I became acquainted with the group. I was especially struck by Lieutenant Norac, a monk of the Pierre-qui-Vire who gave blessing with his right hand while "administrating justice" with the left (Note # 17). A man of remarkable organizing qualities, he and Captain Dubois were an incomparable team.

A second rendezvous, this time successful, was arranged with Léon. I was able by answering his questions satisfactorily to convince him of my identity. I turned over the allotted sum of money to him and was accepted (Note # 18.)

We divided the work. As I had to blow bridges in our sector, I made arrangements, immediately making our four sabotage teams ready, and assigning the work between them.

At that time the most important bridge was on the road leading to our Maquis. As I had never destroyed a bridge before, it was a new experience for me. The one in question, was of free stones, low and very strongly constructed. Examining it, I noticed two cracks (Note # 19). I had 150 pounds of explosive with which I covered the width of the bridge under the keystone(Note # 20). That night, as done in practical exercise, we ignited the charges at 0:15. I was sure that the bridge had been completely destroyed, but the next day when I sent someone to reconnoiter the damages they found that the bridge was still there, but completely disjointed (Note # 21). It was evidently not the right technique to use for that type of stone bridge, I decided to place the explosive in three blocks across the bridge. This method worked very well (Note # 22).

Jean Guyot the chief of the small sabotage group was an escaped POW. He had been living at his farm for ten months without anyone suspecting his presence, except his wife and his servants. He revealed himself only when his wife gave birth to a girl. For ten months he had kept a beard and worn spectacles and no one suspected his identity (Note # 23).

Until 25 August the highways and by-ways were crowded with German convoys ranging from two to 40 trucks in size. Our Maquis was insufficiently armed so our activities were reduced to patrolling the roads in requisitioned vehicles carrying Brens, Stens, rifles and grenades.

One of our fellows met his death during a clash with ten Boche trucks. There were five men in the car, four inside and one on the running board (Note #24). At a curve of the road they came face to face with a German convoy. The first truck let them pass, the second forced them to the side of the road, the third truck pushed them completely into the ditch. Four of the men managed to escape with all their equipment. The fellow on the running board could not get away fast enough. He died after having fired two Sten magazines on the enemy. The Boche bashed his head with rifle-butts and emptied a sub-machine gun magazine into his heart. Captain Dubois and I were 300 meters away from the depot at the time of the attack.

The Boche took away the car (Note # 25), firing with anti-tank guns into the hedges as they went. The boy who gave his life covering the escape of his pals was buried near the Maquis with all the honors due to him. He was Captain Dubois' right-hand man and his death was an irreparable loss.

With Captain Dubois and Lieutenant Norac (Note # 26) my work consisted mainly in organizing safe Maquis upon which we could rely. We had good non-commissioned officers. All that was missing to make our group of 150 men a motorized company was means of transport.

One day Léon ordered me to retrieve all the radio sets parachuted in the region. I took one of the armed cars to go to Entrain to an FFI chief called Belleau. His Maquis was in the neighborhood of Entrain, but I had to find out exactly where they were located. Entrain had been occupied by an FTP group under the command of Doctor "Allen" whose second in command, a common-law criminal called "Tatoué," had a price on his head of 100,000 francs. As Belleau had been condemned to death by these men, they were anxious to do the same to me. Thus for the first time I had to reveal my identity. I had a hard time convincing them that I had nothing to do with their private quarrels. It was also the first time I had become involved with the friction existing among different resistance groups.

The town of Entrain had been occupied by a resistance group without direct orders either from London or from the FFI headquarters of the Nièvre. The French flag had been raised on the belfry of the church and in spite of its situation, on a main road, not one German convoy had gone through the town.

According to information received concerning Dr. Allen, we were on the scent of something significant. Allen had worked with the Germans during the occupation. The population of Entrain feared Tatoué who bullied many of the local young men into joining his group. He was considered by all to be the most dangerous, but I thought Dr. Allen was to be feared much more. Plans were laid to do away with Tatoué when it was discovered that he had the strong support of the FTP group under the command of Roland, who promised to have Tatoué transferred to another group. However Roland did not live up to his promise and Tatoué's reign of terror continued at Entrain.

The FTP officers could not understand why I was supplying arms to the FFI and gave them nothing. The factual policy was that any excess of arms were allotted to reliable FTP (Note # 27) groups after the FFI needs were met. To those FTP officers I suggested that they obtain arms from those who authorized their acts of terrorism.

During the first three weeks I traveled about on bicycle. But as the distance I had to cover became increasingly great, I decided to requisition a car. We found a 1938 Chrysler, with a fine chauffeur named Marcel. I spent my time going to different

Maquis where I instructed the men in the handling of weapons, particularly the bazooka.

A significant incident occurred at the Belleau Maquis which was part of our sector. A group of 40 men was to move to a site some 5 kilometers away. The captain gave them a specific itinerary. For reasons known only to himself the lieutenant in charge did not follow the proposed itinerary, but made one of his own. Three hundred meters away from his destination a German convoy appeared. The Lieutenant quickly ordered his men in position placing the bazooka at a suitable location. The Germans advanced toward the edge of the wood. When they were approximately 160 meters from the bazooka the young Frenchman calmly took aim at the first vehicle, an armored car, and fired. The first shot was a bull's eye. Up to that time he had shot nothing but blanks. This magnificent shot resulted in the capture of 25 prisoners and the death of about 15 enemy soldiers. The following day this young man was mentioned in the order of the day before the assembled company.

Every German convoy in all directions was reported to our headquarters. They no longer knew where to go as every 20 kilometers they met an ambush forcing them to turn back or to change their route. Each time they encountered resistance they suffered losses. For example, a convoy of 20 vehicles had been reported on the embankment of the Loire, traveling in the direction of Auxerre. Three days later the same unit was reported with fewer vehicles. Several days later after covering 200 kilometers. there was practically nothing left of the convoy.

Shortly after having arrived in my sector, I understood what had to be done in spite of the fact that it had not been explained to me. In addition to the destruction of bridges, our objective was to force the withdrawing German units to move through the Morvan instead of through Auxerre. For our purpose the Auxerre route was unsuitable for the following reasons: The Nevers - La Charité - Auxerre highway stretched through flat country, affording no opportunity for ambush. Furthermore, the Maquis of this sector were weak in number. On the other hand, the Maquis in the Morvan district were in full strength, well organized, and a considerable number of SAS were stationed in the area. In addition, the terrain lent itself well to ambush.

Captain Dubois, Léon and I worked out a system of mobile defense aimed at directing the German withdrawal to the east bank of the Loire. To accomplish this purpose we set up the following objectives listed in order of importance:

Detail information on the column movements within and beyond our own sector;

Close liaison between sectors, between districts, between groups;

Rapid and secret execution of movements through "motorizing" our own combat groups;

Liaison between FFI and SAS groups in the region;

Liaison with advance units of the American Army.

On 25 August, the German occupation troops left Cosne where we had established our headquarters. Before leaving they blew up four of the six bridges that we were supposed to destroy - in fact one of them a half an hour before I was to set off the charges. Only three bridges remained on the Loire between Gien and Nevers, one at Briare (canal bridge), another at St. Satur and the third one at La Charité.

Our plan was to force the Germans to withdraw along a certain route which did not include the road over the bridge at St. Satur. We positioned a group of Maquisards armed with a PIAT and three Brens on the east bank of the river. Aided by the contractor who had supervised the construction of the bridge (made of cement) and a saboteur, I gave the order to mine the bridge with 300 lbs. of Composition C explosive making certain that it was well done. The bridge was inspected three times and if deemed necessary changes were made. A guard stood by the fuse day and night with instructions to light it at the slightest indication of an attack.

With a civilian vehicle bearing the tri-colors (French Flag), the Germans did a reconnaissance from the west, the Cher side. Before turning around they threw grenades at the guards killing three of the them.

When I reached the bridge at La Charité, I discovered that the Germans were there ahead of us and they were guarding it vigilantly for they were well aware that it afforded their only remaining passage to the north of the Morvan. They had established a bridgehead on the east side of the river in a radius of ten kilometers. We on the other hand, assisted by the neighboring Maquis, encircled the bridgehead between Pouilly and Mesve. The Germans tried to penetrate our positions. Once, at one in the morning, they succeeded in completely cutting off one of our advance units at Charanton. The only way to dislodge them was to push them back with mortar or machine gun fire. Having neither, Captain Dubois and I drove the 40 kilometers to Briare to awaken the captain commanding a company of the 4th SAS. By four a.m. his mortar group was already in position forcing the Germans back. Of the enemy numbering approximately 2,000, 26 of these were killed. The adjutant in charge of the SAS mortar group was mortally wounded and died the same night singing like a hero.

Thinking they were in combat with advanced units of an Allied armored division, the Germans withdrew. Later I learned that they did not know that we were only 150, ready to hightail at the first counter-attack.

To the east of La Charité, between Clamecy and Vary, Captain Davis ambushed an important convoy. In the process he lost two Jeeps and five of his men were reported missing. Four were quickly discovered, and I sent two men in search of the fifth. I also wanted a report on enemy losses. The results the ambush were unbelievable. Three trucks were burned, 40 enemy dead, perhaps more. Apparently the convoy had turned around and was awaiting reinforcements. Subsequently, to prevent further attack by the resistance, the Germans surrounded their convoy with French civilians from neighboring towns. The next day, not a trace of the Germans nor their remains were to be found. One of my scouts lost his life trying to bring back some very important papers. As for the fifth missing man - we found him and turned him over to his friends.

During this period I maintained a liaison with the American Army through a French officer at Briare. I sent him daily reports on the position of German units and their movements. The situation was becoming increasingly critical. German troops continued to pass through La Charité. Léon requested an RAF bombing raid and Captain Davis sent an identical request to London. For my part I went to see the closest American command and asked for the bombing of this bridge. A colonel, realizing the seriousness of the situation, did because I saw the message he sent asking for a bombardment of the bridge. No reply came. Then I went to see the G-2 of the 6th Armored Division and explained the situation. I hoped that he would order an artillery bombardment in my sector, but nothing happened. Seven days went by - still nothing. Our planes came over, shot up convoys, even shot up our cars so that I had to apologize and make excuses for them to the FFI. The Sancerre group who had two cars destroyed and three of their men killed, while a German column one kilometer away passed untouched, was very unhappy.

Finally the bridge of La Charité was blown up - the Germans themselves destroyed it. German Army troops were followed by groups of SS units. These two elements of the German Army fought each other, the regulars on the east and the SS on the west side of the bridge. This was followed by a temporary disappearance of German troops in our sector. The town of Nevers was liberated and an infantry battalion of the PG (Note # 28) from the Nièvre reoccupied the city. Captain Dubois answerable only to Colonel Roche did maintain his command with limited responsibility.

Next was the story of the 20,000 prisoners. The feat alone seemed extraordinary. Of these 20,000 prisoners, 2,000 escaped to Germany by their own means not wanting to be taken to the U.S or England. Some of these armed escapees on their way to Germany defended themselves, and in the process killed Frenchmen before being caught. Some French people criticized the terms of the surrender which allowed the German prisoners to proceed to the Loire with their weapons. They were hoping to eliminate a few German prisoners before they could reach the POW camps set up by the U.S. Army. On the day of the liberation of La Charité, returning from G-2 of the 6th Armored Division I stopped at Briare at the PC of the FFI. There I was told that they were ready to blow up the canal bridge. I hurried to the bridge and stopped them as they were about to light the fuse. The order written on a piece of paper probably torn out of a note book, with an illegible signature, supposedly had come from General Patton. Based on the existing situation I was aware of the uselessness of this destruction. I gave the order to reset all charges and to double all "cordtex" (Note # 29) lines, instructing them not to blow the bridge before my return. Then I hurried in the direction of St. Satur foreseeing a similar situation there. As I thought, a group of SAS was there with an American captain who had just given the order to destroy the bridge. I asked him how the rest of the SAS were going to return to their base without a bridge to cross the Loire. He replied -by the Briare bridge. If the Briare bridge was also blown up what would they do? He assured me that this bridge would not to be destroyed which reassured me. Then I told him the whole story (Note # 30) which I suspected he only half understood.

The St. Satur bridge was blown up that evening. I was certain, and events proved this to be true, that the destruction of this bridge was the greatest mistake that I observed during my stay in France.(Note # 31)

The Germans had laid mines nearly all along the length of the Loire. Prisoners were used to take them away (Note # 32). In most cases these mines were booby trapped.

When I left Cosne the prisoners were quartered in the prison of the neighborhood (Note # 33).

During my stay in France I also took part in the reception of seven drops.

S/René J. Défourneaux

Comments on the Notes

After reading "my" report, it was impossible for me to accept the document as having been written by me. Some of it was accurate, but the bulk of the report must have originated from someone else. More likely there was a mix up of reports coming from two different perhaps three different sources. Subsequent reports of incidents appear to indicate that in the region there were other agents dropped in the general area. These might not have been under the authority of SOE/OSS, but under the control of the French BOA. The following are my comments related to the above report.

1. When on the night of 8/9 of August 1944 I landed in a field recently covered with sharp posts there was no reception party. I had no idea where I was, I could have been 10 kilometers or 100 kilometers from my destination.

2. About 10 minutes after removing my parachute harness and my jump suit I was initially met by two IndoChinese then taken approximately 250 meters to an individual wearing a Captain's uniform whose name could have been "Michel" hence "Mike" in the report.

3. To my knowledge there was no other plane dropping supplies on that DZ that night. The Mission Reports of the Carpetbaggers indicated that only two aircraft made drops to Licensee on that date, one from Squadron 788, the other from Squadron 36. Unfortunately the coordinates of the drop zones were not indicated on the MRs. I had no idea as to the materiel collected by the group and its disposition. On the morning of August 9th accompanied by the farmer I returned to the drop zone and recovered my two suitcases.

When they first saw me this group, including the captain in charge, was as surprised as I was. The "Eureka" was a relatively new instrument requiring training to operate. I was the only one in our group familiar with this instrument. I am certain that they had no idea as to the utilization of a Eureka nor did they know the name of that instrument, and I doubt if the plane I was on had been equipped with the sister unit called "Rebeka."

If the first French officer I met after landing was in fact Captain Mike I have never met his wife as I didn't know that he was married. If managing parachute drops in the Yonne region was his and his wife's function, he kept it from me. At that time I have no idea as to the meaning of "BOA".

4. I did not leave the money I was carrying at the farm for safe keeping, because for security reasons I did not intend to return to the farm. The funds never left my hands until I turned it over to Léon.

5. The day after my arrival I was moved to a wood where the group was bivouacked. It was the captain who was ignorant of my arrival. He was probably not associated with the FFI and certainly not with BOA. I do not remember "Dédé" and the specific ride to his hideout about 20 kilometers away from the farm where I spent my first night.

6. On my way to meet Léon I do not remember having met a German unit. This is completely unlike my recollection.

7. My assuming the position of a "political refugee" is news to me. Realizing that I was so-to-speak in the "wrong place," I resigned my self as being "lost," but not as a "refugee."

8. I did instruct some of the members of the group in the use of the equipment they had collected, but as they had no radio contact with London, it would have been difficult for me to have a conversation with their radio operator!

9. I did see two women in the maquis' hideout in the woods. I had no idea as to the color of their hair as their heads were shaved. Both had their backs against a large tree and had their hands and feet tied. Both had burn marks on the inside of their bare legs. I saw maggots on one of the women's legs. The only pill I had with me was an L-pill designed to end it all. I doubt if I would have given it to someone else. I had no other pills with me at the time. The two women disappeared before I had left the group. I was told that they had been judged guilty of collaboration, treason, and for these reasons they were executed and buried in unmarked graves nearby.

10. I am not aware of this incident.

11. I do not recall seeing women in the Maquis hideout, nor did I see any sexual activities during my stay.

12. I was not impressed at all with the first group I contacted. They seemed to be doing the very things we were instructed not to do. I could not figure who was in charge. They were very disorganized, and the turnover was constant. I had the feeling that the man in charge was incapable of maintaining a leadership position. They never questioned me about my mission. I kept asking new members if they had seen or heard of a " Léon." The reply was always to the negative until a doctor, who periodically visited our hideout, told me that during a meeting at another district west of ours he had spotted an individual who fitted Léon's description.

13. There was nothing of the sort with that group.

14. Not only I do not recall "Deux Fouets," but I conducted no investigation in the Nièvre because at that time I was in the Yonne area. The sergeant, Laboué, and Mr. Phillipe are unknown to me, nor do I remember the incident mentioned in the report. The story of "François," the Gestapo agent is news to me!

15. I was taken to the Maquis Dubois by the doctor who had made the contact. I did not meet members of Licensee at Cosne because the town was occupied. I met them near a fountain on the square of a small town, perhaps Annay, Entrains, or perhaps another.

16. The meeting had been arranged at a specific spot. We did not have to look for anyone. Léon met me after Captain Dubois and he is the one who locked me up until he was certain of my identity.

17. This remark was made to me by Father Norac when I asked him jokingly if, as a priest, he did not feel bad killing Germans. His reply was: "Not at all, I give them absolution with my right hand and shoot them with the left." I believe that he was joking. He probably told that joke to many others.

18. I gave the money to Léon immediately upon meeting him, before he locked me in the pig pen.

19. The bridge had no cracks. It was in perfect shape.

20. The plastic explosive was held underneath the key stones with the equivalent of two-by-four pieces of lumber supported by other pieces of the same size.

21. According to Captain Dubois the following morning he sent a dispatcher on the road warning him to be careful because there may be a huge hole in the middle of the road. When the dispatcher returned and told us that the bridge was still intact we immediately went to see. I do recall that the morning after the first explosion several of us riding bicycles approached the bridge expecting a huge crater. We were surprised and shocked when we saw a small bump in the center of the bridge, and the trees on either side of the road completely devoid of leaves.

22. It was London who suggested that we pile the explosive on the top of the bridge and cover it with sand bags. It was done with superb results.

23. I do not remember who told me the story of Jean Guyot, actually Jean Guillot. He was a great fellow, probably one of the best resistance leaders in the area.

24. The vehicle in question was a Dodge, and I doubt if it had running boards!

25. The Germans did not take the vehicle. It was retrieved and repaired.

26. The name was Lt. Norac, Real name: Father Caron of the St. Benoît Monastery.

27. This story about Allen and Tatoué does ring a bell, but I have no positive recollection.

28. I have no idea what "PG" stands for! Could be PC *Poste de Commandement,* or command post.

29. Cordtex or possibly Cordex is probably the explosive cord to link charges.

30. He was very skeptical of my involvement, and reported it to the U.S. Command.

31. The local people who were hoping for a new bridge had their wish realized, and in 1988 they, including the architect who designed the new bridge, thanked me for doing the job for them.

32. To expedite the removal of the mines, elements of the local French resistance decided to march German prisoners across the mine field causing casualties and some fatalities. This was contrary to the Geneva Convention, but some of the people I was with didn't give a damn.

33. The prisoners who were in the local jail were also subject to the wrath of some of the members of the resistance who had been objects of the attention of the German occupation forces. Before the liberation of Cosne we were visited by a British officer, Captain Wilson, who had read some of my reports and wanted to see for himself the prison and prisoners' condition. He suggested that it would be wiser if none of the prisoners were allowed to return to Germany.

A copy of this report was forwarded to Vic Calvat and another to Roger Tartrat for their comments.

Comments From France

While I was copying the document at NARA, Brad (Lt. Col. Bradbury) who was also doing research for the Air Force Academy suddenly appeared behind me. I didn't know that he was visiting NARA at this time. He was very much interested in what I had found. I suggested that perhaps the microfilm records had information that could be even more interesting to both of us. I wanted to check on two other SOE/OSS operations for two friends, former OSS agents. The documents related to both operations were listed on microfilm rolls at NARA. And I also wanted to check on Virginia Hall's operation called "HECKLER" which might reveal who was responsible for Léon's transportation to France. Was it the US Army Air Force or the Royal Air Force?

While viewing rolls of microfilm frame after frame, most of them related to the Carpetbaggers' operations, I noticed a document which appeared to be out of place. Brad noticed it also, and when I rolled back the film to that particular frame, I could not believe what we saw. It was the document which had been given to me by the Town Council of Cosne-sur-Loire at the time of its liberation from the German occupation, the same document I had presented to the Mayor's assistant in 1988! (See document, page 66, *The Winking Fox*.)

This particular microfilm roll had nothing to do with me or my operation! What was it doing there? The actual document had been in my possession since September 1944. The two copies that I had made were for my own use. How did NARA obtain this document? And what was it doing in that particular microfilm roll? This is a mystery which will probably never be resolved.

In reply to my request for Kiki's comments concerning my alleged report to SOE, I received the following:

Translation of a report from Roger Tartrat

The files of BOA checked by Michel Pichard indicate five successful operations for the following DZ: Anguille (at Annay), Barbillon (at Arquian) and Rouget (at Entrains) on the following dates: July 24, 1st and 25th of August and 6th and 11th of September but nothing on the 8th of August.

It is noted that "Pain" (Alain de Beaufort, OPS officer on P3 from March to July 44, was arrested on the 27 of July with Jarry the DMR (Rondenay). Thus the BCRA could not logically have records from Pain after mid-July and therefore could not have the results from the moon of August.

On the other hand, the records of the Service Historique de l'Armée (SHA, Historical Service of the French Army) indicate the following dates for the drops on the DZ Anguille, Barbillon and Rouget:

July 24, DZ Anguille, (Annay)

August 6, 8, 11 DZ Anguille, (Annay), August 20, Barbillon (Arquian), September 12, 16, 18, DZ Rouget (Entrains)

In addition one drop August 8 on DZ Montrevillon (Morvan) Source FTP and at Teigny for the Maquis "Le Loup"

My notes:
(That is probably incorrect because on the night of the 8th of August, Dubois and Léon were at DZ Anguille, but I was dropped on the wrong DZ. The Carpetbaggers MR #1513 indicates another operation of the 8th of August also for Licensee, it may have been for the Montrevillon DZ or the Teigny DZ. Unlike the FFI, the FTP, which were under the control of the communists, had no radio communication with London.)

Also on the 8th in the region of Cosne drop of Lt. René Julien Défourneaux (Dairyman) assistant to Lt. Duprés (Source SOE Licencee)

(I did not show up on that date! Léon's report to the French Command states that I joined him on August 10, but his SOE report indicates my joining him was on the 16th of August which is probably correct. Among all the Carpetbagger's mission reports in support of Licensee only one indicates the drop of a "JOE" on the night of 8/9 August 1944. No other Joe was dropped during the entire activity period of Licensee.)

BOA Region P3 Nivernais-Morvan, 1944
DZ: Barbillon 2 km north of Arquian
Utilized By: Capt. Dubois (CO)
Capt. Léon Prevost (SOE)
Lt. Défourneaux (SOE)

For mission "Licensee"
Code letter (D)
On August 8/9 OK
On August 20/21 OK

All confirmed by BCRA
Personal messages:
"Les strophes sont sans fin"
"Il glapi de plaisir à vous entendre"
"La poule couve un asticot"

BOA Region P3 Nivernais-Morvan 1944
DZ Anguille 2 km south of Annay (at Lorien)

DZ selected by Capt. Dubois serviced by BCRA under code designation "Anguille" will be recorded in September 1944 in the same area but never utilized.
Code letter: "L"
24/ 24 July OK
Personal messages: (From BBC)
"Le singe et la giraffe s'emboîtent le pas" (Same as in 1943)

BOA Region P3 Nivernais-Morvan 1944
DZ: Rouget- Glycerine-Trainer 168
Selected in July at 2 and 4 km North of Entrains (At the Castle of Flassy and aux Percherons)

Selected by Capt. Léon of SOE for the Maquis Dubois of OCM and the Maquis of Entrains in support of mission Lisencee (FR Section of SOE)

(Note the misspelling of Licensee)

Code letter: "R"

On September 6/ 7 OK
On September 11/ 12 OK
On September 18/ 19 OK

Personal message:

"Le canard était amoureux"
"François aime chanter"
"La paloma s'écoute"

Kiki's Mission

I met Roger Tartrat (AKA Kiki), former French resistance leader, in 1988 at the reunion of former members of the resistance of the Nièvre at Cosne-sur-Loire. Since then we have been in communication and on several occasions I visited him and his wife Jeanine. I knew that he was doing research on the activities of the French Resistance for the *Amicale des Réseaux Action de la France Combattante* (Association of the Resistance Networks of Fighting France). His research involved the identification and the location of every drop zone used by the Royal Air Force and the U.S. Air Force in support of the Resistance in the Yonne and Nièvre region. It included the drop zones in support of SOE and OSS operations as well as the operation conducted by the French equivalent, the BCRA (Bureau Central de Renseignement et d'Action). His files, meticulously written, were neat and most complete. They included the drop zones of Operation *Licensee* to which I was assigned. However they did not reveal the exact location of the field where I landed in 1944. The people who had been close to the field were not expecting me, thus they did not feel obliged to report the incident. Kiki as well as Capt. Dubois, the chief of the Maquis expecting me, knew that there were several freelance operations in the area, and that people were not always aware as to who was or was not official or recognized by the Allied Forces. Those who managed to acquire supplies destined for other groups did not broadcast their luck for fear that they would have to return their catch to the legitimate customer. For several years while roaming the area where I might have landed, Kiki asked local people if they knew something about a resistance group having rescued an American parachutist, but either people did not know, or did not want to tell. His last report dated June 1998 was disheartening. He suspected that I had dropped in an area close to the town of Clamecy which is not in the department of the Nièvre, but in the adjacent department of Yonne.

In the afternoon of September 24, 1998, I received a telephone call from Kiki. This was most unusual, and by the sound of his voice I knew that he had something important to tell me. He asked:

"René, where did you go after you parachuted on the 9th of August, 1944?"

"I was taken to a farm and was offered a dusty storeroom on the second floor."

"What was in the room?"

"There were a lot items on shelves, and a small metal cot."

"What were you carrying?"

"I was carrying a 32 Colt and a money belt with a quarter million francs in large bills."

Then he explained that at the village of Lainsecq, close to where he suspected I had parachuted, he had asked several people if they had known an American having been rescued in the area. The reply was negative until he mentioned it to an old lady who replied:

"Of course I knew him. I was the one who gave him his first meal, after he landed."

Kiki, never expecting such a reply, was shocked. Incredulous he asked her to describe this "American."

After describing me, she continued telling Kiki about the steel cot, and that it was so small that my feet stuck out in the end. She knew about the money belt, because when the German column passed by the farm, I had hidden it on one of the shelves. She claimed that as I was leaving the farm without it, she ran after me thinking that it was ammunition! Her eyes opened wide when she saw what it was.

"What about the three girls who were in the hallway when I left the store room?"

"They are still at the farm. They remember you. I gave them your address, and they would like to hear from you."

"Who are these people?"

"Her name is Andrée Blondet, she is 92 years old, and is the widow of the farmer who sheltered you when you landed in August 1944. She is sharp as a tack, and has an unbelievable memory. Her husband, who was a member of the resistance and who had breakfast with you the morning you arrived, passed away a few years ago. André Cagnat was the captain whom you met under the oak tree. He died in Indochina in the fifties."

I could not thank Kiki enough for his unbelievable detective work. In addition to the information he obtained, he promised to take photographs of the farm, the room where I spent one night, of the small cot, and of the farmer's wife and daughters.

Although it first appeared that Kiki had hit pay dirt, one thing bothered me. How did she know that my feet were sticking out of the cot? And how did she know I was an American? To my recollection, the woman I met the next morning was never near the room where I was unless as I was sleeping, she could have opened the door and looked in. I was not so sound asleep not to have heard her walking on the creaking floor of the farm. As for me forgetting the money, and leaving the farm without it, that is very unlikely because the delivery of the money was the most important part of my mission. From my accent she might have thought that I came from another region of France, but she could not have known that I was American, as I most certainly did not tell anyone who I really was. I stuck to my cover story and mistrusted all those I did not know, even Léon who was not aware of my nationality until we parted company.

Kiki's next move will be his search for the field where I landed to determine if the sharp poles were still there. If these had not been placed by the Germans, the local people must have done it.

As soon as Kiki hung up I went to my computer and wrote a letter to Madame Blondet whose address Kiki had given me. I also sent a copy of *The Winking Fox,* dedicated to her for her courage and determination. In retrospect, I should not have because there were too many facts revealed about my adventures of that period.

Translation of a letter sent to Madame André Blondet

24 September 1998

Dear Mrs. Blondet:

What a surprise! When Kiki (Roger Tartrat) called me yesterday announcing that, not only had he discovered the farm, but also the individual who had sheltered me on the night of 8/ 9 August 1944 when I arrived in the middle of France, I could hardly believe him.

For the last ten years I have been searching for the area where I was mistakenly dropped by the American Air Force, unfortunately without success. Thanks to Kiki who found you I hope to have the pleasure of meeting you, to kiss you and together share our memories.

Since our short meeting much water has flown under the bridges. While you have never left your country, mine during twenty-two years had moved me from one end of the world to the other. Finally I ended up in Indianapolis where I now reside with Ginny, my spouse since 1963, and where we raised four boys and two girls.

To give you an idea of my adventures, by surface mail, I am sending you the book that I have recently published. If you cannot read the text the pictures will probably be of interest to you.

We expect to come to France next spring. I will not fail to visit you. However, I would prefer a bed other than the one you offered me in 1944!

Most affectionately,

S/ René J. Défourneaux
Major, U.S. Army (Ret.)

Shortly thereafter I received the following letter;

Translation of the first letter received from Mrs. Andrée Blondet

Le Jarloy, September 25th 1998

Dear Friend:

For me you are a friend of long ago. I remember well the night when Mick, Bieler and Cacane brought you to our home. The night was dark. That evening my husband had gone to a parachute drop of containers, those which included you. I learn from him that you almost fell in the fish pond of the Bauvais Castle. It occurred in an uncultivated field perhaps plowed. Perhaps there were pickets and wire to keep the sheep from wandering in the park. The son of the farmer is still alive, and perhaps he will know where you landed. In those days we were not talkative; all clandestine actions were conducted quietly. We were at the mercy of traitors. I do not recall the date of your arrival. I must have written it on a note book later on, and it was probably taken by my children. Our last daughter was born on Christmas day 1940.

Your friend Kiki was informed by a former member of the Maquis DÉDÉ whom I never had the occasion to meet. There are no longer veterans of the Maquis in the region. My husband was 72 when he died of coronary failure following an operation on January 24, 1977.

Alone but with my children, I am delighted to know that you have returned safely to the United States and that you are in good health.

I believed that you had learned French and that you were older. At that time your parents were still alive. Perhaps the fact that you parachuted in the wrong place saved your life. General Patton's army was decimated in Normandy. On your way over, I believe that you had flown over burning towns. You cannot imagine the surprising happiness your friend had produced for my entire family and to me. I believe that if my legs had been more nimble I would have jumped with joy.

I would be very happy to see you. I remember the tall soldier that you were, but not your face because you were with us for such a short time.

I send my best remembrance and perhaps I shall see you soon.

Your friend who hopes to meet you again.

S/ Andrée Blondet

This was difficult for me to believe that a 92-year-old woman could write such an interesting letter even before she received mine. Yet I began to have slight doubts concerning her recollection.

I do not remember three men escorting me to the farm. Only one individual guided me to it.

I do not remember dropping near a pond, nor close to a castle.

She did not actually remember the date I landed near her farm,

She believed that I had learned French, and that I was older. As a native of France having left the country only four years earlier, I handled the French language with more ease than English which I had only recently learned.

She also believed that I had flown over burning towns. This fact was only revealed in my book, and I have never told anyone. Also she did not mention that before leaving the farm her "husband" and I went to look for my two suitcases.

Then on the 2nd of November, 1998, I received her reply to my letter.

Translation from a letter from Mrs. Andrée Blondet

Le Jarloy 19 October 1998

Dear Sir and Friend,

I received your letter following the visit of our friend Kiki. I well remember your arrival during a night of August 1944. At that time practically every day my husband went with a horse and a cart to the parachute landings, but these were only for arms and supplies. We put up young people and fed them with our own products never asking their name nor where they were coming from or going to. If we were captured, even tortured, we would not have been able to say anything. There is a resident of the Beauvais farm who knows that you fell on the posts of a vineyard near a large oak. The area is well known, but the oak tree or the vineyard no longer exist.

The maquis of Dédé was located in the woods of Saint-Sauveur near the farm of Des Vernes. Since those days two families have succeeded each other. The day you parachuted my husband must not have seen you as he did not participate at your reception. I believe that he had arrived after you came and that I was alone, and our children were in bed. I bedded you on a cot too small. I gave you some kind of cover, you were very calm. We kept French agents during the entire month of August. It was on the 24th of August that the hitlerites (Germans) passed by and executed two young men they found in a barn. There was no other execution because a German soldier who was prisoner came out and said to the chief, that according to the Geneva Convention he did not have the right of killing those that helped the wounded. He left with them. There was another who hid in a barrel and remained at Clamecy. He was a musician, an organist at the cathedral of Koln.

I still remember the shape of your face, you are the one on the right in the picture. In him I see the young man that I received. Tomorrow my older son and his wife will come. He does not remember you, but my third son has maintained a souvenir of a tall soldier impressive by his height, and my entire family will be very happy to see you again.

I hope that my letter will find you as well as your family in good health.

I have not yet received your book. My little one will translate it because she has been in England and speaks English fluently.

I send you my best wishes.

S/Andrée Blondet

Her second letter caused me to question her account even more .

At the spot where I landed there were no visible means of transportation. There might have been, but I did not see it.

I did not see my host until the morning. The individual who escorted me to the farm knew his way around and he probably had placed others where he guided me.

If according to my report I had been picked up by "Dédé" I would have been 20 km from the farm of Le Jarloy!

Apparently several agents had been at the farm during August 44. It is conceivable and probably very likely that Madame Blondet is confusing me with someone else.

Why did Madame Blondet remembers certain facts precisely while others related to me are so vague?

Late November I received another letter from Madame Andrée Blondet. She describes in greater details her recollection of the night of 8/9 August 1944.

Translation of Madame Blondet's third letter

Le Jarloy, November 17, 1998

Dear Sir and friend:

I received your book and my granddaughter has translated the first part when you arrived on the night of 8th to the 9th of August 1944. You were carrying a great amount of money in a cartridge pouch; 30,000 bills of 20 francs bearing the effigy of Voltaire. I hid it for you in a neighbor's home in some linen to be repaired. There I also hid members of the resistance as well as parachutists from whom I never heard again.

In the book called The History of the Resistance it is written that on the 8th of August two individuals were arrested and taken to the Maquis of Boutissaint. They were accused of having informed on the resistance. Doctor Fayen was a member of the group who at Clange (Saint), captured a truckload of dead sheep and flour sacs destined to the black market. They drove it to the forest of Rousseau for the Maquis.

Your friend Kiki has a better book than mine in which your arrival must be included. The book that I have The Cross of St. Andrew, was written by the same author, Robert Bailly, and was edited by ANACR-Yonne.

You must have been shocked at the sight of these burned women even with cigarette butts. Here, after shaving her head, they sat a woman on an ant hill. She was accused of having relations with the Germans. A man was executed by a firing squad because the postman at Auxerre intercepted his letter in which he denounced all those on the main street including us.

A local woman, a butcher who entertained Germans at her table at Brienon, was executed in her kitchen because some people of Brienon had been arrested, tortured and executed. Her family no longer lives there.

I do not remember hearing comments about the women you have seen. I must check with André Robert of Saint-Sauveur! He was at the Maquis of Boutissaint.

The members of the resistance arrested were tortured, beaten with cut timber, killed or sent to concentration camps from which they never returned. That is why these women were maltreated and shot. In those days it was horrible.

Dear Sir I send you my sincere friendship

S/A. Blondet

Note: I was carrying a money belt not a cartridge pouch, and the bills were more than 20 francs. The total amount was greater than 30,000 francs. The money belt never left my sight. I did not know these people and had no reason to trust them with anything. She claims to have housed other individuals, and was involved with a neighbor. She was probably confusing me with someone else. On the morning of the 9th of August I only met a man and a woman, and was taken immediately to a maquis in a nearby forest by a third party.

Then shortly before Christmas 1998, I received another letter from Madame Blondet.

Fourth letter of Madame Andrée Blondet

Le Jarloy December 18th 1998

Dear Sir:

I have received your year-end letter and have had the visit of "Zidore" the maquisard who received you when you landed in the thorn bush at Beauvais.

Yves Pasquier who resides at Cosnes close to Kiki told me that he pinned a badge on your tie. He asked me to tell you that you should come next May to participate at the reunion of the regional Maquisards who had known you.

My husband did not participate at your drop. We learned that all the drop zones were surrounded by the Germans stationed at Taingy on the high ground overlooking Beauvais. They were under the command of a Polish officer who let them do anything they wished without intervening. No doubt they were those who have passed by after your arrival. A Frenchman wrote a book about an English soldier ejected from a plane shot down. There were seven aboard. He entered the home of an old couple who never locked their door. The maquis came to pick him up. I went to see the lady who did not know what happened to the man once he was taken by the Maquis. I gave you coffee perhaps with milk. I thought that it might have been malt, barley or wheat roasted which gave it a cookie flavor. I fed you the evening you arrived? I did not have much, but I always had ham and eggs, or I made some crepes.

"Zidore" thinks that he knows what happened to doctor Fayen. I will see him again.

Mr. and Mrs. Tartrat sent their wishes hoping that we shall be reunited in May with the local Maquisards.

I send you my best feelings of friendship.

S/ A. Blondet.

Note: I have never heard of Zidore but Pasquier was not entirely unfamiliar to me. Yet I do not remember anyone pinning a badge on my tie.

After this series of correspondence from Madame Blondet I began to have strong feelings that what she was describing was not exactly as I remembered. I was certain that once I visited the area I would be able to judge if her recollection was accurate or imagined or perhaps secondhand!

Searching for the First Tracks

After our last trip to France in 1996 I was so busy with my book, that I did not plan to go back to France for three years. By 1999 so many things had happened since our last trip that I felt that we might as well go to Europe while we can still walk and drive a car.

We had toyed with the idea of taking one of our grandchildren with us, and when our daughter Noëlle inquired about the possibility of taking her son with us, we immediately agreed.

On June 26, 1999 Ginny and I left Indianapolis and flew to Boston to pick up Brecht 15, the oldest of Noëlle's children. Together we settled aboard a British Airways 747 whose attendants treated us royally.

For Brecht this was his first travel aboard a wide-body aircraft and it was his first trip to Europe. Laura Golmar, one of our stewardesses must have mentioned it to the captain because he invited all three of us to his command post, a rare occurrence nowadays! The cockpit of the aircraft has more lights than a Christmas tree. I signed one of my books and gave it to the captain who seemed quite surprised, but very happy to get it. This was certainly a thrill for Brecht who will not forget this trip for a long time.

We landed at Orly where we picked up a Peugeot 306 and drove to our first stop Saint Cyr-Ecole located on the outskirts of Paris near Versailles. St.Cyr-Ecole has a military school called St. Cyr, the equivalent of our military school of West Point, but its campus does not compare. It is relatively small, and looks more like an industrial plant than a military university.

A four-day tour of Paris including the Eiffel Tower - my first time, would you believe it -the Seine by bateau mouche, Notre Dame, the Louvre and the Arc of Triumph was most enjoyable for us, but especially for Brecht. In the Place de l'Etoile, inscribed on the northwest leg of the Arc of Triumph I pointed out to Brecht a list of names. These were Napoleon's army generals, and the first name on the list was that of General Desfourneaux one of my ancestors. As I was explaining this to Brecht two American tourists were listening. Both husband and wife were school teachers much interested in French history. They wanted to know how I knew what I was telling Brecht. At first they thought that I was joking, but after showing them my passport, they were quite impressed.

Before offering us a great dinner, my cousin, retired General Marc Défourneaux who resides close to Versailles, took us on a guided tour of the park of the castle, and the following day Brecht and I returned alone to the castle to see how the French kings used to live.

From Saint-Cyr-Ecole we drove to my home town of Delle stopping at Baccarat to admire the crystals, and the church with windows rebuilt with American dollars as war reparation, and to Eguisheim to pick up a couple of cases of good Alsatian wine to share with our cousins.

We stayed in the very comfortable home of Michel and Lucienne Eglin, two of my many cousins, and from there we went to Switzerland where I spent most of my youth. Brecht was fortunate and impressed to see the homes of his great-great-great-grandfather, his great-great-grand-father, his great-grandfather and where his grandfather was born. The homes of four generations on mother's side. The home of my grandfather was so small it is difficult to imagine how they could have raised fifteen children in such a small space!

Four days later, after visiting relatives both in France and in Switzerland, we were on our way to St. Germain Laval on the upper Loire region by way of Montrachet in Burgundy to attend a ceremony honoring the crew of an Air Force B-24 that had crashed in the town of Mably. Vic Calvat and his spouse Jacqueline met us at the Hotel des Tourists at St.Germain-Laval. To get together with old friends and to discover new ones was delightful.

I had no idea as to the kind of ceremony I was to attend as the representative of the Carpetbaggers honoring the crew of a US Army Air Corps B-24 which had crashed in the area, but neither did the organizer! If he had, he most certainly did not tell me which placed me in a very awkward position. I decided not to worry about and play it by ear. Because she did not understand what was going on, Ginny, my dear spouse who did not speak or understand much French, was convinced that I was holding something from her. At 10:00 am on the 4th of July,1999, the day of the ceremony, following the car of one of the participants, we reached the Mably's town hall where many people were already assembling. We learned that it was not where the ceremony was to be held! So, after a while, back in our car, we joined a convoy of vehicles and left town for the countryside. Several miles away, following a dirt road, we reached a field where a French flag was draped over a flat panel. Several people were already there, and approximately a dozen were carrying French flags and a single American flag. Ginny had the presence of mind to bring a small American flag in case there was none to honor this unfortunate American crew!

I was waiting for the start of the ceremony when the organizer, Joseph Tournaire, said to me: "Now it is time for you to begin the program." What was I supposed to do? "You and the Mayor's representative will remove the flag while we pay our respects." "Where is the Mayor's representative?" "Ho! sorry we forgot to introduce you to Mr. Solnon!"

Mr. Solnon, who was used to their way of doing things, did not appeared perturbed. We shook hands and together we proceeded to the fence to remove the French flag draped over a plaque posted on the edge of a field. I had trouble removing my side of the flag so Mr. Solnon helped. It was a short observance and after a while we were told to return to the town hall of Mably. When we arrived, the *salle des fêtes* (social hall), located in a building across the park from the town hall, was already filled with guests. On long tables were plates of snacks and bottles of wine were lined up. After everyone settled down Mr. Solnon made a few remarks followed by Serge Blandin who was the representative of the Carpetbaggers in France; also Joseph Tournaire the organizer of the memorial. When it appeared to be the end of the official part of the ceremony, I decided that I did not come all way from the U.S.A. without telling these good people why I came. Thus I took the microphone and spoke in glowing terms about those brave airmen who dropped me behind the German lines in 1944.

We left the following morning on the direction of Nevers, a town which had remarkably sinister memories for Vic. Since the end of WWII, Nevers has seen many changes. When we reached the city Vic could not find the building where the HQ of the local resistance had been located. The local gendarmerie (police station) was no help either. The policemen at the station were not even born when the Germans were the masters of the town. Their knowledge of the city's history was from vague to non-existent. However, they were very familiar with one building, the jail! The same jail where Vic had spent months because of trumped up accusations against him.

The prison at Nevers

Marker on the prison wall at Nevers
Translation:
From 1940 to 1944 more than 1715 patriots
were incarcerated in this prison,
36 left it for the firing squad,
413 for Nazi concentration camps.
Passer-by remember

Vic Calvat AKA Captain Dubois

Who ate the fourth pork chop?
or
The recruitment of Vic Calvat

It took a while for me to find out who was really Vic Calvat the famous Captain Dubois. I knew that he had been a captain in the French army and that his rank was not fictitious as in the case of many other resistance fighters. Prior and during the war he, his wife Eliane, and their daughter Nicole resided in Paris. Having been discharged after the French capitulation his main concern was the survival of his family. In those days food in Paris was very scarce and in June 1940 when he was offered the job as a caretaker of his cousin's castle and property, he immediately accepted and moved his family to the town of La Celle-sur-Loire in the Department of Nièvre.

Even though throughout France there was a general shortage of food, his new situation was an improvement over that of Paris. The German occupation forces had established a system of rationing, until then unknown to the French people. However, in true Gallic manner they accepted it, and violated it just as readily.

The fish ponds located in the property Vic controlled attracted local people who wanted to better their diet. One day the foreman of a small nearby factory making rubber products came to his door to ask for Vic's authorization to fish in one of the ponds. Vic knew that the factory made rubber bicycle accessories under the trade mark "Remember." His own bicycle, his only means of transportation, had long been without tires and was in sad need of parts and repairs. But in those days rubber was no longer available, and only a few tires were made and sold under the counter to the privileged. Vic immediately recognized his luck and invited the man to fish in the ponds, asking him if by chance he could provide him tires for his bicycle. The man replied that Paul Fougerat, the son of his employer, was a school friend of his, and that he would be happy to meet Vic as he and his wife were about the same age and both were very friendly. Things occurred as anticipated and according to Vic the man was worth one hundred fishing permits.

Thus Vic met Paul and after a quick aperitif served by his charming spouse, Yvonne, and with enough "rubber" for his wheels, he left with a luncheon invitation for the following Sunday.

It was at that Sunday luncheon that Vic met Jean Guillot and his wife Eugenie, owners of a farm close by, both Paul's childhood friends. While Paul was a fine delicate intellectual Jean was a tall rough, down-to-earth individual speaking mostly in the local dialect. While he was intelligent, and sure of himself, nothing scared him. He spent part of his military service in Morocco where he learned a few farming tricks which mystified his neighbors. In the region he enjoyed a certain prestige, and as an escaped German prisoner, although he was observed everywhere, no one dared to report him to the authorities.

From that day on a strong bond unites these three families and periodically they meet for meals and to exchange information and gossip about the people of the region. Very quickly Vic had become a respected member of the community.

As it were one morning, the three friends found themselves in the meadows of the castle each having brought what was necessary for a picnic which was their main preoccupation. Paul was struggling with a basket full of wine bottles and a pot full of pottage prepared by Yvonne. Vic was responsible for the homemade bread with flour from Jean's wheat fields. Jean brought a flask of homemade alcohol, some farm cheese and superb thick pork chops to satisfy heavy laborers: four pork chops!

Their fishing net in place, their lines in the water, they occupied themselves with the preparation of the food.

After a little fishing and much eating and drinking, during which Vic and Jean shared the fourth pork chop, Jean suggested that he and Vic row their boat to the middle of the pond where the fish would surely be more abundant while Paul, his eyes closed, was snoozing, his head resting on a rock.

"I noticed that you do not like to see the Boches in our community?" said Jean casually while looking at his bobber floating quietly on the surface. "Can we do something to chase them?"

"Yes when the time comes if we are needed" Vic replied.

"Should we be preparing for it now?" continued Jean.

"Certainly, but prudently," suggested Vic.

"Well, let me tell you. With some trustworthy fellows I have hidden the war material abandoned after the retreat. You are an officer. You could help us maintain this equipment and teach us how to use it?"

Jean then explained to Vic that he was involved with a non-political full military net, then added "Above all, this must stay between us, nothing said to the wives."

. Vic, who had basically the same idea but did not express it to others for fear of provocation, immediately agreed. Subsequently he discovered that Paul had been part of the group from the very beginning, but in the event he had refused for security reasons, he did not participate in Vic's recruitment.

On the way back to their respective homes, on a narrow path they met a person whose reputation as a drinker gave him the nick name of "Boit tout" (drinks anything) carrying under his chin a small barrel full of home made booze. Incapable of resisting his offer all tested the content of his barrel. Jean and Vic were able to return home via the fields, but Paul's unsteady condition on his bicycle was not ignored by his neighbors including his wife Yvonne who at their next gathering mentioned it to the group. But it was suspicious Eugenie, Jean's spouse who asked the most pressing question. Who was the fourth individual who had consumed the fourth pork chop? In unison all three wives repeat the same question: "Who ate the fourth pork chop?" The men were stupefied! Majestically, Jean confronted the three women: "That is a secret."

Yes, they had a secret, but not the one that intrigued the women. Later on, with the help of the wives who were brought in the plot, Jean's farm became the base of the organization controlling the maquis of the northern part of the Nièvre, where the first radio communications with London were established, where parachute drops were received, and where asylum was given to those involved in clandestine activities. Jean and Eugenie fed them and hid their equipment, and from his cellar after a few glasses of the red wine, Jean directed his group in nightly sabotage.

I was not aware of this until one morning, after spending a night on top of Jean's hayloft I was awakened by Eugenie holding the sharp point of her pitch fork on my throat. We became close friends, and Jean was no doubt the best Maquisard of our group.

When I left Vic Calvat in October 1944, I was not aware of his problem with the local command of the FFI/FTP. I knew that Léon was bitterly anti-communist, but only later was I told of his death. Shortly before I left him he asked me an unusual question. He said:

"If the British Intelligence Service ask you to work for them, would you?"

This was an unexpected question, and probably because I was never asked, this proposition had never entered my mind. As an American officer I had been transferred to the British Army and was under the command of a British officer, but no one had suggested my employment after the war was over. Then I said:

"Did they ask you?" He did not reply. I continued.

" If they would ask me, I suppose I could get away with it, but you better be careful. The French services are not easily fooled; they play for keeps."

I am not certain that he took my advice, but sometime later I learned that Léon had died in a car accident. I felt that perhaps the French had discovered his new allegiance and did away with him. Until I met Vic Calvat I was certain that Léon had been assassinated. Now I am not so sure.

Vic's story was so compelling that I imposed upon him to write it for inclusion in this book of research.

The Trials and Tribulations of Captain Dubois

At All Risks. Without Assurances
By Vic Calvat AKA Captain Dubois

As the Crow of Lafontaine

Why did I accept the job that I was offered? I, who up to that time was so self-possessed. My job was to gather information about the enemy and to instruct young folks who wanted to fight the invaders, when the time came. As the steward of an estate, it was a comfortable cover given to me by my cousin Pasquet! Thus I had the time to circulate throughout the region seeking useful information, collecting weapons and ammunition abandoned by soldiers during the disengagement of June 1940.

Under the circumstances, what is it to fear when protected by Jean Guillot? His neighboring farm had been transformed into a logistic retreat protected by a devoted, well-compartmentalized group, dominated by his exceptional personality.

That is why, proud to have a rare bird within his group, Jean recommended me to one of his friends who introduced me to a sad-looking young man who, assuming a mysterious appearance of someone who knew much, initially had said very little. Eventually he informed me that the FFI Headquarters of the Nièvre had charged him with the recruitment of individuals who would dare take over the command of the resistance groups located in the northern part of the department of the Nièvre. How many rejections had he received before trapping a stranger such as I, and in the process eradicated his discreet cover! Not many candidates solicited for the position were available! This was easily understood because, in the past, all those who had ventured into this situation had landed in prisons, had been tortured, or had faced the firing squad of Nevers for an early morning execution. The most experienced members of the local underground had been denounced. Rumors that the area was rotten to the core had reached my ears.

Consequently, it was the skill of my visitor to convince me that only incompetence and imprudence had taken these unfortunates to their doomed destination.

"But you, as an officer, you are not subject to that kind of blunder. Unknown to all in the area it will be easy for you to avoid the traps of the Nazi services." Then he added :

"It is time for a specialist such as you to take over and relieve the amateurs who up to now had volunteered."

Nonetheless my fears did not vanish. Quietly in a calm voice the clever young man convinced me that my legitimate anguish was proof that prudence would inspire the effectiveness of my actions.

"In any case, you are the only officer in the region capable of assuming this position. You will never forgive yourself if you do not accept it. So many have successfully faced the dangers of clandestine activities."

"Chante canari" (canary sing) is a local saying. I believe that flattery would not affect me. Vanity, this insidious vice, lowered my guard. The refusal that I presented to the recruiter was not explicit enough. He left me flashing a small, falsely-grieved smile. The clever fox was certain that he had earned his cheese. He understood that the pretext of consulting my spouse before making such a grave decision was ridiculous and that I was already in the kneading trough rolling into the flour.

For a long time I forgave myself with the excuse of having fallen in the net of a graduate psychologist, and it was probably not the first case of this skillful officer in the service of subversion. To my thorough disappointment I soon discovered that actually it had been a unique mission assigned to a modest corporal of the Headquarters Records Section.

Better Than the Ostrich

Thus, on my way to Nevers, 50 km away, I took the train at Cosne to meet the commanding officer of the FFI in the department of the Nièvre. I was accompanied by an unknown individual furnished by the Nevers HQ. His bogus name was Alfred. He bragged that he had recently managed to escape from the last Gestapo round up, but his own boss had not been as lucky. Having been involved with the resistance for a long time he knew practically everyone in the local Maquis. He was taking me to this mysterious high ranking officer who had a tremendous responsibility in the conduct of the Secret Army.

I imagined him hiding in a discreet lair, difficult to reach, well protected with a camouflaged entrance. I visualized him writing his coded orders under the dim glare of a small discreet lamp. He must be a cool individual with the expression of a warrior, his facial traits brutal as if cut with an ax, his voice brusque, his glance forthright and inquisitive.

These mental aberrations of my imagination were responsible for my first surprise. Without a single misleading detour, Alfred guided me to a public park in the center of the city. German soldiers were everywhere. Others not in uniforms, but having a certain military bearing, appeared more observing. Ignoring their presence, a huge man framed by two average individuals was walking slowly in the central lane of the park. While strolling slowly he spoke with a fourth individual of average age who, despite his civilian attires, looked very military. Walking backward in front of the fat man he appeared listening. After a brief exchange the average man discreetly disappeared.

That was the moment my escort was waiting for. He pushed me toward the trio. The massive person in the center accepted my presentation without stopping. High on his puffy face his small shifty eyes seemed to ignore me. In a few steps I learned that he was Commandant Moreau, who had been given the command of the FFI units of the Nièvre by General Koenig. Thus our group was a section of a military organization placed above the various political nets of the region.

Then, not certain that he was addressing me, he said:

"You will be in charge of the Northern Zone. Take command of all the ill-assorted groups, even the small FTP (Communist) groups. All are in disarray, and are waiting for you. Alfred who knows them all will guide you. Meet me in one hour on the Loire bridge. You are brave to accept this difficult mission. If you do not mind you will be identified as Dubois, thus I will not have to redo the dossier that I had prepared for Colonel Dufrene who prefers another position." (Wise fellow! my comment.)

Thus my pseudonym who did not have the same initial as my real name - as it was the common practice - was to mislead the bloodhounds the Gestapo would send after me!

I was flabbergasted and ill at ease. Having used innumerable stratagems, deception, and discretion to be invisible, was I now dealing with a senseless individual, or was I witnessing a subtle scheme? However, this was not the end of my surprise. As agreed, one hour later I found my new boss on the quay of the Loire.

Surrounded by approximately twenty individuals without apparent precautions, in a loud voice he described to us the customary way to communicate with him according to necessities. Oh! the good Germans!

"Soon," he continued, " they will no longer see us as terrorists. Thus when captured there will be no summary executions. We will be treated as prisoners of war protected by the Geneva Convention. To take advantage of this, every Maquisards will wear an arm band bearing the letters FFI. Here is a sample for each one of you."

And to top this foolishness, we were to pocket a clealy written copy of our instructions to pass on to our groups!

If stopped here by the Gestapo and searched, how can we justify the contents of our pockets? Faced with such beatitude and absurdity caused in me an anxiety of panic proportion. Hurriedly I reached the railroad station, a storm raging in my stomach. I crashed into the toilets of the first bistro. A mice pursued by a cat could not have gone faster. Quickly disposing the compromising material, my pocket emptied, my heart having returned to its normal rhythm, I boarded the train, refreshed by this timely escape from a stupid and risky plan. I did not intend playing the resistance game the way these crazy people did. Taking advantage of the distance between Cosne and Nevers, I decided to conduct my affairs in my zone according to my usual way.

A Trail Paved With Broken Eggs

Circling around Cosne, the indispensable Alfred took me from group to group. Where was I to settle down? These groups had been constituted under the banner of various nets. The disastrous campaigns of previous months had cut them off from their bases of operation. Their components were disoriented, and for many, they were placed on inactive status. It seemed that I came just in time as the safety rope for which they had prayed.

But of course each wanted to remain faithful to his own persuasion while accepting the advantages of a strictly unified military organization that de Gaulle desired, and that I represented. In fact the socio-masonic obedience of Nevers had suffered very little from the activities of the Gestapo. It took advantage of the situation to take over several battered groups. Commandant Moreau, a regular army officer on inactive status, was placed in charge of the operation.

In my sector I had the tough job of bringing all these people together. Because I did not belong to a specific group and could not produce reassuring references, I was often received with suspicion. As for Alfred, he was differently appreciated because of his participation in past incidents of which I was not aware. So many discussions, so many glasses raised higher and higher so as to be accepted. It was a success when I was told:

"OK to follow your instructions provided the team of Paul not be included. They stink!"

That is then that I earned my rank as a diplomat and tested the tolerance of my liver, because in France, in our countryside, one must not ignore the virtue of a "Goutte" (small glass of alcohol). A glass filled several times and emptied with small appreciative swigs in the discreet shadow of a basement resulted in the acceptance by the most suspicious maquisard. I believed that the best asset for a candidate prior to elections is his capacity for alcohol.

During the first phase of my mission, risks were minimal and all those to whom I revealed my interest appeared to be OK. However I learned later that, during my visit to a small maquis well hidden in a deep forest, it was the result of one vote of confidence that allowed me to depart alive.

A failure was to affect the final outcome of the episode. This small FTP group so-called "Disoriented" by Moreau was in fact the personal guard of an important communist leader, a teacher in a village near Cosne. The drink he offered me was not in friendship. As always with these kind of people no personal exchange would sway their position. All arguments landed on robots which repeated the same slogans imposed by the party:

"We are the only one resisting, the only one fighting. Our organization does not need you."

They insisted a little. They felt a need to redeem themselves, particularly those who before June 1941 had helped the Nazis', their pretended anti-capitalist brothers, to conquer France's middle class! I left the communist leader and his scornful attitude, yet he did not betray me.

On my second visit to those who had accepted my proposition, they were waiting for me, their lifeline, as if I were Santa Clause, one stocking for the weapons, the other for supplies. Unfortunately my bag was full of hot air:

" Have a little patience; the organization is on course," I told them.

Drinks are no longer offered! A clandestine individual deceived quickly becomes restless, ready to eliminate the perceived danger. I felt ill at ease during the subsequent meetings. It was a risk I did not anticipate, but I understood their concern. The recuperated rifles to be used in small acts of sabotage were fine, but the Maquisard who left his job and was in hiding had to feed his family.

Warned of the consequences, Commandant Moreau, himself lacking the means, suggested that I "requisition" funds from public coffers (Post Offices and Tax offices). These operations disclosed a modest success. Unfortunately, the distribution of the confiscated funds became a source of jealousy within the groups. Many believed that they were not given their fair share, and I suffered their resentments.

When One Wants To Kill His Dog

As I had feared a tragedy occurred. An operation poorly conducted against the Revenue Office of Cosne resulted in the elimination of the group that had taken the initiative. Even though I had nothing to do with the affair, it was said that I gave the operation very little chance of success. The situation was intolerable, but what was I to do?

One of our best men was executed before I was able to intervene. Then a bicycle breakdown delayed my arrival at a rendezvous which allowed a German patrol to arrest one of my contacts. Could it be me who arranged for this trap? Suspicion increases, and if one listens carefully, he will hear that a fellow named "Dubois" has betrayed members of the resistance to the Gestapo. Of course this fellow's real name was "Dubois" while mine was a name given to me by Commandant Moreau.

What a great opportunity for those I restrain to link me to this individual. Thus one afternoon, a group of my men with somber faces came to my room where I laid in bed with a reoccurring bout of malaria. They had already decided on my execution. In view of my calmness, one of them fiercely opposed my immediate elimination. Eventually they agreed to leave, but "only to debate the method," they said without conviction.

Every Man to Himself

Thus my hiding place in the castle grounds of my cousin was brought to light. With my family I had to hide in a small hut that always-far-sighted Jean Guillot had set up. Ah! If I had imagined that in addition to the Germans I was obliged to protect myself from my own Maquisards! My mission was becoming impossible.

Despite my distaste for this kind of meeting, I went to confront Commandant Moreau, still the park surveyor.

"Without the weapons I have hoped in vain to obtain, I cannot assure either my authority nor my security," I told him. "Herewith I return my apron." (Give my resignation.)

He replied: "Indicate a field and everything you need will be parachuted."

Almost reassured I was on my way back when Capt. Egelee, Moreau's assistant, caught up with me. His father, the railroad station master of Cosne, was my friend. Was it for this reason that he sympathized with me? He wanted to tell me something personal.

"I understand the difficulties of your position. In all confidence I must warn you that the position of the Commandant is not secure. In fact in no way can he supply weapons for your needs, neither for his own. His promise of help is to make you be patient."

Well, right then I ran out of patience. I no longer wanted to risk my life and that of my family under these conditions.

When Salvation Comes From Heaven

I was about to announce my resignation when a liaison agent informed me that a British officer who parachuted in the Cher region was looking for me. I met him at the home of retired Colonel Vaissereau who was helping the resistance as best as he could.

The man whose pseudonym was Léon had come just in time. The legendary Diane of the Buckmaster net was to extend into my sector the activities of Mission Licensee, the net she had created in the center of France. Captain Léon and I were charged with its organization. Once our operations plans were established, he could have weapons and supplies parachuted immediately. I consulted all the groups that had joined me and all unanimously agreed to follow me in this new assignment which took us away from the domain of Commandant Moreau who with his FFI unit, had withdrawn to the Morvan mountainous region southeast of Nevers.

His decision to bring under my command all the FFI groups in my zone were to be at the disposal of the Licensee mission with full autonomy, eventually proved to be very important.

On Solid Ground

In no time two maquis were created, each with its own drop zone, in addition to the one set up by of Jean Guillot. In the process Capitaine Dubois makes many people envious and a few critical comments were heard.

"He sold out to the British, and he receives his orders from London." As far as I was concerned that was the way to comport oneself as ally. This way we would be able to help the landed troops more efficiently with a minimum losses. With Léon and Julien, an American officer instructor who joined us in spite of a fancy parachute drop, I took command of the north of the Nièvre region. The open fields were not suitable for clandestine operations. Nevertheless, we were able to conduct sabotage and guerrilla operations thanks to the equipment dropped by the U.S Air Force, and the RAF.

It Was Too Beautiful

In early August Commandant Moreau convened all the leaders of the groups under his command at his CP hidden in the Morvan mountains. Among those present I recognized a few. The communist leaders were also there. I was kept away from secret - often stormy -meetings. Complaining about the lack of officers I was able to select one among the volunteers lined up before me.

If only for this selection I did not regret my trip, and congratulated myself for my choice -a man of the cloth, former scout, capable of starting a fire in the wind with three matches, important capabilities for the head of a Maquis! In addition he behaved as a knighted monk worthy as a Templar.

But this reunion had another purpose. It was characterized by a process favored by de Gaulle who wanted the FFI and FTP (Communist) together to form the Unified Movement of the Resistance (MUR), connected to him under the command of General Koenig. De Gaulle had sent Jean Moulin, known for his Marxist sympathies, to the communists leaders to seduce them. Under Moscow's orders these communist leaders were not to mix with capitalist troops. They agreed to comply only in regions where they were in the majority thus placing the others under their authority. It was not the case in our socialist region of Nièvre but.... nevertheless!

I soon learned that at that reunion Moreau had given the communists what they demanded - their complete control of the Loire valley. This capitulation was the first step to their takeover of the department as soon as it was liberated. At the same time they all agreed to be under the command of

138

Moreau on the condition that he remained far enough in the mountains of Morvan with his faithful FFI Maquisards.

To comply with the agreement he had with the communist leaders, he ordered me to withdraw from the Cosne region, to join him with my FFI units and my equipment, and to allow the FTP to settle where I was! With the unanimous support of the chiefs of my groups, and the cautious warning of Léon, I categorically refused to comply. In acting so I respected the engagement I had taken with the Licensee Mission which required my response and my support in the northern zone of the Nièvre. Did Moreau forget that, incapable of helping me, he had agreed to it? With a clear conscience I was ready to face the coming storm.

Beware Of Still Water

But what bothered me the most was his silence. Moreau neither disagreed nor approved my decision. In fact he was perhaps happy that I had saved a portion of what he was forced to concede under the pressure of the commies. As long as I was armed I was certain that the FTP would not try to drive me from my sector. Very irked, as they usually were, they would dream up an underhanded retaliation.

I was well supported by the Buckmaster network and too engrossed in the conduct of military operations to be concerned about what was going on in the local command of the resistance. Being far from Nevers, I did not see what was going on there after its liberation. Only an unexpected occurrence would alert me.

At the Nevers Headquarters where I was summoned, when I met Moreau who had assumed his real name of Roche, he was wearing the brand new stripes of colonel. I expected to find him triumphant, the liberator of the Nièvre at the head of the FFI. Why was he sitting behind his desk, sloped in his chair, embarrassed? He did not face me hoping that I would not see the shiny badge on his chest: The insignia of the FTP! Head lowered in a small voice as to apologize, he mumbled:

"They forced me to put it on; otherwise they would not let me be the head of the General Headquarters. I accepted in order to preserve the Union."

Alas, he capitulated only when confronted with this demand. Around him all the key positions were in the hands of political commissars. Now they are in position to make me pay for obstructing their plan.

To the Assault

The moment appears to be auspicious for their first attempt. My area had been liberated, and the Licensee Mission was terminated. With those who wanted to pursue a military career I was alone at Cosne for the administrative liquidation of our net. The others had gone home. In order to organize new combat units with volunteers they found a perverted solution. Taking advantage of the occasion, they try to convince me to link my unit to that clumsy Napo, the chief of the Nevers Maquis who also wanted to eliminate me. It was known that our men were ready to fight this group because there were some old businesses to settle.

Deception is the strategist of discord. When we met we looked askance at each other, then Napo and I established an armed peace almost cordial. In fact I was ready to leave the area to join the French intelligence service where another mission was awaiting me. If I was out of the trap I was not out of the woods and the commies had their eyes on me.

This time the trap was effective.

At Nevers, Roche had convened the staffs of all the units recently formed. As I was resigning I thought that my presence was unnecessary, but Napo insisted that I accompany him saying:

"You may take this opportunity to say goodbye to HQ."

Did he know what was waiting for me?

In the course of the conference everyone seemed to ignore me which was not so unusual. For them I was a marginal leader who received his orders from London. The meeting terminated, I went to take leave of Moreau. Sorry Roche. Alone with him in his office he seemed ill at ease. As usual when with me, his gaze was elsewhere. In addition, that day he must have feared the consequences of the decisions he had been forced to take, and that I would soon discover. He stood up, shook my hand and with a failed smile showed me to a door.

"Pass next door, the clerk has papers for you to sign."

With a tap on my back, a tap I thought to be friendly, he pushed me into a darkened room and moving back he closed the door. Two tough guys waiting there grabbed me and a third roughly extracted the pistol from my belt saying:

"I am Lieutenant Badaire, head of Security, I arrest you by order of the Colonel."

"Where are you taking me?"

"I am to lock you in a cell at the prison."

I realized then that I was without defense, at their mercy, and that they would take advantage of the darkened cell to get rid of me. I who thought that my only concern was for the Nazi! I must assure my survival. I had to improvise something quickly and effectively.

I felt that they feared me, and what they were doing was troubling them. So when Badaire turned me over to the head of the guards, calmly but loudly I said:

"I anticipated this arrest and I willingly lend myself to it, but if I am discovered dead in my cell as a "suicide" all the members of the headquarters starting with Roche will fall victim to my secret commando team. Let it be known that I gave orders to that effect."

The Plot

I had been in this prison before for routine investigations, but only on the first floor where visitors are allowed. As in all such establishments narrow stairs lead to a series of balconies upon which cells opened. A guard in front and one behind I climbed to the first level. A place had been saved for me. A turn of the key, a door with peeling paint opened. I thought that I was entering a narrow darken hallway when in fact it was to be my cell. The escort behind me moved back, the creaking sound of a bolt, and I was locked up.

When I became accustomed to a feeble light from a dirty small window located high up on the wall I had the impression of living a bad dream. Was I back in the middle ages? Was I drawn in the bowels of an anthracite mine? And what a smell! Against a wall a narrow shelf covered with a paillasse (straw mattress) flattened by the preceding tenants; perhaps members of the resistance tortured before their execution. In a corner a hole stained with excrement from which escaped a slight air current with a noxious smell; my private latrine! I felt as if I had been dunked into a cesspool. I assembled all my energy to surmount a retch and maintain my composure.

That is when I recalled the strange sight I had noticed shortly before climbing the stairs. Men that I knew well were occupied at housekeeping tasks. With Lieutenant Michel they composed a team of fighters that I had decorated for their bravery. Later I had to arrest them so that they could appear before a judge for their alleged savage executions of collaborators whose guilt was uncertain. This had occurred after the liberation of Cosne. When they saw me, as expected, they should have saluted me, or at the least made a small sign of recognition. On the contrary when they saw me between two guards they froze, petrified with astonishment. The more I thought about this the more I found this bizarre. A little later I learned the reason.

At first my attention was attracted by a small scratching at the door. Then I saw a piece of paper that someone was sliding under it. My eyes had become accustomed to the dark and I was able to read:

" My Captain forgive us for what we did."

What did they do that I was not aware? Soon thereafter I learned what it was. It was time for lunch. Michel had volunteered to serve the meal. As he was passing the mess tin full of house stew he had time to whisper :

"They told us that you had gone to England forever, and that we must declare that the orders to commit these assassinations came from you. We did it in the hope of being soon liberated without prejudice."

Thus I discovered the snare they used to justify my arrest. I imagined the anxiety of my wife, and the indignation of my men.

Cleverly Napo managed to calm those of my men who, weapons in hands, wanted to spring me out of the prison. Blocked in this dungeon I began a stay "incommunicado" for which no one had given me a reason.

Nevertheless a few days later, my door slightly ajar for a few seconds, I noticed a woman who, seeing me, waved a friendly sign. She wanted to make sure that the pie she had made for me and brought was duly delivered. I immediately recognized Napo's girl friend. I mistrusted him and wondered what did his sudden frankness hide? The affected marks of friendship that he had displayed towards me made them suspect. Weakened by the detestable diet of the establishment, I hesitated before this appetizing pastry so easily acquired. Was some poison under this attractive golden crust? Pained I finally decided and threw it into the hole of the latrine. My life was worth a lot more than a pie.

How long will they leave me in this rat hole? Was I forgotten? No, a second pie arrived. If it were to poison me they must have included a greater dose. This pie took the same route as the first.

After the third week I had taken the complexion of a corpse buried alive. That is what she noticed when my wife was authorized a visit under a discreet surveillance. It was with pride when she announced that, thanks to her efforts undertaken at Paris, two inspectors properly accredited were to come to Nevers and ask Roche for an explanation. Being officials they would be heard more seriously than Léon who attempted the same proceeding. Threatened with a fate same as mine, under the protection of his Colt professionally drawn, he was able to retreat to his vehicle. Eventually they lost his tracks in the capital.

A Step Aside

During the preceding four years the prison guards had to cheer up the members of the resistance turned over to the attention of the Gestapo. They did not comprehend why patriots again were locked up now that the Boches had left. They handled them with more concern than the traitors who had let themselves be caught. Thus I felt a certain veneration when they opened the door to a non-commissioned officer whose actual rank I do not recall. He had the insignificant appearance of a subordinate who follows orders blindly, otherwise he would have known that his mission revealed the embarrassment and the retraction of Roche in my affair. He was charged with my transfer from the odious dungeon to a room at the Hotel de France, also occupied by the General Headquarters.

Without encountering a soul other than sentries along the way I was taken to a room on the upper floor of the Hotel. After the cave where I wallowed this room was royal luxury. View of the sky through a large window, a clean and comfortable bed, a john worthy of the reputation of the hotel, and an officer's menu with room service! No outside promenades, but my door remained opened for a while long enough to allow me to pace the large hallway. Why this solicitude?

At her first visit obtained with much difficulties, triumphantly my spouse indicated the reason: The inspectors she had brought from Paris, although not able to obtain my release from a cell, had insisted that I be treated with the respect accorded to officers. But who had organized this plot against me?

It was unexpectedly that I was put on the right track. Another internee was staying on the same floor of the hotel. The orderly responsible for our surveillance considered his duty annoying and useless which enabled us to have long conversations. Our common fate, the exchange of favors furnished by our relatives, had quickly created a sympathetic atmosphere favorable for confidence. Yet, up to that time we did not navigate on the same boat. However it was confirmed that for different reasons we were victims of the same pack, a core of commissars of the French Communist Party.

These moles, having remained hidden in their professional occupation until the liberation, had since then come out in the open. They imposed themselves on the General Headquarters of the Nièvre relegating to Roche the pusillanimous role of figurehead. For them, as political members, their goal was to eliminate those who in combat had acquired a prestige that embarrassed them. To reach their goal they were not short of stratagems.

The method used with my neighbor revealed what was in store for me. He was an imposing individual in height and personality.

"They dared locking me up, I, the simple resistance fighter known as Laripette, also known as Captain Levengeur!"

Choking with indignation, his tale sprinkled with profanities, he detailed his situation. While aware of my opposition to the behavior of the Communist Party of which he was member, he did not hesitate to reveal the underhanded tricks fomented against him by the group with whom he had fought impartially. His unfortunate situation was caused by his acquiring an important promotion within the FTP over the selection of some of his companions.

With the rank of Captain he had been the chief of their "Patriotic Militia" (this designation depreciated before the invasion of USSR by the Germans) He had to be eliminated to permit the civilian cadres of the CP to take it over.

One day, an uninvited officer rushed into his office. That was Badaire. (a name he pronounced only while spitting on the floor.)

"Do you realize" he explained, "a guy who remained hidden in his factory, who was never seen in the field now that the Germans have left, he parades with the rank of Lieutenant! And it is he who pretends to establish order at home, so as to weed the rotten apples from the Party! According to this garbage I am one of them! I grabbed this miserable person by the neck daring him to accuse me of anything. But for his two stooges I would have strangled him, and he would never have the nerve to wave under my nose his accusing paper full of lies. I was gagging!"

Who was capable of confirming these accusations? Stupefied, he soon found out. As he launched into denials punctuated by twirling with his long arms, Badaire let one man who had been left behind enter. Poor Laripette could not believe his eyes: Jojo his best friend with whom he had fought for months, it was he who confirmed his detestable indictment!

White as a sheet, looking at his feet, Jojo did not look good.

"He seemed so miserable that the thought of crushing him left me," regretted the accused still under shock.

"He must have been invited by two pistols that showed him the way." Before getting in the car, broken down under the killing stare of his friend Jojo managed to whisper:

"They forced me to do it for the good of the Party."

Le Vengeur, whose real name was Matriolet, justified his nickname in declaring before me:

"Fight for your honor, never pardon your accusers regardless of their mea-culpa, their repenting genuflections."

In this type of affair others, even more unmanageable, have fallen for more elaborated stratagems.

As for me, up to then, no question was asked, and no explanation was given. Weeks passed punctuated by many requests addressed in vain to Roche. I was wondering what role was he effectively playing. Christmas was coming. I was determined to spend these holidays with my family. I reminded Roche that up to then I had accepted my incarceration, and I hoped that, before the end of the year, I would not have to go home without his authorization. By return message he informed me that I was free to leave. Was it a trick? Undisturbed I abandoned my neighbor and returned to Cosne thanks to the kindness of one of the few drivers circulating on the roads those days.

My spouse verified the plundering of our house by the Badaire team. My sophisticated secret agent equipment, my archives, even my personal correspondence all were gone! Thus the festivities occurred in a climate of indignation and rancor.

Soon after I rushed to Paris where I met the two agents who had tried to free me from the prison of Nevers. They were no longer interested in my case. They would not benefit from it as much as they would in black-mailing black market dealers.

Nevertheless they mentioned an incident outside of my case which interested me. They had returned to Nevers to locate and arrest an industrial

144

spy who had sold documents to the Germans. They knew that he had left the capital in the direction of the Nièvre. In Nevers, entering the Hotel de France occupied by the FFI Headquarters, they addressed themselves to the first officer they met.

"We are looking for Raoul Battard, have you heard of him?"

"Unknown here" the officer had replied without disconcerting himself. He quickly understood that he was dealing with amateurs, because actually he was Battard. He had found sanctuary under the protection of the Badaire team! Who would have found him hiding under the name of Captain Revére, the HQ finances officer? Quickly however he had evaporated at the surprise of Roche who was ignored by his associates.

By luck, many years later, I accidentally bumped into Roche in the Paris Metro. He recognized me, and without embarrassment, smiling, he gave me a tap on the shoulder before disappearing in the crowd.

In Paris I found Léon. He confirmed that discharged from the Buckmaster net we were automatically incorporated into the DGER (French Intelligence Service.) We were to wait for a meeting that would acquaint us with the nature of our new task. I returned to Cosne to prepare a move to an apartment that I had prepared in Paris. This family obligation proved to have been disastrous, The Nevers gang on the lookout was waiting for this moment.

Three days after my return, late afternoon, two gendarmes knocked at our door. In their shiny boots they appeared ill at ease.

"Captain, we are sorry. We have orders to take you to the brigade downtown."

My spouse and my mother-in-law understood that again they will have to fight an enemy that did not come from the other side of the Rhine. My little four-year-old daughter must not worry about this intrusion, so cheerfully I greeted the visitors.

"Thank you for coming to pick me up. I was waiting for you. I'll pack my bag and we'll go together."

The poor gendarmes, often accomplices of the resistance and despite their embarrassment, played the game. Skipping the handcuffs, chatting along the way, they quietly took me to their chief. The rare passerby paid little attention to the dignified trio.

Livid, with irrational gestures, the adjutant received me in his office without looking me in the face. We had known each other well in the past having often exchanged information, and resolved together thorny affairs. That evening I believe that he would have preferred to be elsewhere, but he was a conscientious and obedient soldier.

"Excuse me, captain, it's regulation. Do not worry, but I must frisk you."

As prescribed by the book he patted me lightly from head to toes, then he said:

"You must take the train tonight so that you will be at the prison of Dijon tomorrow morning. Two of my men will accompany you."

As he did not cuff me, I told my wife who had rushed to the station not to ask for help.

I believe that no one at Cosne noticed that Captain Dubois who had liberated the town a few weeks earlier was walking the street between two policemen as a felon captured red handed. This spectacle had been favored by my communist persecutors and their socialist accomplices, but they did not dare to come from Nevers to enjoy it. They still feared and did not risk a trip to Cosne where I had warned them not to come.

At the station we discreetly took the train for the 100-kilometer trip to Dijon. My mother-in-law, who for a long time dedicated herself to my healthy subsistence, in no time had prepared an emergency snack to satisfy my gluttony for a week. I appreciated her gesture doubly because these happenings did not cut down my appetite, and to be able to calm it because of the loving attention brought back a normal ritual to this brutally degrading situation.

In the middle of the night we had to change trains. It was cold on the platform where we were to wait more than one hour. My companions who up to then had given me some latitude held me tightly between them. I took this as a sign of kindness to keep me warm. Passengers standing before us, while stamping their feet, insulted me despite the rebuffs of my guardians. Curiously this humiliation coming from strangers did not affect me. I was satisfied to see that these hostile voices were directed at the brigand they believed I was.

Early that morning we reached the prison of Dijon, seat of the Military Region. As dictated by the routine procedure, after photos, finger printing, and the lifting of my pocket knife, my necktie, and cigarette lighter, I was ready for the pen. As in all jails there were three galleries linked to a central point. A guard, indifferent as to his client, dragging his feet, took me to the balcony of the first floor. Stopping before a door, he peaked in the small spy hole, and deliberately he introduced his key into the lock. Opening the door he announced:

"Here is some company." Three "Ahs" of satisfaction escaped from a cloud of cigarette smoke. The door closed and I am assailed with questions:

"Who are you? Where are you from? Why?

"Dubois; Maquis leader; Someone hates me."

"Then welcome, we are all in the same boat. We need a fourth for our bridge game."

From the very beginning they were friendly. Of course they had nothing to reproach themselves. The military success of each had caused jealousy of others. They were there because they were embarrassing to someone. I was

146

tempted to believe them. As all other communists they were looking forward to the future power grab of their great leader, Maurice Thorez. He would recognize their merits and immediately he would liberate them with honors. They had been locked up for several weeks, and were still waiting. From them, by chance, I would quickly learn the tricks of prison survival.

At first sight our residence was not a pleasant one: Two double cots in a space large enough for one; A low table which we had to climb over occupied the narrow space between them. A high small window shed enough light over the few personal objects that were left here and there so as to make prisoners feel at home. In a corner a small cheap mirror hung over a sink minus a faucet. For water, an old rusty bucket. Once a day each prisoner in turn would go to the ground floor below to fill the bucket. This same process was used for emptying the used water. No, I could not believe my eyes! Near a stack of used paper cut at the correct size a soiled bucket with flaking paint for relieving the bowels of the four occupants. Its filthy wooden cover let escape odors that a strong dose of chlorine attempted to correct.

This depressing comfort was no reason for the jovial humor of my companions. The large photo of a naked goddess pinned to the wall must have contributed to their moral comfort. Ah, when they are freed they will know how to catch up after this long period of incarceration. Waiting for that moment they organize, taking advantage of every opportunity.

Thus a trip to empty the bucket of night soil permitted the exchange of news with their neighbors on their same floor having the same duty.

Trivialities communicated by Morse code in tapping the floor or the partitions were not without interest to some of the unknown tenants. A mandatory daily short promenade in the exiguous court yard, and seldom was the Sunday mass missed. It was usually rushed through by a hurried officiate, but seriously attended by authentic miscreants.

One week passed without news from anyone.

"If you do not want to be ignored, get a lawyer" my companions told me in unison. Following their advice I hired Maitre Lenoble. He had a good reputation which must account for his busy schedule. I found that he did not reply to my call very quickly. Finally one day the door opened. "Calvat, to the attorney."

Maitre Lenoble was waiting for me in a small room. He looked serious and his presence was reassuring. He accepted and agreed to handle my affairs, begging for my patience because the prosecuting judge was loaded with cases. Meanwhile at Cosne my spouse, listening to the advice of influential friends, went to see a star performer of the local bar. Too late I had already retained Lenoble. I congratulated myself for quickly, under respectful escort I was taken to the office of the prosecuting judge near the Military Tribunal of the region. Sitting behind his desk, staring at me attentively, he greeted me without hostility. After having stated my name and identity, I protested my incarceration done without a stated ground.

"This is only to have you here when we need you" he replied as if he was to be forgiven. On the assurance that at the hotel I would be at his immediate disposal, my attorney asked for my freedom which was firmly refused. After this rebuff, my defender, aware of his uselessness, disappeared for several months. During that time I had to answer many questions concerning Lt. Michel's men who were now in the same prison.

It was almost with pleasure that I rediscovered the warm camaraderie of my companions who anxious to know, with little optimism, the speed of the prosecution. Alas they were right. Days passed. Long weeks followed in the silence of the judicial system.

The only thing left for me was to submit to the routine of the prisoner who tries to fool his own impatience. The intensive bridge games interrupted with reading made the time go faster. The distribution of the miserable stew in a metal bowl, which used to be white, gave us the opportunity to share the sweets sent by good souls. It was the time to mask the odors of the chamber pot with a heavy cloud of strong tobacco smoke.

The most depressing was my spouse's visit. We saw each other only through a screen for a few minutes wedged between others glued on both side of the partition. In this brouhaha it was difficult to hear or understand each other. Returning to my cell, nostalgic, I kept the image of her smile composed before the unhealthy whiteness of my face deprived of fresh air. Because of this inconvenience we decided to forego the visits which imposed a difficult trip for her.

To the others I appeared quite privileged when the judge asked for me a second time barely two months after our first meeting! The others waited in vain. As I entered his office I understood that despite their denials the first accusations of Lt. Michel's killers still made me responsible for their misdeeds.

" Why believe them when they charged me? You can see that there is a conspiracy against me." I tried to be persuasive when casually the judge asked me:

"Where is the parachuted money?" Shocked, abruptly I replied:

"Ask Buckmaster."

Haughtily, raising my voice, for that cutting reply without argument had abruptly closed the session. In retrospect I wondered how inwardly my interrogator had appreciated my departure. I had the time to mentally reflect on this question. Fortunately my co-internees, all with equal humor, never morose, were not disagreeable to live with. Bridge games occupied most of the day to such a degree that we played by instinct without much concentration.

Curiously, we who spent our life in the fresh air, in the wide outdoors without restraints, finally we had become accustomed to restrictions and measured the least of our movements. Packed in our small space in a restricted atmosphere we faded away. We gave up the expectation of calls from the outside. The time had brought us to a certain resignation; we no longer counted the days. Our life began to look normal in a world of our own. We no longer looked forward to the letters of our families with the same eagerness as we did in the beginning. Our families had a distant existence which to us appeared more and more strange. We no longer wished that one of us would end his detention for fear that it may upset our equilibrium.

One early morning an unexpected event woke us up. Under our very window in the court yard a rifle salvo followed a short time later by a single pistol shot! Damn! An execution at the foot of our building!

Often we thought that traitors responsible for the death of our comrades should not avoid the firing squad. But to discover that one of these, so close to us, of whom we knew nothing, could fall without warning provoked in all of us a vague malaise.

Shocked, for a while we had no words to treat this event. Then our door was suddenly opened. Contrasting our torpor an excited military individual had rushed toward me: "Captain, I was in charge of the squad. I take this opportunity to come to see you and ask you if you need anything."

My companions were surprised when this unexpected solicitude did not result in a courteous "thank you" on my part. I did not recall having had contact with the individual as I did with all the members of my cadres. He did not belong to my organization. Wearing a warrant officer's bands indicated that he was no doubt a regular army officer recently integrated into a communist unit. His task had been probably to ensure that I was still incarcerated and a sad condition.

Actually a prison wall is never air tight. A prisoner on our floor extremely attentive with a considerable freedom of movement let us believe that he was one of us, a victim of an unfortunate argument. Citizen of the city, he had no trouble befriending one of his former neighbors employed at the prison. Thus with the help of his wife who was running his business, a channel of communication was established, enabling us to obtain all the extras appreciated by prisoners, including unchecked mail.

I had advised my spouse regarding accusations brought against me during the latest interrogations. Alerted, members of my unit who had remained at Cosne, had collected a large quantity of signed affidavits affirming that I had been flatly opposed to savage cleansing. In addition, through the intervention of Léon who was out of reach in Paris, Colonel Buckmaster had sent to the French authorities a protest against my unjustified incarceration. I had learned from my attorney, who suddenly had become interested again in my case, that these documents had reached the judge responsible for my case.

From the very beginning I wondered who was the judge who would handle my case. He wore the rank of captain, but not the bearing of a fighter, rather the appearance of an accountant. Where did he come from? Perhaps he was a recently recruited professional magistrate? Perhaps a redoubtable political commissar responsible for dirty works? Or, which would be even less reassuring, was he member of the militia, unrelenting killers of the members of the resistance, a lost free-mason now exonerated by his FFI "brothers" who operated at Never under the obedience of Roche?

I was not able to obtain information concerning him, I was to be satisfied with my interpretation of his demeanor. He displayed neither contempt nor aggressiveness toward me, the accused.

I was summoned at the end of my fourth month of incarceration. He appeared more at ease behind his desk. With a slight smile he showed me the thick incriminating dossier given to him by Security services of Nevers' Headquarters. I was accused of larceny and extortion. All this was poorly established and I was able to clear myself easily.

I realized that he believed me when he roared in laughter reading the most outrageous accusation: "You were seen robbing underwear in a town store and selling these in the market!"

He took the joke with the care that this smuttiest story requires stating: "I will not ask you to respond to this," and he threw the report in the waste basket. His reaction comforted me. This magistrate was not part of the plot. But was he aware of its scope? Was he aware that it had been pieced together by a willingness to do me harm?

This was the opportunity I was hoping for. He must consider me the victim of a conspiracy and I must provide him the reasons. Thus gluing myself to my chair in a measured and serious tone I declared: "In order for you to have a complete view of this affair I must reveal what is underneath. However what I can reveal must not be included in the official record. If you accept what I say to you, it will be for your ears only, a secret sealed between officers. Also I must insist that you ask your clerk to leave the room."

Not at all concerned by my request he begged his secretary to leave us alone. He appeared very attentive and encouraging. I could then unmask the conspiracy.

"You must know the reasons which led my accusers to mount this plot. In addition to my position as a commanding officer of the Forces Françaises de l'Intérieur, I belonged to an allied intelligence network which directed me to remain with my units in the northern area of the Department of the Nièvre. Thus I had to refuse to relinquish the area to communist units which had extracted this requirement from Colonel Roche. His headquarters, infiltrated by commissars of the Party of Moscow, have created these monstrous slanders to get even with me. I know that you have in your possession petitions that will exonerate me and a commendation from Colonel Buckmaster concerning my conduct as one of his agents."

Then haughtily I added: "I always had the means of avoiding arrest, but I accepted my incarceration so that I may face my accusers and exonerate myself before the justice for which I fought."

Judging by his manner I saw that he had taken in serious consideration all that I had revealed to him. Carefully he put away his documents as to give himself time to think and dismissed me with a look which seemed to say: " Now I understand many things." I wondered what would follow this meeting. Better wait with an empty head.

As far as a surprise is concerned, that was a surprise! The comrade of Dijon, the one who was so devoted, so sympathetic, the one who was so useful, ready to help as only one of us could be, well, this St.Bernard did not have his place in the haven of patriots. We could not believe it, but the tribunal had just condemned him to a long prison sentence for his collaboration with the enemy. He must have been laughing at our trust and gullibility! Frustrated, sorry we had to say good bye to our supplier of forbidden supplies.

One more day we had to silently chew our resentment, while outside the entire world was "rejoicing": It was the 8th of May, the vanquished Boches had signed the armistice. The fighters will soon return to their wives. When will we? In prison one day is the same as the next. We had contributed to the victory, but no one seemed to remember. It was the end of all hopes for the Nazis and the jailed traitors near us. A feeling of frustration and of injustice drenched us in nostalgia for the first time.

One more week! We had to admit the common fate of the prisoners unconsciously created a solidarity that unnoticeably brought them together. Thus we could not imagine that this neighbor in the cell next to ours, so pleasing and obliging, could be anything but a poor resistance fighter who as we was victim of a trumped-up accusation. But one evening he, usually so calm and retiring, returned to his cell excited and boisterous after a courtroom appearance He was besides himself with joy and happiness. No doubt we thought he had been acquitted and soon would be freed. As we were about to congratulate him, we looked at each other perplexed when we heard him repeating: "I got life without parole! I got life without parole! Why was he happy to end his days in jail? We learned than he had killed a gendarme and that often he had imagined his head dropping in the basket of saw dust of the guillotine.

I had forgotten my attorney who had learned what the judge intended to do with my case. Thus after he returned to the court, the judge summoned me immediately and indignantly he said: " I do not understand why you are still detained. The court has no case against you. In agreement with the prosecutor I signed a "Non-Lieu" (nonsuit) and your "Levée d'Ecrou"(release) three weeks ago. I will take care of your discharge immediately."

The next day I left my companions whose feelings were split between their appreciation for my release and the regret for not being able to join me. Included in the formalities required to vacate the establishment was an order to report to the General commanding the military region, which I did immediately.

Small, thin and accompanied by a tall captain, the General received me. Without preamble he announced in a satisfying tone: "I delayed your release to give me time to review your military dossier. Having done so I have the pleasure of informing you that in appreciation for your actions against the enemy you have been promoted to the permanent rank of second lieutenant."

I could not believe what I had heard. Controlling my indignation, I snapped to attention and with a spectacular salute before saying with a sugary smile : " General I am touched by this kind gesture. However I must tell you that I was a lieutenant before the war and that three different army services have promoted me to the rank of Captain. I could have told you personally without waiting three extra weeks in prison."

Taken aback he looked questionably at his assistant. I then explained to him the reasons the Nièvre HQ went after me. "Ah! I understand why Roche neglected to introduce you to me during my visit at Nevers." Looking at his assistant he added: "In the end, perhaps this Resistance has done more damage than good." That is what was believed by the regular Army.

Back to action from the British SOE services I transferred to the DGER (French Intelligence Service.) These mandatory recruits coming from elsewhere were not greeted with enthusiasm. Were they submitted to a quarantine?

I insisted that the mission to recoup at Nevers the documents and material of sabotage taken by the Badaire team. I considered this an essential and complementary operation to the court decision. For me it represented a rehabilitation in the eyes of all. But it was considered a useless provocation and I was forbidden to retrieve my belongings. I was forced to abandon them to the gloating communist thugs. There also the ground appeared to me to be shaky and that is why I decided against a further military career.

Returning home after months of incarceration and faced with an uncertain future was not a relief without malaise. As if a long and difficult journey had ended with the pride of having reached the objective. Before me appears a great void where your loved ones have been during your absence. There, were they have organized their existence without you, as you were not missed. An effort was necessary to hide your feelings that you are disturbing them in their routine, that you came late, perhaps too late.

When Duty Is an Adventure

One can understand the internal forces that prompt you to fight the invader of your country. But is it bearable to face the snares of those who were supposed to be your fighting companions?

I exposed my life to the effectiveness of the Gestapo, to the treachery, the ambitions of those who wanted my post, to the coup fourrés of those I impeded, to the lack of concern of the amateurs, the imprudence of the braggers, my own mistakes.... for the sole guarantee, "Luck" the chance the supreme hope of the fighter.

S/Vic Calvat, Alias Dubois

Return To the Alledged DZ

Another Communist Plot

With the Calvats from Nevers we proceeded to our next destination crossing the Loire River over the new bridge of St.Satur. I had laid the charges to blow the old one in 1944. In 1988 when we returned to the area for the first reunion of the Maquis Dubois we visited the town of St.Thibault on the Cher side of the Loire, west of the bridge. We were all pleasantly surprised to receive the accolade of the population including that of the architect who had directed the reconstruction of the bridge. It seems that the people never did care for the old structure and the architect probably needed a job!

Ten years later, accompanied by one of my grandsons, it felt good to again cross the Loire on the new bridge on our way to the nearby town of Sancerre. We checked in at the Panoramique Hotel overlooking a valley covered with vineyards. We knew the inn well having stayed there before.

The following day with Vic and Jacqueline we picked up Kiki and Janine at Le Boulleret and together went to Lainsecq by St.Sauveur-en- Puisaye then to the small hamlet of Le Jarloy where Mme. Andrée Blondet was expecting us. We reached the farm close to 11:00 am and already a few people had gathered in the court yard where we parked our vehicle.

As we approached the group one of the men addressed me as "McCormick." At the time I thought nothing of it because this name was given to me by the members of the Maquis Dubois, the resistance group to which I was assigned during the war. I had learned of this nickname only in 1988 at the first reunion of the group at Cosne-sur-Loire which has been renamed Cosne-Cours-sur-Loire. The man's face was common and at first unfamiliar to me, but it seemed that I should have known him. To those assembled he gave the impression that we were old friends.

The man's right hand was missing! I would have remembered such an infirmity if I had met him before, even 55 years ago. Coming close to me and pointing to his lapel he said:

"Why aren't you wearing the pin that I gave you?"

I looked at the pin he was wearing which appeared familiar to me, but I could not remember then where I had seen it before. I did not reply, but began to wonder where and when I had seen either such a pin or a similar design, when suddenly I recalled that several years ago I had received a letter from a group located at Clamecy, a major town close to where we were. This group of former resistance fighters had invited me to a celebration stating that I would be their guest of honor. In the letter was a 2 inch round badge made of leather. Imprinted within a circle was the letters N and M and a cross of Loraine with two wings or feathers. I did not know the meaning of this object which had a safety pin on its back side. I was very familiar with the initials FFI (Forces Françaises de l'In-térieur) and FTP (Francs-Tireurs Partisans), but NM was foreign to me. Not knowing what to do I had called my old friend Vic Calvat, the head of the Maquis Dubois, and asked him about this invitation. He replied to me that NM meant National Maquis and it was a communist organization masquerading as

NM3 Badge

a legitimate resistance group which had not been recognized by the Allied Forces. He stated, "They are trying to justify their existence by using you to show that they had played a significant role in the resistance." Vic suggested that I do not attend the ceremony and to ignore the invitation, which I did.

This individual whose name I learned later was Yves Pasquier apparently was the one who had sent the invitation on behalf of a local veterans group, former members of the National Maquis. What was he doing in the farm where I was to meet Madame Blondet and her family?

More people arrived at the courtyard including Madame Blondet's children and grandchildren, and finally on crutches came the 92-year-old grandmother who supposedly had served my first breakfast after I parachuted

**Madame Andrée Blondet and Roger Tartrat (Kiki)
at the farm of Le Jarloy**

into a field nearby on the night of 8/9 August, 1944. We hugged and kissed as all French people do. She no longer resided at the farm, but at her daughter's home, close to the farm now run by her younger son.

It was a typical French farm with an enclosed court yard. However, the outside of the building in relation to the road was not oriented the same as the farm I reached that early morning. Nothing seemed familiar to me. The entrance I had used in 1944 was in the back or the side of the house and when the man who escorted me opened the door we were facing stairs that lead directly to the second floor.

When, with the rest of the guests, I entered the kitchen nothing looked familiar. The position of the stairs did not correspond to my recollection; only a long table seemed to fit. Of course most, if not all French farm houses, have long tables in their kitchen! I dismissed this thought thinking that perhaps they had remodeled the house, but when I went upstairs again nothing looked familiar. I clearly remembered that the upstairs could be reached by two sets of stairs, the one I had entered in the night and the other leading to the kitchen I used in the morning. I was told that much had been done to the upstairs including the building of a bathroom and a toilet. The room I had occupied in 1944 had a window overlooking the road. This room did not have such window. The son who lived in the farmhouse said that the steel cot was in

**Vic Calvat, the author and his wife Ginny with
Madame Andrée Blondet at Le Jarloy**

the attic and that it was difficult to get to it. I wanted to see if my feet would stick out in the end, as I was told they did. But I didn't recall this to be so.

Mme. Blondet announced that when I arrived at her farm in 1944 I was so tall that I banged my head on the low beams of the rafters. I must have shrunk because as I walked underneath the lowest beams of the ceiling, none came close to my head! Either I shrank terribly, or the floor dropped several inches!

Champagne was served and the one-handed man spoke a few words giving the impression that he and I were old friends. I did not know what he was talking about, but he appeared to have played an important function in my adventures with the resistance -adventures of which I had absolutely no recollection.

Robert Blondet, the oldest son of Madame Blondet, then announced that they had a surprise for me. They had been saving it for 55 years! The surprise was brought in and I recognized the object immediately. "We saved your parachute!" someone announced.

"My parachute?" I looked at the strong bag with two rings in its base and what appeared to be white silk protruding from the top. It was a parachute all right, and I must say in perfect condition, but it was the type attached to containers. These people did not know that my actual parachute had been made into undergarments by the local girls in the Licensee area of operations. Why did they keep this parachute which by itself was useless while most of the parachutes used with containers during the war had vanished?

My next thought was: "What happened to the container attached to the parachute, and where is the material that was in the container?" But no one knew not even the one-handed man. Up to that point Vic had been very quiet, and obviously not pleased with one of the guests. I noticed that he was quite perplexed and when we were away from the group he said: "I did not know that there were containers in the aircraft that brought you, You were supposed to come alone!"

"My dear Vic," I replied," in my plane were 12 containers plus ten large packages including my two suitcases."

I was told by the captain I met under the huge tree that the field would be cleared before morning.However I did not inquire further as to the actual disposition of the containers and packages.

When, a few months earlier, I was assured by Kiki that indeed he had found the farm and the wife of the farmer who had met me on that specific day, I had no reason to doubt him. Generally speaking, her initial story matched what I had told Kiki. Her letters began to worry me because some of her statements did not meet my recollection. I felt that once on the site, after seeing the farm and meeting the people concerned, I would know for sure. Instead I had stronger doubts but kept these to myself.

Every one at Le Jarloy knew that I wanted to see the field where I was deposited by the fine crew of the B-24 called *Miss Fitts*, a well deserved designation. If I remembered correctly it was no more than half a mile from the farm. However we drove about two miles and when we arrived at the place where I had supposedly landed, instead of hedges and poles, or a vineyard as I was told it was, in its place was now a huge wheat field with no hedges, no poles and no trees. I was assured that what I have described as a large oak tree was in fact a pear tree which had since been cut down. The topography of the area could have been the same, but so was a multitude of other places in the area. The local press was there and of course there were interviews including that of the one-handed man who gave his own version of what had happened, but no one paid attention to him. When every vehicle moved on I followed, but noted that we were not returning to the village the way we had left. We took a different route and at one point the head vehicle piloted by the one-handed man stopped along the way close to a high wall perpendicular to the road. Everyone disembarked and moved close to the wall where a plaque had been affixed. A small metal fence outlined an area below the plaque making it a kind of memorial. On the plaque two names were inscribed and the fact that these two individuals had been executed by the Germans at that very spot. The one-handed man seems to be in charge of this operation and after describing the incident, he stood at attention while one of his friends or associates deposited a bouquet of flowers on the ground below the plaque. Then we all returned to the village and the farm. I asked Kiki who these two fellows were who had been executed. No doubt they were resistance fighters? "No," Kiki said, "they were members of the local communist party who had done some stupid things and had been caught by a German column passing by. They executed both. The Germans did not bother the wounded resistance fighters who were in a makeshift hospital under the care of a German surgeon." I was wondering if these two fellows where the ones mentioned in Mme. Blondet's second letter! The more I watched this one-handed man the more I began to wonder! What was his role in all this?

When we returned to the farm, the kitchen being too small for the crowd and the sun having returned, drinks and snacks were served in the courtyard. It lasted a while. I thought this was a great reception. Having seen all I wanted to see, it was time for us to depart. We were about to do so when the doors of the barn were opened wide revealing a long table upon which was a feast almost impossible to describe.

For the next three hours tasty food was served and the finest wines consumed. Then a cake was brought in and of course the icing was red! Two flags one French the other an American adorned this masterpiece.

This was too much for my dear spouse who could not hold her tears. The one-handed man stood and spoke about a past unknown to me. Then the mayor of the town praised the USA. Vic followed with a few words, but I could tell that something was bothering him for he was not his usual self. When my turn came I thanked the good people for their great welcome and promised to return. After much kissing we left,

Madame Blondet with author and the cake!

but not before Vic, taking the one-handed man aside, gave him a piece of his mind. "I fought for the red, white, and blue, while you bastards only fought for your red masters, and you lost!" What was all this about? Apparently Vic had not forgotten the months he spent in jail because of the accusations of Pasquier's friends.

Returning to our hotel, I felt that something was really wrong. I had the feeling that someone had pulled my leg and that whoever he was he had done a number not only on me, but on all of us. I knew it was not Kiki's doing, nor was Madame Blondet responsible, but I strongly suspected that Pasquier, the one-handed man, had something to do with it. Kiki, Vic and I had long discussions concerning our suspicion, but we reached no reasonable conclusion.

A few days later with Vic and Jacqueline, we left Sancerre on direction of Valençay to admire the memorial erected in the memory of the members of the F-Section of SOE who gave their lives for the cause. All those mentioned on the table of honor were agents who had died in combat for the liberation of France. Incidentally, we were told that during their entire occupation German troops never occupied Valençay!

After a short stop at Boston we returned to Indianapolis on the 15th of July. On the 10th of August I received a letter from Kiki. He had received mine, while he was out of town visiting one of his children. He replied to my questions concerning Pasquier including his address. Apparently Pasquier, who was 20 years old in 1944, had been a member of a resistance group in the Yonne region, probably a Maquis FTP. Kiki had known him prior to his investigation at Lainsecq, but only briefly. Kiki was on his way to other reunions of the region, while there he would try to find more about my transfer to the Maquis of Annay.

Valençay monument honoring all Section F, SOE agents who died for the liberation of France

While Kiki had not seen Pasquier since 1988, he was surprised by his visit shortly before our recent July arrival in the region. Looking over an old correspondence file, I discovered that on February the 18, 1990, in reply to my inquiry, Vic Calvat had written to me the following:

The invitation of Pasquier inspires great suspicion as to his true purpose. The information that I have at this time leads me to believe that it is an episode of the grand scheme by the Commies to guarantee and glorify the achievements of their maquis. They want to include these in history as if they were the sole actors in the frame of the resistance. Pasquier was not one of us. He is a friend of Jean Escalier who brought you to us after your parachuting into the Morvan, but who has yet to reveal where. It involved a maquis called "National Maquis" created under the protection of "The Front National" (Communist Party.) Under this appellation they were able to recruit many regular military officers who were not aware that they were serving political commissars disguised as innocent patriots.

both Pasquier and Escalier were members of a group who
plotted against me in retaliation for their inability to evect
me from Cosne. Shortly before Maco's (Max Dessons) death,
they suddenly became very friendly with my wife who
thought that they were after her charms. But soon after
Maco had passed away they requested her to give them
the weapons they believed he (Maco) had hidden. As a
polite request did not bring the expected result, they
switched to threats. Since then she has kept a rifle handy.

    While offering the possibility of your presence at their
ceremony, ask Pasquier to provide you information about
the maquis who received you in 1944. This information
he had refused up to now to divulge or give to me.
S/Vic

Thus Pasquier obviously knew of me because he is the one who invited me
to Clamecy and who sent me the badge of the National Maquis, which a few
days after our return from France I found in a drawer. How did Pasquier obtain
my address? I did not correspond with him as Vic had suggested. Certainly Vic
had no contact with him, and had no reason to give him my address. The only
individual who might have given him my address was Pierre Bon, the shipwright
of Cosne to whom I had given my business card in 1986.

How did Pasquier manage to be a guest at Le Jarloy and why he was there
are questions that need to be resolved!

After reading over the letters Madame Blondet sent me, and listening to
her accounts, I have the feeling she was repeating what someone had told her,
and that she mistakenly took me for someone else. Possibly her farm was not
the farm where I spent my first night in France, and she probably was not the
farmer's wife I had met that morning.

In reply to my suspicions, Kiki sent me the following letter:

Boulleret, September 9, 1999

My dear René:

    Forgive the delay in replying to your last three letters.
    Vacations are ending soon and we have many friends
and family, to visit, and Janine is very tired.
    Let us examine some facts:
    You did not remember Pasquier who was at your first
reception at the Cosne Town Hall in 1988 because in those
days he had both hands. He had an accident much later.
    At the reception of Cosne in 1988 Vic had mentioned
your nickname "MacCormick," and Pasquier was there and
he has big ears. In the area he is known to have penetrated
veterans organizations to which he was not entitled!

It is at this reception that he could have given the insignia you mentioned and that this is the symbol of the movement called National Maquis whose origin I ignore, and whose existence I did not know prior to June 6, 1944. It has nothing to do with FTPF, a Communist group to which Pasquier belonged in 1944, a group which has left unfavorable souvenirs in the region of Clamecy-Entrain.

As I did not remember this individual, I was very surprised by his visit two weeks before your arrival last July.

He came on behalf of Mme. Blondet with a letter that you had sent to her, and of whose content I was not aware. This letter was to be used as his introduction to me.

At that time I did not know the date of your arrival in France.

He told me that he was the one who had received you when you parachuted in 1944 and that he wanted to attend the reception at Lainsecq.

I replied that I was not the organizer and I had no right to invite anyone. I do not know who invited him, but I noticed that at Le Jarloy some old maquisards who were there appeared surprised by his presence.

When I first contacted the Blondets no one in the family mentioned him.

Finally, I am slightly disappointed with the conclusion of this adventure, but not surprised as the Blondets have received and sheltered many people including maquisards during these times.

It is therefore not impossible that this brave woman, 55 years later, could confuse you with one other agent parachuted because Mic Pailler the head of the Yonne regional BOA had his CP at her farm between June and September 1944.

She may be forgiven.

I do not know Pasquier's relationship with the Blondet family, but I am now convinced that he has influenced the grandmother. I will try to find out, but will not mention my suspicion to her.

In reply to your last letter of September 28, when Pasquier came to my house two weeks before your arrival in July it is I who told him that you had been received by two men with slanted eyes and that you thought: "Shit, I have fallen in China!" which was what you wrote in one of your letters to me. That is when he told me that it was he who watched you drop. After helping you he took you to

Yonne. It was Bon who suggested to me that this fellow (Pasquier)could provide me with information. He (Pasquier) greeted me very crudely in a dark hallway of his apartment and he refused to answer my questions. I did not insist and could not have recognized him later.

During the twenty two months of search for your DZ I have never heard a word about Pasquier in the Yonne region. The last contact, which by luck enabled me to find Madame Blondet, was Louis Moreau of Lain, 10 kilometers north of Lainsecq through the intermediary of Madame Gaufillier whose parents are farmers at Champ-martin-d'en-bas had also helped the crews of bombers in distress.

I do not know who invited Pasquier to the reunion of Le Jarloy.

It is certain that Pasquier did not actively participate with the reception at Le Jarloy because, when I told her the date of your arrival, the daughter-in-law of Madame Blondet told me: "You are invited with your spouse, and we will take care of everything. We are used to it and the Mayor wants to participate." She never mentioned Pasquier.

Confusion or not, the Blondets and their friends are brave people who have done the maximum with sincerity. After 55 years they deserve our respect and we must regret nothing.

I will do my best to learn more very discreetly. We shall visit them in a few days.No news from your friend Blandin.

With our best souvenirs, Janine joins me for a friendly kiss to both.

S/Kiki

If indeed, between June and September 1944, BOA had a CP at the farm of Le Jarloy, and if Mic Pailler had been the one in charge it is inconceivable that he would have been without communication with his HQ in London. The people I first encountered on the 9th of August, 1944 had no radio, they did not expect me; they were positively not members of BOA. The fact that they were there in an area not designated as a drop zone is a mystery. Until they were told, Léon, and Vic had no idea where I was and neither did the local BOA.

If according to Kiki, Le Jarloy was a BOA Command Post between June and September 1944, Pasquier would not have been with that group as he was with a FTP-controlled maquis.

If Le Jarloy was a command post, there must have been a constant movement of personnel - some BOA agents parachuted either by the RAF or U.S. Air Force. On the night of 8/9 August, 1944 only two aircraft were dispatched to my region in support of *Licensee*. The second aircraft did not unload at the Anguille DZ where Capt. Dubois and Léon were waiting for me. The crew must have made a drop at the one indicated by Kiki. (See Page 114.)

This letter confirms my suspicion that Pasquier has been involved not only at Le Jarloy, but in 1988 at the Town Hall of Cosne .and that he has in a roundabout way pointed Kiki in the direction of the Blondets. But how and why?

While thinking about my first contact with Vic and the reunion at the Town Hall of Cosne I now remember him (Pasquier) at the Mayor's reception of Cosne-sur-Loire. He was the one who told everyone that, as the driver of a Jeep, he and I had ran into a German patrol, and that because of his sangfroid, and quick thinking and splendid reaction he managed to get us out of a jam. He sounded so convincing that I did not question his story. I've been scratching my head ever since, and could not remember this incident at all. In retrospect I should have asked him for details, but his story seemed so real, and he appeared so heroic, I did not want to demolish his short moment of fame.

When I met Bon in 1986, I was aware that during the war he was not with us, the Maquis Dubois, but I did not know that he was a friend of Pasquier. Whatever Pasquier learned about me including my address must have been from Bon because I had given him my business card. After the reunion at Cosne the local newspaper carried an article about me revealing many aspects of my past activities.

The same day Kiki wrote the above letter, Madame Blondet did the same and it came a day later. The following is a translation of her communication:

Fifth letter from Madame Blondet

September 8, 1999

Dear Mr. Défourneaux:

I took some time to reply to your letter. I fell in my room. My daughter-in-law found me a while later without much damage. I am happy that you returned sound and safe. Your grandson as well as Madame Desfourneaux have appreciated our food. For us every day it is simple. We are happy to have offered you a good meal. It was only the things that we produce.

The night of the 8 of August 1944 I learned from my sister-in-law that I had made you an omelet. Eggs beaten with oil were cooked in a skillet.I did not remember. In the

the morning it was barley roasted in the oven of the range as we had no coffee. We had nothing. As far as the bread was concerned we had wheat to make flour and baked the bread in the oven with ration cards we had very little and the baker did not bake much. I saw the war from 1914 to 1918, then the war of 1940 to 1944. In 1916 we lost a young man who was not yet 20 years old. He was a teacher at Douaumont. The veterans of Algeria have just gone there. It is a very sad trip. Long time ago I took it.

I've just learned that the day you arrived here, the 8th or 9th there was a big battle in the woods of Boutissaint. I did not remember you were lucky not to have gone in that direction. My son Michel found out that it was close to us, approximately 10 kilometers.

Our life has become very calm, these are only bad souvenirs. We go toward a united Europe. I hope that we will have no more conflicts.

Today as every day the sun shines, the water is rare, there is no grass in the fields. We give corn to the cows. The cistern is empty. Fortunately we have public water. Large sources of water have been impounded, only the vegetables lack water. We water them with hoses. Our tomatoes are beautiful as well as the flowers and the roses which resist the heat. The farmers cannot plow their fields.

I have nothing else to tell you. I recover from my fall and my left elbow has been stitched and the scar is almost gone. Helene puts mercurochrome on it and it is still sensitive.

I send you and your wife and grandson all my friendship as well as that of my family.

Your friend who does not forget you.

S/Andrée Blondet

My Notes: According my recollection and the Air Force mission report I was dropped at 1:30 am. After spending some time with those on the ground, half an hour to fortyfive minutes, I was taken to a farm. It was approximately 2:30 am when I reach the room where I spent the rest of the night. By that time it was the 9th of August, 1944. No one made an omelet for me, but I remember the terribly tasting coffee, and the hard dark bread. I do not recall having had an omelet in my entire stay in France during the war.

There were only two individuals in the kitchen when I came down from the second floor that morning, a man and a woman, both in their forties.

As for the so-called "battle" ten kilometers from our location, if this had been the case I would have heard about it and would have remembered.

I am more than ever convinced that Le Jarloy was not the farm where I spent my first night in France during the War, and that I am the victim of a scam (dupe). But why?

———————

Puzzled by the efforts to convince me that Le Jarloy was the area where I landed on the 9th of August 1944, and determined to find the reason behind it, I asked Kiki to continue his research. The following is his reply to my request.

Kiki's letter dated February 25th, 1999

Dear René:

In response to your letter of 17th and 22nd of September 1999 I have reviewed my personal BOA files of the P3 region which included the department of Yonne.

Jarry (Rondenet) of the DMR, and Pair (Alain de Beaufort) of BOA, his assistant whose CP was at Lormes in the Morvan since June 6, were responsible for all the BOA operations for the FFI and NM3, which included the P (Paris) region, and all the Sub-divisions P1, P2, P3.

At that time the F-Section of SOE had been integrated with BOA in agreement with the War Office and the BCRA concerning all operations on French soil.

You were one of the nine OSS agents integrated into Section F of SOE.

The Service National Maquis came from the CNR (Conseil National de la Resistance) same as SNR Service National Radio, a kind of state within a state ignoring compartmentalization rules, with an aggravating particularity; no one knew under whose authority they operated.

Created in June 1944, against the wishes of General Koenig, commander of the FFI, in many ways it depended on many sources including its financial dependence from the BCRA.

It was understood that this organization's control by the CNR was against the trend. A rushed recruiting left it open to penetration which posed serious problems (note from Michel Pichard, head of the Northern Zone of BOA in his history of BOA).

Mic (Michel Pailler), the actual BOA Operations Officer for Yonne named by the DMR Jerry Perrisian, professor of mathematics, had settled in the Yonne with his spouse Marie Louise AKA Miquette who was also his BOA assistant. However I do not know if he was a reserve captain.

Deux Fouets, the Maquis leader whom you mentioned, was in reality De Foë (Nicholas Solivélas), responsible to the National Maquis 3 as an inspector of the five or six Maquis of the Yonne. It was he with Mic Paillier, head of BOA, Yonne, who took care of you.

The FTPF, Roland, le Tatoué and the maquis of the Front National (Bellot) were also in the area.

It was true that Gestapo agents had infiltrated all the security services of the Yonne as early as 1943. The nets Jean-Marie, Donkeyman of SOE were penetrated and manipulated by the Abwehr and the SIPO of Dijon.

Many arrests were conducted in October 1943 in Yonne and in the Nièvre region where many BOA nets were smashed.

These penetrations were responsible for the arrest of Jarry and of Pair on the 27th of July 1944 at Paris and their execution on August 15th. All this has been confirmed by the records of the French military tribunals from 1946 to 1949 as well as by reports from Abwehr and SIPO agents.

As far as Pasquier is concerned, I visited Mme. Blondet in November and asked her how long she had known Pasquier. Her reply was short and clear: "At the same time you did, at our reception."

In fact, he was twenty years old in September 1944, and based on this fact I doubt that he was in the Maquis of Yonne before early 1944, and I also doubt he held a responsible position with the BOA. He is not well liked by those I met who knew him. He asks many questions and infiltrates himself in every commemoration of WWII. [1]

The IndoChinese who were at your reception and the Marine captain were former military, demobilized at the armistice after the occupation of the free zone in November 11, 1943 and picked up by the NM3 in June 1944. They conducted training of the young recruits and helped the maquis' operations in the P3 region.

I found nothing concerning Mr. Phillipe who took you to the Maquis Dubois, but Vic told me that he met him at the reunion of Maquis leaders at Ouroux (Nièvre) on the 4th of July 1944, and that he came from Clamecy. You should ask Vic.

Virginia Hall of SOE and her radio Denis Rake, having returned by Lysander at the end of April, 1944, then to Chateauroux, probably escorted "Léon" from the DZ at Yvois-le-Pres, of Col. Colon's (Arnaud de Voguë) Maquis of the Northern Cher, to Annzy via Léré in July 1944. This was told to me by a friend who was at the CP of Colon and who knew her at that time. He remembers that she had a prosthesis and that she was an American who had been at the American Embassy at Vichy in 1942. She died after the war. [2]

The last news of Mme. Blondet is not very good. She no longer leaves her bed and she has periods of unconsciousness. Every day a nurse comes to help her. She no longer recognizes the people around her. I was lucky to have seen her before her present condition. [3]

The main actors of that period having disappeared, I personally feel that that now is the time to forget the witnesses of your SOE adventure in France.

I hope and wish that my modest help will be useful to clarify your souvenirs. Janine joins me to kiss Ginny and you affectionately without forgetting Brecht.

Your Friend:

S/ Kiki

Notes:

(1) Pasquier is still alive. He has left his footprints everywhere, but no one has challenged him. He does not reply to my questions, which leads me to believe that he does not want to face facts. When she told Kiki that she first met Pasquier at the reception in July 1999, it was not true. In her letter dated December 18,1998, Madame Blondet stated that she had a conversation with Pasquier probably at Le Jarloy and he had given her his address. How did Pasquier learn about her without speaking to Kiki?

Virginia Hall's official report states that on 21 March, 1944, accompanied by Aramis, she returned to France by rubber boat landing on the coast of Brittany. Virginia Hall as Léon was a radio operator. In the Department of the Cher she did meet a maquis leader called "Colomb."

In her report, Aramis was not with her when she went to Colomb HQ, and no mention is made of a "Denis" or "Rake." These names do not appear on the Glossary of Code names and code Words used by SOE/OSS. They might have been BOA radio operators.

(3) Madame Andrée Blondet passed away on June 4, 2000 and was laid to rest at her native village of Lainsecq.

Pierre Bon

On October 11, 1999 I received the following letter:

Letter from Pierre Bon

Cosne/ Loire
October 7th, 1999

Dear Comrade:

Following your letter of September 23, I have researched my area between Bleneau, Lavau, St.Amand, and St. Fargeau.

I found traces of parachuted individuals, but these were part of a British group.

My comrade Yves Pasquier had mentioned the spot where you were dropped. I am very glad that the field where you landed on the French soil was found. He (Pasquier) even specified the particulars as he was present at your "jump."

On the other hand I almost have to reproach you for waiting 55 years before trying to find the people of that period, and what was left over from the drops.

As far as I am concerned all I possessed was turned over to the military authorities "commissariat and the police" more than 20 years ago. In my possession I had a BAR, several submachineguns, American carbines, including cases of ammunition related to all weapons as well as grenades, two parachutes half burned (as we had to destroy them).

Same as you, I have nothing left except souvenirs. Receive my sincere friendship as well as to your spouse.

S/Bon, Pierre

Notes:

Bon appears to have forgotten that I had contacted him in 1986 for the purpose of finding the members of the resistance group with whom I served while in France during WWII. I had left my card asking him to contact those who were part of my group including Captain Dubois. He never did. At that time, only thirteen years earlier, Bon displayed his souvenirs which included a Sten submachine gun plus other items including a red parachute in perfect condition. In 1988 when I came to Cosne with Vic, Bon was at the Town Hall, and after the reception he, Vic and Kiki with their spouses joined us for dinner at a local restaurant. Kiki and Vic were reminiscing and my own adventures were mentioned. Bon heard it all. He knew that I had asked Kiki to find the people I had met when I reached my destination and where I had landed.

It appears that the link between Pasquier and me is Bon because neither Vic nor Kiki had contact with him (Pasquier) until 1999. Whatever Pasquier learned about me was at the Town Hall reception of Cosne, and from Bon who heard a blow-by-blow description of my arrival in France on the night of 8/9 August 1944.

Pasquier learned from Bon that I had charged Kiki with the search, and that the suspected area where I jumped was near the town of Clamecy in the Department of Yonne. Kiki was directed to Mme. Blondet by a contact of Pasquier, and not through his own efforts. Kiki did not know this even after contact had been made, and if Pasquier asked him to be invited to the farm of Le Jarloy it is because the Blondets had not done so.

Apparently, the communists were unable to get Vic Calvat. Now they are hoping that a gullible American will help justify their imaginary resistance against the invader they initially helped against their own countrymen.

A Tough Little Guy

In October, 1996 after our return from the Colorado Springs Carpetbaggers reunion, I received a telephone call followed by a letter from James Heddleson, whose plane was shot down in the Haute Loire in 1944. He spent the rest of the war at St.Germain-Laval helping the local maquis. Because we have been friends since an earlier Williamsburg, Virginia reunion he felt obliged to tell me the following story.

The year before at a meeting of the Air Force Escape and Evasion Society at Toronto, Canada, he met a William Randall, a former POW and his son Richard. They told him that they were in contact with Michel Bloit a former American "Joe" who resides in France and who is a well known porcelain dealer. This came about because collecting porcelain objects is Richard's hobby.

I was familiar with the name "Bloit" having noticed it in the directory of VOSS. The only OSS agent with whom I was familiar was Michel Block, a young Jewish fellow who, as I was, had been recruited by OSS in Northern Ireland in early 1944. He was one of the nine members of our group of Americans who were transferred to SOE, trained in Malaig, Scotland, and at Ringway near Manchester, England for airborne operations, and we were commissioned at SHAEF on the same day. I had lost track of Michel in Europe, but found him again in Kunming, China, in 1945.

In Paris in 1990, at a meeting of the *Amicale Buckmaster*, I met Colonel Pierre Fayol, the author of *Le Chambon-sur-Lignon sous l'occupation,* who informed me that he was related to Michel Block, but he did not elaborate. Colonel Fayol, FFI regional commander of the Haute Loire, was familiar with Virginia Hall, the organizer of my own sector, and of Michel's operation called *Freelance.*

When I saw his photograph included in Jim Heddleson's letter I realized that Michel Bloit was indeed Michel Block who had taken a different name probably because of anti-semitism still prevailing in France.

With his address provided by Richard Rendall I immediately contacted Michel who promptly replied, sending me photographs of both of us including two other agents taken in England in 1944. The picture on page 22 of *The Winking Fox* is one of these.

In May, 1944, when I decided to return to France as an OSS agent, I took a calculated risk. I knew that, unless I was captured red-handed, my chances of survival were not entirely hopeless. I could have avoided the unpleasant attention of the Gestapo with a good cover, but being a Jew Michel knew that he could never hide that fact, and if he were caught by either the Milice, or the Gestapo, it was curtains for him. What prompted him to jump in the middle of the German Army was for me difficult to understand. He had many reasons for not doing it, but his gratitude for a country who had given him and his family a refuge was I believe his motivating factor. Even more amazing is what happened to him after reaching his destination.

The following are excerpts from Michel Block's own field report on file at NARA under War Diary, Vol 3, Page 910 to page 926 (F-Section, Freelance).

"The plane left the airfield around ten o'clock at night on 31 August. I had been added just the day before to a team of four. Major Lord obtained the authorization to drop blind from Captain Grell if no light was observed on the ground. The trip to our destination was quite comfortable in the big B-24.

Around 0130 hours the dispatcher gave us the running-in signal. I jumped as number four. I didn't see any light during the descent, and didn't have much time to look around because of a bad twist in the ropes. Once on the ground we were supposed to wait for a flashlight signal or the reception committee. I was becoming impatient when I heard on the road bordering the field someone whistling the "Marseillaise." Pistol in hand I started to walk toward the whistling and found Major Lord, 2nd Lt. Macomber, and Raoul Duval surrounded by about ten Frenchmen in civilian clothes armed with pistols and Stens. One of them was in a gendarme's uniform. We had dropped into a maquis patrol 500 yards from the small town of Lurcy-Levy and roughly 40 kilometers from the reception committee. The surrounding area was somewhat heavily controlled by the local maquis. The nearest German unit was located at St. Pierre-Moutier, 40 kilometers away."

Michel was not actually a member of Major Edwin Lord's team; he was to join Hubert, another SOE agent, who had jumped earlier. He was assigned as an advisor to a maquis battalion and while making an inspection of its composing units from an OP he saw a vehicle bearing the Swiss flag moving about German positions. Finding himself in the middle of a 20,000 German retreating column, he and the French officers managed to avoid capture until a runner brought them the news that about 5,000 Germans wanted to surrender, but not to the Maquis, only to the Americans. A meeting was arranged with a German colonel and at 1530 hours on the 12th of September, 1944, a German staff car bearing a white flag stopped at the designated bridge of Mornay and out came Colonel Burgert and an interpreter. With Michel and two French officers they went to a small nearby café. The interpreter introduced the colonel who made a snappy "Heil Hitler." As a representative of the United States and of General Bradley, Michel hesitantly shook his hand.

After reading the terms of surrender to the colonel, who unconditionally accepted them, he showed him on a map the road his troops were to take to reach the designated prison camp at Orleans. After another "Heil Hitler" the colonel left to inform his boss General Elster.

It was ironical that a young Jewish refugee who because of the war became an American officer would accept the surrender of an entire German column composed of over 20,000 well-armed men and equipment. But the decision to let these German troops keep their weapons until they had reached their destination, the prison camp, was hard to swallow by the French resistance fighters.

The Author with Michel Block (later Bloit) in London, 1944

Michel's report states:

"The Germans had threatened to burn the town. I understood the inhabitants' happiness over such a successful end. But I must say that the Maquis boys and officers did not like the armistice as much as the people of Sancoin. They could not understand why the Germans didn't surrender to them and why they kept their arms. Most of them wanted to continue the fight. I had to spend a lot of time explaining to them that they were fighting, not to make war, but to chase the Germans out of France and be in peace again, and that fighting now would only delay the process by keeping in France American troops immobilized by those Germans, now prisoners. They seemed to understand"

I remember this incident well, because the people I was with also let me know that they were very unhappy about this decision. At that time I had no idea that Michel had been involved with the surrender of these German units. The US Command had been told that if the 20,000 German prisoners were disarmed not many would reach the prison camp. The resistance would make sure that they didn't.

Michel made another interesting comment in his report:

"As far as the political situation, parties, and organizations are concerned, I came across only one, the FTPF (Francs-Tireurs et Partisans Français), a maquis unit with a separate staff from the FFI proper. Those FTPF are communists; they formed the only political party making propaganda, printing leaflets and posters, setting up recruiting agencies. I talked to their leader in Montluçon and found him to be a very intelligent but bitter man. He told me that the only thing that should be done now is to wait for the return of the prisoners from Germany, and then hold a general election. Meanwhile he recognized that only de Gaulle could govern France. I must say that I was very much impressed by the FTPF discipline compared to that of the FFI units.

Author and Michel Bloit, St. Cyr-Ecole, July 1999

Some people at Monluçon told me that the FTPF were storing big quantities of food, weapons, gasoline and ammunition for future political use. I absolutely cannot prove this statement in any way."

When I went to France in June 1999, met Michel at St.Cyr-Ecole, near Versailles where we spent a couple hours talking about the past. For both of us it was a wonderful reunion, but too short. We had a schedule to maintain and could not delay our departure from St.Cyr-Ecole, and Michel had urgent family commitments.

The Agony and the Deliverance
of Louise Maria Mariet

While in Laos between 1957 and 1963 I met some very interesting individuals. Many were members of the French Military Mission who, following the SEATO agreement, had a specific function with the Lao Army. One in particular was Captain Henri Michel whose brother Ferdinand had been in Kunming at the time I was there in 1945. Ferdinand Michel was then Military Attaché at the French Embassy of Phnom Penh.

At the time I was writing *The Winking Fox* I was contacted by Elizabeth McIntosh, the author of *Sisterhood of Spies*, who wanted to introduce me to her friend Patricia Lane, the daughter of a former OSS agent in Indochina. Having heard that I had been in Indochina during the war, Pat who was working on her doctorate at the University of Hawaii, wanted to speak to me about my experiences, and obtain names of others who had been in the area at that time. I gave her the name of Henri Michel and an address, hoping that she would locate him. She contacted Henri, his brother and other French veterans of Indochina, but had mixed feelings about the French officers involved in that area during WWII. They were reluctant to bring up unpleasant memories, especially to a stranger such as Pat. Her contacting

Henri Michel, author, Ferdinand Michel, and authors's wife at Nancy, France

Henri Michel on my behalf resulted in bringing me closer to him, eventually leading to meeting him and his brother in 1997 at Nancy, France.

Henri Michel, now a retired colonel, was a veteran of the French conflict (1946-1954) against the Vietminh, and while in Laos had many contacts among the Thaï refugees. He introduced me to many of these including His Excellency

Lt. Henri Michel, May 1947 at Van-yen

Bak Kham Cui (Bac Cam Qui), the chief of the Black Thaï nation in exile near Vientiane, Laos. Bac-Cam-Qui had offered me three thousand well-trained former Thai soldiers to fight our way into North Vietnam. His offer was promptly rejected by CIA and the U.S. Army as well as our State Department.

During the time I knew Henri Michel in Laos and subsequently through correspondence and face-to-face in his home, he never mentioned his past experiences. He occasionally would make reference to his having been in Vietnam, but in vague terms. For this reason I was quite shocked when he sent to me a copy of a speech he had given to the French Retired Officers Association. The translation completed, I promptly sent a copy to the Library of Congress.

The following is a story that will probably surprise many historians and scholars who have had their own views regarding the Vietnam conflict. This narrative is only one of the many stories that have been ignored, not only by the French, but the rest of the world. It involves people that I have known, some that I have worked with, as well as those who have risked much to help the war efforts of the United States in South East Asia.

Coming from the 9th DIC as a volunteer to relieve one of his comrades of the French Troops in South East Asia, on the 19th of December, 1946, Lt. Henri Michel found himself at Dien-Bien-Phu at the command post (CP) of the Colonel commanding the northwest Sector of the Tonkin region during the general attack of the Vietminh.

With the exception of Than-Uyen the overall military disposition had withstood the enemy attack. This very important post controlled one of the oldest roads leading to the Red River valley toward the valley of the Black

177

River. After reaching the Khau-Co Pass (alt. 1,700 meters), this route leads to the basin of the Black River in the heart of the Thaï Provinces at Lai-Chau, or Son-La, eventually to Dien-Bien-Phu.

The colonel entrusted Lt. Michel with the mission of organizing a powerful unit consisting of thirty European and thirty IndoChinese soldiers. The latter were experienced native troopers close to his heart because they came from the company commanded by his own brother Ferdinand at the time of the recapture of Dien-Bien-Phu. Supported by six Bren guns and a 60 mm mortar, this combat unit was to display exceptional aggressiveness in order to reoccupy the military post of Than-Uyen then, to secure the Khau-Co Pass.

He and his unit reached Lai-Chau, the capital of this province, where they obtained reinforcement, then the personnel and the ammunition were loaded into ten large canoes. These were to take them to Qui-Nhiai, approximately 50 kilometers downstream, under the protection of Partisans of the Black River. This group, known for its formidable aggressiveness, was composed of White Thaïs who assured the protection of the navigation of this important line of communication. This unit was under the command of Captain Pere of the IndoChinese Guard, assisted by Deo-Van-Phat, the son of the local province Chief.

During the preparations, Lt. Michel had long discussions with Captain Pere concerning the situation in the region where he was to operate. He obtained valuable information concerning the population, the terrain, and the areas of operation of these partisans. Significantly, he learned that Chief Warrant Officer Mariet, commanding officer of the IndoChinese Guard at the Post of Bao-Ha on the Red River, on the 9th of March, 1945, had been forced to abandon his post at the time of the Japanese takeover, and that he entrusted his spouse to the protection of a local Mandarin family. Madame Mariet, a very obese person, had been unable to follow the column on the mountain trails leading to the Chinese province of Yunnan.

Monsieur de Pontiche, advisor to the Chief of the Province, who participated in the discussion during the briefing, confirmed that it was unlikely that Madame Mariet did survive, because according to local information the population of the valley of the Red River was heavily influenced by the Annamese who appeared to favor the anti-French political movement known as "Vietminh."

Informants sent to that region after the return of the French Army in the Tonkin region reported that the Mandarin family charged with the protection of Madame Mariet had cooperated with the Vietminh. They failed to perceive indications of her survival. This latest information deeply touched the lieutenant because, a few months earlier at Dien-Bien-Phu, he had discovered his brother who had been missing from March 1945, following the Japanese massacre of the Garrison of Lang-Son where his brother was stationed. He and his entire family believed that his brother was gone. But he found him!

Against all logic, because of his own personal past quest, the idea that this person could still be alive never left him.

Except for the lack of training of the young French troopers assigned to his unit the trip to the combat zone was conducted without major problems. The mountain trails in tropical forest, heat, humidity and attacks by the multitude of leeches in the tall grassland were new to them. Guided by local partisans after a three-day march in combat formation in case of possible ambush, they reached the unit that had to abandon Than-Uyen. Their bivouac was in the middle of a jungle approximately ten kilometers from the post they had deserted.

After a prudent reconnaissance and a prolonged binocular observation of the area the following day, 1st January, 1947, Lt. Michel launched an attack. They secured the post without firing a single shot, and in the heat of the operation the Khau-Co Pass, eight kilometers further, was reoccupied. A few rifle bursts were exchanged with a group of Vietminh who apparently did not expect this unit so soon.

In a few days the post was reorganized, and the defense of the Pass reinforced. With sporadic harassing fire, the Vietminh seized the initiative during the night then again during the day. In retaliation the lieutenant conducted two successive raids on Minh-Luong, 15 kilometers beyond the pass. He was highly surprised by the favorable welcome of the population who returned to their village within an hour after the arrival of his unit. Approximately ten individuals spontaneously made themselves available to him. Separately he charged each one with the job of obtaining information regarding the French wife of the post commander, who had remained in the area after the 1945 Japanese attack. Despite the incursions, encouraged, the Vietminh increased their harassing against the Pass, this time with a Bren gun. Then Lt. Michel decided to conduct a raid on their rear base at Van-Ban to show the local population that the Vietminh were not yet masters of the region. Thus he conducted an extremely daring incursion 35 kilometers into Vietminh territory during which they were able to capture their Bren gun, causing them losses but without a single casualty in his own ranks.

Returning to their base at Minh-Luong he was obliged to give his exhausted troupers a rest of 36-hours. Individually he contacted the informants he had dispatched throughout the area. Because unbeknownst to the others each one provided him with identical information, he felt that he was being used! In reference to Madame Mariet, their response was identical. "Madame chef de post de Bao-Ha, lui mort"!! *(The spouse of the post commander of Bao-Ha is dead.)* These responses were too identical to fully convince him. Compared to his own personal estimation acquired in the course of the different skirmishes, notably at Van Ban which lasted several hours, the informants' assessment of the Vietminh forces was grossly exaggerated.

A few days after his return to Than-Uyen the new colonel commanding the sector called him to his CP at Son-La and announced the arrival of one of his friends a fellow military student who was to replace him at the head of the unit. At the headquarters of the sector, the successive raids conducted by Lt. Michel were considered as excessively daring exploits. He was just lucky in these operations! The French intelligence service had information identical to that given to him by the informants at Minh-Luong. They were so convinced that any attempt on his part to persuade the intelligence officer of the enormous exaggeration concerning the power of the Vietminh facing Than-Uyen would have failed. He did not insist because his audacity no doubt would have been more hazardous than the raid he conducted at Van-Ban.

After several operations along the Colonial Route N° 41 between Son-La and Moc-Chau, some of which were as daring as the one at Van-Ban, (this time with the congratulations of the Battalion Commander) in June, 1947, exhausted and ill, he was taken to the Lanessan Hospital of Hanoï to be treated for a severe case of amebic dysentery.

At that time he had the pleasure of the visit of an Air Force Chief Warrant Officer Marcel Marin, a friend of his parents who invited him to cocktails at his home. During the reception he was surprised to meet Mr. Mariet, a friend of CWO Marin. This cocktail party had been organized specifically for this meeting. As were all the people he had met earlier at Lai-Chau, Mr. Mariet himself was convinced that his spouse was no longer of this world. She would not have been able to survive, and informants had brought back no clear evidence that she had. Of course the Lieutenant reported in detail what he had experienced at Minh-Luong, then at Van-Ban, but in good conscience he could not accept the reports of his informants. As for the military information they reported, they seemingly tried to manipulate him. Consequently, if it was unlikely that Mr. Mariet's spouse was still alive. Michel could not swear that she was dead.

Still hospitalized but physically in better shape, on the 10th of July Colonel L'Hermite requested his presence as soon as possible at his CP at Son-La if his health condition permitted!

Madame Soulage, head doctor on the officers' ward, refused to sign his release but he managed to sneak out of the hospital, and on the 17th of July he parachuted at Ban-Connoi, 25 kilometers from the air strip of Na-San - his initial destination. Because of bad weather reports and a heavy downpour, the pilot had failed to reach his target.

He had never jumped before! When unexpectedly he arrived at Son-La the astonishment of the local people reached its peak, and the surprise was general. Forthwith the Colonel ordered him to Binh-Lu to organize a new company-size unit to be part of the 2nd Thaï Battalion created at Phong-Tho. When he arrived preparations for an important offensive towards the Red River were in progress.

As a part of this initial operation in September, 1947, he found himself fully committed on the trail leading from Binh-Lu to Chapa through the Lo-Khi-Ho Pass when, without providing any detail, Battalion Commander Lavergne suggested that he proceed immediately to Than-Uyen and take command of the 6th Company.

Mounting two horses in succession and covering 60 kilometers in 36 hours, he reached Than-Uyen by early afternoon. When he arrived he learned that during an attack, the 6th Company of the 2nd Thaï Battalion had been caught in a major ambush while moving into the Plaine of Van-Ban. They had been forced to withdraw to their starting position leaving behind the body of one of their officers. The lieutenant commanding the company also had been medically evacuated. The morale of the unit was at its lowest. His reception was very cold, probably because his reputation as a "driver," although untrue, had preceded him evidently as far as Than-Uyen. He was aware that a few months earlier his old Vietminh adversary had the luxury of encircling the military post for a few days. But thanks to the necessary intervention of an airborne platoon, the garrison was relieved.

While receiving a thorough briefing on this unfortunate operation regarding the post of Van-Ban, Michel gathered that, according to the unanimous opinions of those present, the strength of the adversary was estimated to be 600 fighters. Remembering the information he had received 10 months earlier by his informants and after learning that one of the full strength company had been knocked out, he was far less certain of his own opinion. He decided to give all platoon leaders a one-week rest, and specifically to the commander of a company of Méos, to enable him to verify their information. This company occupied the high ground above a 1000-meter elevation, and his main mission was to cover the post of Than-Uyen to prevent an eventual surprise offensive through the summits. The Méos truly prevented all penetrations of the upper region of their territory by the Vietminh.

Alone he visited the chief of the village who was openly pleased to see him again. He too was very worried about the situation and offered his help to determine more accurately the real strength of the adversary. A few days later, receiving information much different from that which he had received earlier, he examined the company's various courses of action as its mission had not changed. The other companies of the battalion had captured Cha-Pa and were proceeding toward the Red River. The 6th Company was to unconditionally control the large trail from the Khau-Co Pass towards

Bao-Ha so as to prevent enemy elements coming from Yen-Bay to attack the right flank of the 2nd Battalion.

Utilizing the full strength of the company, Lt. Michel launched the offensive. Knowing the usual positions of his adversary, he hit them with 81mm mortars before overtaking them. The effect succeeded and they found themselves at the entrance to the Plaine of Van-Ban after only a few insignificant skirmishes. He remembered well the topography of the area. At the cost of strenuous physical effort two platoons penetrated the thick jungle covering the steep slopes bordering each side of the valley from one end to the other. With the support of two mortars they harassed and overwhelmed the enemy's defense. Surprised by his assault with two platoons at the bottom of the valley and unable to react, the Vietminh, after a few ineffective shootings, hurriedly moved back in complete disorder under a barrage of the 60mm mortar supporting the platoon of Lieutenant Mingre on his right flank. The important Vietminh base of Van-Ban was occupied late that afternoon without a single casualty in their ranks.

Surprised by the results, he decided to pause to rest his men. Expecting a counterattack, he did not dare move farther. Major Lavergne, the Battalion Commander, confided later that his message from Van-Ban advising him of his success had "comforted him immensely."

As a result, the colonel commanding the sector, equally surprised by this success, sent Major Lambert to his position to make certain that he did not take unwarranted risks. Thus, while waiting for this ranking officer, he continued seeking information to find out where his adversary had withdrawn. As it were, he was surprised to face again one of the informants he had sent to Minh-Luong in January. While his main interest was information of an operational nature, the informant declared point-blank "Madame chef de post Bao-Ha lui pas mort"!! (The spouse of post commander of Bao-Ha is not dead).

He immediately accepted this good news, but suspected that the individual had not come only to deliver this "message."

After spending two days with his unit Major Lambert realized that Lt. Michel did not act without due consideration, and by a message without ambiguity he reported this fact to the Colonel. Subsequently the Major joined them as the offensive continued up to the crossing of the large trail towards Lao-Kay by Vu-Lao. Following a second leap they occupied the last pass giving access to the valley of the Red River and the important village of Ban-Khen, *fief* of their adversaries.

During another rest period, they searched for a connection to locate the enemy while at the same time conducting reconnaissance in the mountainous area of Pou-Mao, on the right bank of the river. It was at Ban-Khen that an individual, hesitatingly and appearing unsure of himself, approached Lt.

Michel telling him that he had been sent by Nguyên-Dinh-Tan, the local chief of the Vietminh to deliver a message. This opponent who faced him during almost a year wanted to surrender with the remainder of his unit. He wanted Lieutenant Michel to guarantee his safety, and in return he would personally surrender Madame Mariet safe and sound!

This surprising information reaching Michel only a few days after having heard from his informant at Van-Ban that Madame Mariet was still alive, incited him to be very suspicious as he knew very little about his adversary and had no idea where he was. His reply was immediate. Overcoming his emotion, bluntly, leaving no room for a possibility of discussion, he replied that, when Madame Mariet is under his control, only then will he guaranty the safety of this Vietminh chief. He feared falling into a trap but he immediately felt that his duty was to save this woman before anything else. The following day the same individual brought him the accord of his adversary and a guide to point the way for CWO Soubielle's platoon which had been selected to pick up the person in question. At his CP, with two platoons on full alert he was ready to send them help if need be.

Early afternoon the lookouts advised him that a party was coming towards their position, and that they were transporting someone on a stretcher. Thinking that it was Soubielle's platoon returning with the body of a dead comrade, the IndoChinese NCO impulsively assembled his men who were resting in the blockhouse, and lining them at the entrance of the village they presented arms to the person on the litter. Great was their surprise when they realized that the body they were saluting was a European woman, alive!!!

It was the 7th of November, 1947! Madame Mariet had left the Post of Bao-Ha close to the 10th of March 1945. Since that date she had not spoken to a European. As soon as she arrived at Lt. Michel CP at Ban-Khen, the women of the village came running to see her. They had been forewarned by the emissary of Nguyên-Dinh-Tan who was a native of the village.

The soldiers surrounded her expressing their surprise and their joy. Only a few staff members were aware of the true purpose of the operation. Everyone approached this very aged woman, who with the help of a long stick, walked in the village. It was a heart-rendering sight. Crying with happiness, incapable of speaking a single word, she stared at one after the other. During the three-hour trip from Lang-Liem to the CP she had been happy to meet CWO Soubielle, a fellow Pyrénéan (A native of the Pyrénées region of France).

For 32 months in a virgin tropical forest she had lived alone in three consecutive bamboo huts. She successively occupied these as she was moved further away from the village of Lang-Liem, and always to a higher elevation in the massif of Pou-Mao at an elevation close to 900 meters in the region occupied by the ethnic population known as Man.

Lieutenant Peuchot, the medical officer, examined her immediately and was surprised by the vitality and energy displayed by this woman who nevertheless appeared very old (perhaps older than 70).

Settled in the only European-type house in the village which had become Michel's CP, she rested a while.

The next day a few women of the village came to take her away and help her freshen up. They brought her a long skirt the same as theirs, and a jacket too long but warm. Footwear had to be found; unfortunately we only had military boots. A woman from the village brought her a pair of soccer shoes with cleats! He never knew where they came from. These were small, but fortunately they were light. With a large thankful smile to the giver, Madame Mariet immediately put them on.

That same evening by radio Lt. Michel reported the event to the Battalion CP, who had moved to Lau-Kay, and to the Colonel commanding the Son-La sector. He asked them to contact Hanoï and to alert Mr. Mariet whom he knew was there. Strangely he received no response from either concerning his request. None from his Battalion commander nor from the Colonel. No one in their respective CP had been aware of the probable existence of this woman. Arriving at the time of an intense operational activity, perhaps his telegram did not attract particular attention.

The following day the unit's own outstanding communication specialist, after matching his frequencies and orienting his antenna correctly, managed to contact Hanoï HQ directly, asking them to advise Mr. Mariet that his spouse had been found. This NCO radio operator, proud of his exploit, came to show him the Q.S.L. (response accepted and understood) he had just received from Hanoï.

Now it was up to the doctor to resolve the first problem concerning their guest's readjustment to a balanced diet. This woman had eaten nothing but rice for more than two years. With a few cases of individual rations that they had kept for the wounded, the doctor prepared menus which progressively replaced the rice. Their field pharmacy included vitamins and one bottle of Champagne!!! This diuretic was normally intended for those afflicted with an attack of pernicious malaria, referred to as "irritable" malaria. This remedy could be effective in relieving blocked kidneys. When the bottle of champagne was opened all those present took one swallow in the company of Madame Mariet who over a period of several days consumed the rest.

This woman displayed a distinct contrast between her physical aspect, placing her age in the seventies, and her remarkable lucidity, her quick and precise responses, her sharp eyes, and her smile revealing a strange and surprising youth. To ask her age never entered the Lieutenant's mind. Her emaciated body, the curve of her spine, her forward-stooping shoulders accentuated her hunched appearance. Her relatively slow and uncertain gait left no doubt as to her advanced age. The doctor certainly must have asked her, but they never discussed it so evident was her venerable age.

During her stay at Ban-Khen, all the Europeans visited her. She was happy to be able to talk to the soldiers about their families, and about her adventures as all were eager to hear her story. They appreciated better than anyone else what life in the jungle entailed, and for a woman surviving alone in the jungle was to them unimaginable.

Of course Lt. Michel spoke with her often, but she was the one who asked the first question: " What happened to the Japanese?" She was not aware that the war was over, that the aircraft flying over her to drop supplies to the battalion could be other than Japanese! She had noted that recently air activities had clearly increased.

She had lost track of time and was only aware of day and night. She lived in a small hut built approximately 10 meters from a spring. The walls were made of juxtaposed bamboo lattice and a thatched roof she periodically had to repair. She had a small machete given to her by the woman who brought her food every other day. In the center of the shelter was a small fire she kept burning with dry wood she collected nearby. To chase the insects which at time were numerous with smoke, she burned green leaves. Thus she had built a reserve of dry wood to activate the fire and create higher flames, especially at night when she heard a tiger roaming the vicinity of her shelter, which had occurred on several occasions.

Because of the danger she could only identify by ear she never slept at night. She rested during the day on a kind of raised cot made of branches twenty centimeters from the ground. She periodically renovated and improved her "paillasse" with grass.

On several instances, hearing a group of monkeys passing through the tree branches, she came out of her hut to chase them away. Wasn't she surprised when small bales of rice fell from the sky. The monkeys had stolen these from a nearby rice field. Scared by the presence of this human they took off, dropping their bounty.

She knew how to cook paddy in a section of bamboo closed on one end. This non-decorticated rice was healthier because of its vitamin content.

Each day Madame Mariet would relate the numerous stages of her agony. In March 1945 she was taken by trail directly from Bao-Ha to Ban-Khen then to Lang-Liem in four days of march at the rate of 15 km per day.

She was convinced that she had been saved by her feminine intuition. In fact once, but she could not exactly state when, a man came to her hut. Very likely he was a Thaï. Up to that time he was the only man she had seen.

The behavior of the man intrigued her. He held his machete (normally it should have been in its scabbard attached to his belt) and imperceptibly tried to place himself behind her as he was speaking.

Intuitively she felt that he had come to kill her. Courageously, facing him, with a daring which surprised her, she lifted her arm in his direction, and showing him her rosary said to him: "If you kill me my blood will fall on your family who will be persecuted to the last person." The man was probably an animist. Under the menace of this symbol represented by the rosary, and the superhuman aggressiveness of the woman, terrorized he immediately ran way.

Later on, because of her diet of glutinous rice, she developed a case of beriberi. This illness is caused by a serious lack of vitamin B resulting in a case of edema over her entire body. When she was lying down on the right side, her right leg and arm would swell and become enormous and her left side would appear skeletal. In turning over, after a few minutes, an inverse phenomenon resulted. The Thaï woman of the village of Lang-Liem, who was her only connection, seeing her condition, immediately contacted a Tho woman who by suction began to extract liters of serum from her arms and legs. Beforehand the epidermis was chafed with a fragment of porcelain coming from a broken "Khe-bat" (small bowl to eat rice). A knife could not to be used to make the incision on the skin, only a rough instrument to scratch it so that the liquid of the edema could be sucked through scratches. At the same time she was to consume only paddy, non-decorticated, a variety of mountain red rice, cooked with many raw green plants such as mint and wild sage. Both women brought a few water mint plants which they planted in the nearby spring for the continual daily use of Madame Mariet. The beriberi caused loss of sight in one of her eyes, but she was saved from this serious and deadly illness with local indigenous medicine.

Weakened and emaciated by this grave illness, she had trouble moving about and only seldom did she venture slowly ten meters away from her hut to search for dry wood. The Thaï woman of Lang-Lien brought her a tea pot and dried herbs including a little tea to make a beverage after prudently boiling the water collected from the spring. In her condition, a case of dysentery would have been fatal.

On numerous occasions, Michel expressed his surprise and congratulated her for the courage she had displayed, and when he dared ask her where she had found her energy and this internal fortitude, she invariably would show him her rosary saying: "It is in my faith and my desire to see my children again." She told him that she had two children, 11 and 13 thirteen years old. She was not worried about them because a few months before the Japanese attack they were sent back to France for their schooling.

Michel told her that in June he had seen her husband at Hanoï and that he was very much concerned about her. He explained to her the accomplishment of the communication NCO who despite great technical difficulties had managed to contact Hanoï directly and inform her husband.

He described to her all the events which had occurred in Indochina since the Japanese attack on the 9th of March, 1945. It included the existence of the anti-colonialist political movement known as Vietminh which had instigated an armed action against the French. They were at this very moment in the process of fighting.

The arrival of the Vietminh chief was announced a few days after the liberation of Madame Mariet. To be prepared for all eventualities a significant military defense had been put in place. Impressed by these precautions Nguyên-Dinh-Tan showed up only two days later. Madame Mariet recognized him immediately and appeared happy to see him again. She knew him well at Bao-Ha. Prior to the Japanese attack she had nicknamed him "The secretary" because he spoke French exactly as the French did. He only had a light singing accent and a slightly nasal twang as have most Asians. They spoke together for a long time. When Michel informed her that he was the local chief of the Vietminh, she was not surprised. She insisted that the one and only logical reason for his surrender was: "He is as French as we are!! He was a brilliant student in Hanoï!!!"

In her written account she stated: "The following day, 7 November 1947, at sunrise the forest appeared to have an air of celebration, and I had the premonition that someone would come to look for me that very day".

Michel remembered this detail very well and asked her how had this air of celebration manifested itself in the forest. She replied that for a long period a cloud of very small birds had made a circle over her hut, and that she had never witnessed such comportment of birds before.

Whoever knows life in these equatorial regions understands that these small birds called "mange-mil" live in large flocks, and at time display spectacular aerial ballets while chirping in happiness when they find a cloud of insects!!

A different kind of problem soon presented itself. Now that this individual had been found, it was necessary to attend to her still clearly precarious health. The doctor attended her with great care, and progressively her strength increased. About ten days had passed and neither the Sector CP at Son-La, nor the Battalion CP at Lao-Kay, had manifested any interest in the welfare of Madame Mariet. New messages were sent, some vitriolic stating that: "The agony endured for more than two years by this person had seriously damaged her health. As a result her medical evacuation must be considered as soon as possible."

Finally Michel received two communications from both headquarters. The landing strip of Lau-Kay was still unusable - *in those days the expeditionary force did not have helicopters capable of conducting evacuation* - the nearest landing strip where Madame Mariet could be transported was located at Than-Uyen, a three-day march from Ban-Khen through the Khau-Co Pass. The dry season was somewhat late. The ground of the dry rice paddies was not sufficiently hard to support the landing of light planes such as the Morane 500, the type in service in the Tonkin at that time.

Previously in early January, 1948, the ground by then being fully dry and hard, in leveling the small dikes of a large rice field near Ban-Khen they were able to build a landing strip for light aircraft. After their medical officer had left, they were able to evacuate several wounded with light aircraft.

But now the only possibility of evacuation was to transport their guest to Than-Uyen. Near the 25th of November Dr. Peuchot told Michel that he feared a worsening of Madame Mariet's health if threatened by a serious attack of malaria. At the high altitude where she had been, malaria did not itself present a danger, but at 300 meters where she had been taken, despite the treatment she received, a malaria attack was possible. Her general health, although little by little improved, no doubt would not have overcome this added trouble. For Michel as well as for the doctor the situation was distressing. Thus they decided on an evacuation by stretcher to Than-Uyen. In agreement with the doctor, Michel designated his secretary Corporal Chef Michalowski to escort their patient. Madame Mariet mustered considerable efforts to walk as much as she possibly could and let herself be transported when it became absolutely necessary. In every village kindly porters took turns carrying her. Michalowski exerted himself selflessly to satisfy all her needs and to resolve all problems with total devotion. His particularly delicate escort mission was accomplished with good perception. The last stage of the trip was the most difficult because although there were a little more than 20 kilometers from Minh-Luong to Tan-Uyen, the climb to the Khau-Co Pass was steep, and there was no hamlet to rest in between the two villages.

The old post at Tan-Uyen had become the rear base of the company, and WO Avrin, treasurer of the company, had become its commander. In terms of food, he had combat rations in reserve, allowing good nutrition.

They were linked to that rear base only by "Coolies-tram," or runners relaying messages from village to village. To cover a distance of approximately 80 kilometers messengers took 36 hours. When a white feather and a piece of charcoal were attached to the message, the runner ("Paille Men Men" phonetic spelling) were to go very fast as a bird during the day as well as at night without rest at the relays.

All the exchanges of information concerning the air evacuation of Madame Mariet were conducted in this fashion with Michel's CP. All the "Coolies-tram" knew that the messages concerning Madame Mariet were to move at top speed. He was surprised by the remarkable functioning of this transmission system! In the past Michel had used it to communicate with his platoon leaders, who at the time were at one day's march away.

It is only fair and just to render homage to the natives who participated in this particular relay chain for almost three weeks.

Even though he was able to report to the command the arrival of Madame Mariet at Than-Uyen, it was necessary to wait for the weather to clear up to accomplish the evacuation. Between Na-San and Than-Uyen, ridges as high as 1800 meters as well the passes are often covered with fog. A fuel reserve had been set up at the military base so that pilots could refuel for their return trip to Na-San.

After waiting approximately ten days, too long and causing much distress, the anticipated airplane finally arrived and transported its dear rescued to Hanoï via Ban-Na-San.

Madame Mariet was immediately hospitalized at the St.Paul Clinic where she received the competent care provided by the sisters.

After a few months of rest, in May 1948, she was repatriated to her French home of Miramont de Comminges.

During her stay in Hanoï the spouse of General Salan, commander of the troops in the Tonkin region, as well as other persons she had known in the past, visited her on several occasions. Many "colonials," knowing well the survival conditions in the upper region of the Tonkin, considered her survival a "miracle." The local press described this adventure in details, and naturally no one was interested in those who had been responsible for this happy outcome!

After the dismal failure of the first attack of Van-Ban, the morale of the company was at its lowest. It was with the spirit of discipline, and certainly with a prudent determination, that these combat veterans marched to a new offensive. This new success was due to the orderly execution of their mission, and they knew it. This new optimism quickly replaced their pessimism. The happiness seen in their eyes at the arrival of Madame Mariet revealed a legitimate pride at having personally saved this unfortunate woman.

Visibly, the local military authorities did not attach any particular importance to this event giving it only an *anecdotal character*. On the other hand, because of Monsieur Mariet's relations with the Garde Indochinoise the regional administrators and advisor to the Thaï provincial chiefs were all very much interested in the event.

Nguyên-Dinh-Tan, known to the Mandarin leaders of provinces as the heir of the Chief of the Thaï province of Yen-Bay, eventually caused strife within the recently created Federation of these Thaï Provinces.

In 1951 or 1952, Madame Louise-Marie Mariet born Sens, residing at Miramont de Comminges, received the Croix de Guerre of the T.O.E., and was included in the Order of the Legion of Honor with the rank of Chevalier.

Later as a resident of Nice she passed away May 1st 1973 at the age of 77.

Her exact age which was recently disclosed explains the vivacity of spirit of someone who appeared to be 70 while in reality she was only 51 when rescued November 7, 1947

Madame Mariet is no doubt the last individual discovered and rescued following the Japanese aggression in Indochina.

She related other anecdotes concerning the wild animals such as bears, snakes of all sizes even a black panther posting itself every night for two months in front of her hut.

She described her sadness and distress in her solitude, her lack of nourishment, and her constant fear of being assassinated - notably when being transferred from one hut to another in areas which appeared to her more and more sinister.

Her amazing memory returned enabling her to ascertain certain facts with precise dates even though at her liberation she had lost all notion of a calendar.

After the Japanese she speaks of the Viet-Minh, who were looking for her, which reinforces Michel's opinion regarding the protective role of Nguyên-Dinh-Tan. In fact he had her transferred several times from one location to another to elude them. These transfers were conducted in secret at night unknown to the population of the village of Lang-Liem. Only a few ethnic families of a race known as Man from an isolated mountain village knew of her existence.

Her account includes some implausible facts. At her liberation Michel was surprised as well as all his subordinates, by her ignorance of the existence of the Vietminh movement and moreover, of the Japanese capitulation. She believed that the planes flying over her were Japanese!

Naturally, Michel tried to find out who wanted to assassinate her. He swears that she always replied that she had no idea, while in her anecdotes she deliberately accuses the mother of Nguyên-Dinh-Tan of being the instigator!

She does not appear to remember that it was the platoon of CWO Soubielle who at great risks went to look for her near Lang-Liem. It was in a zone where he had never been, and which was always under the control of mobile Vietminh units.

According to her, through an emissary, Michel had sent her 1000 piastres (local money) as well as a letter inviting her to an evening"dinner" !! Evidently this is unbelievable because he would never have entrusted such a sum to an unknown individual. In reality, he personally gave her that sum at Ban-Khen. She divided the sum as she wished among her benefactors. The idea of "inviting" her to dinner would never have entered his mind. Whoever knows or even imagines our living conditions in full military operation in the jungle, where we shared our meals with our men, this invitation to a dinner under these circumstances may seem shocking and unbelievable.

190

She claimed that at Than-Uyen about "ten soldiers coddled her the same as they would have their mother." Every one of Michel's men were needed for combat. To leave ten in the rear base was unthinkable. In their rear base only WO Avrin, Corporal Chef Puig and a lame soldier were left. Thus it was at Ban-Khen, where there were three platoons, including the HQ Platoon (with WO Thu) and possibly the Platoon of Lt. Dorandeu, where she might have met about ten French soldiers.

Nor did Lt. Michel leave for Bao-Ha the day after her liberation. Michel CP remained approximately 15 days at Ban-Khen and was not moved to Lang-Coc until mid December. Nguyên-Dinh-Tan showed up at Ban-Khen approximately three days after the arrival of Madame Mariet, and

Mrs. Louise Mariet and her daughter in 1951.

it is at Michel's CP that she met him. He was accompanied by his mother whom she did not like. (For good reasons because Michel always had the feeling that she was not entirely happy with her son's decision to change camp!)

Strangely, the events related to her liberation are not in chronological order nor are the places where they occurred. This is understood to those who have observed her physical condition at the time of her liberation.

This anecdote gives Michel the opportunity to state specifically that before the arrival of Madame Mariet he ignored completely her living condition from the 9th of March, 1945 and that he could not have imagined them. As soon as he learned that she was alive, his only worry was to find her and save her, but he was never concerned with her surviving conditions.

She wrote that "he snatched me from the claws of the Vietminh." This is a way of judging the events while her recount demonstrates the efforts of Nguyên-Dinh-Tan himself, the military chief of the Vietminh, to hide her from their searches. If captured by the one or the other she most certainly would not have survived very long.

The operations that Michel conducted at the head of the 6th Company were in the framework of the offensive launched by the entire 2nd Thaï Battalion toward the Red River and only the operation conducted by CWO Soubielle had the sole purpose of saving Madame Mariet.

In February 1948 during the offensive of the 2nd Thaï Battalion toward the valley of the Song-Chay river, CWO Soubielle was killed at the pass on the trail between Bao-Ha and Lang-Pho-Rang.

The informant who contacted Michel at Ban-Khen was Mr. Nguyên-Dinh-Thu the brother of Nguyên-Dinh-Tan. He now resides at Toul, France.

Colonel Mariet, the son of CWO Mariet, quotes the following last paragraph of his mother's account:

"I owe to Lieutenant Michel my liberator, a boundless acknowledgment of indebtedness. To him I owe my salvation. This young leader full of vigor who in January, 1947 unsuccessfully attempted my rescue returned in force in early November 1947 to chase the Vietminh and snatch me from their claws."

S/Louise Mariet - April, 1948

PS: In her recount, Madame Mariet specifically stated that Nguyên-Dinh-Tan knew that Lt. Michel was looking for her. This confirms that the informants of Minh-Luong were in fact double agents.

The Defection Of Nguyen-Dinh-Tan

Nguyên-Dinh-Tan, Chevalier de la Legion d'Honneur with particular citation for war action, son of Nguyên-Dinh-Van and of La-Thi-Kuen (White Thaï), was born at Ban-Khen in the county of Van-Ban (Muong Van) February 25 1924.

His father was the head mandarin of the Thaï Province of Yen-Bay. This province, located on the right bank of the Red River extending from Coc-Leu at the frontier of Yunnan to Yen-Bay on the Red River, was over a distance of 120 kilometers downstream. Its southern boundary was approximately the line of separation of the watershed between the valleys of the Red and Black Rivers. Four important penetration routes toward the Black River permitted the movement of commercial products coming from Lao-Kay toward Phong-Tho through the Pass-des-Nuages (2,200 m), or toward Binh-Lu via Chapa and the Lo-Khi-Ho Pass (1,700 m). (Because of its climate Chapa was a rest area well known to the Colonist of the Tonkin.) A third route from Bao-Ha led to Qui-Nhiai or Lai-Chau by the Khau-Co Pass (1,700 m). Finally, a fourth route coming from Yen-Kay led to Son-La (Muong-La) via Nghia-Lo and the Khau-Pha Pass.

The heterogeneous population was dominated by the White Thaï settled at the southern portion of the valleys. The Nang, the Lao, the Man and the Xha, all ethnic groups of the region, had settled at a lower altitude than any others, remaining halfway down the side of the mountains close to the Lu tribes. Subsequent to the construction of the railroad line to the Yunnan province of China, Annamese came in large numbers and competed with the Chinese in business activities. Lead and tin mines were exploited near Cam-Duong close to the Red River.

This heterogeneous population, the mine exploitation, and the easy access to the Tonkinese delta by rail changed the character of that Thaï

Nguyên-Dinh-Tan and Pham-Van-Duong

province. The designation of Sip-Song-Chau-Thai-Thuong of the days of Auguste Pavie in 1893 (12 Thaï cantons) had become Sip-Hoc-Chau-Thai (16 Thaï cantons).

Compared with the other Thaï provinces, this difference is obvious to a reader familiar with the geography of that area. In fact from their source to their widening in their respective valleys the rivers bear the generic name of "Nam," while downstream where they meet other rivers, they are referred by the Vietnamese word "Ngoi." We find that a great number of Annamese family names have appeared in these areas. The mixed marriages between ethnic groups were frequent, and the majority of these were contracted by Annamese men marrying young Thaï girls, usually White Thaï. Because of the ease of movement, more often than any where else, the children — specifically the sons of the chiefs — went to Hanoï for their higher studies. Invariably they were subjected to the influence of city life, accepting less and less the traditional authority of the local leaders.

A brilliant student in his early youth, Nguyên-Dinh-Tan pursued his study at Hanoï where he was among the students of professor Vo-Nguyên-Giap, who surely noticed him.

At the time of the Japanese attack it was to the Provincial Chief Nguyên-Dinh-Tan that Monsieur Mariet, Post Commander of the IndoChinese Guard of Bao-Ha, entrusted his spouse before withdrawing to China as did the famous Alessandri column coming from Son-Tai. Monsieur Mariet was familiar with the mountain trails because he was a member of a clandestine net which escorted to China American airmen who had been shot down by the Japanese. (?)

His secret activities were surely known to the Chief of the Province who frequently was not ignorant of the activities of his subjects, especially if these activities were clandestine and for the service of the colonial power.

The Japanese committed atrocities against the French and against the IndoChinese leadership equally. At Ha-Giang, a small town on the Claire River near the Chinese border close to Bao-Ha, the Japanese savagely massacred all the French men, women, and children; civilian as well as military.

In hiding Madame Mariet, Nguyên-Dinh-Van was no doubt aware of the serious consequences awaiting him if he was betrayed by one of his subjects. This was possible though improbable in view of the people's hatred for the Japanese.

Immediately after the capitulation of Japan a nationalist movement promoted by the Chinese (extremely interested in a direct line of communication toward the Golf of Tonkin) was established in the region. It was the Popular Party of Vietnam or Viet-Nam-Quoc-Dan-Dang of Chinese obedience, better known to the French under the acronym V.N.Q.D.D. This popular movement could only be anti-French.

When the war was over, the Chinese army occupied the upper region of the Tonkin, specifically the area of Dien-Bien-Phu where the French Quilichini column was compelled to fight a Chinese regular battalion. Thus it was necessary for the Thaï leaders to compromise with this new political movement so powerfully supported by their northern neighbor.

As a result, Nguyên-Dinh-Tan, son of a provincial chief, was enlisted in this movement, becoming its local military leader. It was better to be at the head of these armed militias than to oppose them. This was part of the Asiatic slyness which was practiced by all ethnic groups in the course of their history depending on the circumstances.

In those days, particularly in the Annamese zones, the movement called: "The alliance for the independence of Vietnam," (Viet-Nam - Doc - Lap - Minh - Hoi) headed by Ho Chi Minh, was promoting the independence of the "Democratic Republic of Vietnam." It was the beginning of the Vietminh.

Nguyên-Dinh-Tan at the head of the V.N.Q.D.D. militia, immediately joined the Vietminh whose military chief was his former professor Vo-Nguyên-Giap. To refresh our memory let us not forget that in 1945, the first Vietminh troops parading at Hanoï alongside Ho Chi Minh had been equipped and trained by the Americans under the leadership of Major Patti. (??) Nguyên-Dinh-Tan thus became the commander of the local Vietminh company of Van-Ban.

The Vietminh movement flourished in the valley of the Red River, notably at Yen-Bay. This movement, whose main purpose was the "liberation" of the people, could no longer accept the old leaders. They were identified, found guilty of treason against the people, and executed. That is why Vo-Nguyên-Giap assassinated the father of Nguyên-Dinh-Tan, his "friend." This error most certainly deeply shook up the conviction of Nguyên-Dinh-Tan, who initially appeared agreeable to the Vietminh and who became ipso facto the head of the province.

On December 10,1946, under a general order of the Vietminh, Nguyên-Dinh-Tan captured the Khau-Co Pass, then the Post of Tan-Uyen. Learning that European reinforcements were coming from Lai-Chau he prudently withdrew. No doubt intelligence from Lai-Chau had warned of the arrival of a powerful French column.

After Michel's raid on Van-Ban in January, 1947 and the departure of his commando for Phong-Tho, the 6th Company coming from Lai-Chau occupied the post of Than-Uyen and the Khau-Co Pass adopting a passive defensive disposition. That is when Nguyên-Dinh-Tan conducted a new raid on Thai-Uyen with the help of Vietminh regulars coming as temporary reinforcement from the Son-Chay region. It was the Vietminh company known as Dai-Doi No. 262. The

French company locked in the surrounded post eventually ran out of ammunition and of food. Reserves were almost gone when an airborne platoon supported by a Catalina relieved the garrison and forced the Vietminh to return to their starting base of Van-Ban.

In September, 1947, the general offensive of the 2nd Thaï Battalion advancing in the direction of the Red River convinced Tan that it was not a small element of a local action, and after the events related earlier he decided that this was his opportunity to surrender.

After the liberation of Madame Mariet, Michel having promised his safety, Nguyên-Dinh-Tan surrendered to him. Ten days later an emissary sent by Monsieur Deo-Van-Long from Lai-Chau asked Michel to turn Nguyên-Dinh-Tan over to him. He was to be tried for his activities with the Vietminh. Having given his word, and having nothing to do with the Province Chief of Lai-Chau, Michel immediately sent Tan to Colonel l'Hermite who was in charge of Son-La sector and forwarded a detailed report of the entire affair. One month later Tan was returned to Michel by the Colonel with a few words of congratulation telling me to ensure his protection. The Colonel had spoken at length with Tan, who convinced him of the sincerity of his surrender and of his engagement to their side.

After his repatriation, following almost a three year tour, Michel's successor pursuant to his suggestion utilized Tan in the collection of information and the recruiting of local auxiliary troops, most of which proved to be fighters of high quality. Aware of the attitude of the Chief of the Thaï Federation toward him, Tan remained close to French military with whom he was totally absorbed. He was convinced that to link "his" Province to the Federation was more a submission than an alliance and he has never accepted this concept.

Leading a Thaï commando unit, he continued fighting in the jungle after the French military setbacks at Lao-Kay and Than-Uyen. He managed to reoccupy Than-Uyen and then withdrew toward Phong-Tho. Here he gained the admiration of the patriarch Deo-Van-An, chief of the province, who gave him one of his daughters in marriage to consummate the alliance.

Tan continued attacking the rear of the Vietminh supply columns on their way to Dien-Bien-Phu. At Pa-Tan, on the Nam-Na River, approximately ten kilometers downstream from the confluence of the Nam-So River coming from Phong-Tho, he led a fight that was particularly deadly to the Vietminh, delaying considerably their advance toward Lai-Chau and allowing the total evacuation of the leaders of the Central committee of the Thaï Federation. Monsieur Trancart, a high ranking administrator and advisor to the Thaï Federation, was pleased to address to him a laudatory testimony. Tan had reversed the opinion of the high dignitaries of the Federation who wanted to convict him after his surrender in November 1947.

196

Managing in extremis to be evacuated to Hanoï with the principal actors of his military exploits on July 27, 1954, after the disaster of Dien-Bien-Phu, Nguyên-Dinh-Tan was made Chevalier de la Légion d'Honneur with special citation.

After Dien-Bien-Phu, Michel found him as a refugee in Vientiane, Laos, where he stayed from 1956 to 1958. By then he was extremely disappointed, and had completely lost the drive and passion Michel had seen in him. His second spouse, Deo-Thi-On, who had given him four children, passed away in Vientiane. After the American defeat he took refuge at Toul, France, where in 1967 Henri Michel found him sick and in full denial, refusing to admit the successive defeats of the French and the Americans. Totally unknown and ignored, going from hospital to hospital, in 1963 he passed away in Toul where he is buried, and where his brother Nguyên-Dinh-Tu resides with his family. Pham-Van-Duong, one of his faithful assistants, took refuge at Metz where he is now buried.

These three commando leaders with Se-Co-An, a Nung from the Pa-Kha and Muong-Kuong regions, were posthumously promoted to the rank of Lieutenant. These ranks were recognized only during their periods of command and operational activities. It brought them no future retirement remuneration and they could not be referred to as lieutenant, a rank they had received with so much pride.

As for Madame Mariet, Nguyên-Dinh-Tan had kept the engagement of his father who promised her safekeeping to her husband. Neither the Japanese nor the V.N.Q.D.D. learned of her existence, especially not the Vietminh. When ill with beriberi, she was cared for and healed by local attendants. In this region, where everything is known, to have managed for 32 months to hide and feed as best they could a European woman in the middle of the jungle, unbeknownst to the rest of the population, was an unbelievable feat.

If Lt. Michel is the deliverer of Madame Mariet, there is no doubt it was Nguyên-Dinh-Tan who was her savior.

This information concerning Nguyên-Dinh-Tan has been

recently confirmed with greater details by his brother Nguyên-Din-Tu.

In December, 1947, La-tan, another brother of Nguyên-Dinh-Tan, was killed close to Ban-Khen while he was leading a platoon toward a Vietminh unit which was about to attack the CP of Ban-Khen.

End Note: While assigned in Laos in 1958 I had the pleasure of meeting many of these Thai refugees in their village north of Vientiane. I was particularly impressed by His Excellency Bac-Cam-Qui who offered me a battalion-size unit to attack North Vietnam. This scared the hell out of our command who were certain that this would start WWIII!

(?) I do not know where Michel obtained this information. However the post of Bao-Ha was located close to Lao Kay where according to the following document AGAS-China had agents recruited by GBT as members of an escape and evasion network.

(??) Major Patti was extremely disliked by the French who blamed him for everything they did not like. Major Patti was not involved in the training of the Vietminh, only the Deer Team was involved in this function.

Reflections

Over sixty years have passed since I first set foot on the soil of the United States. I never dreamed that I would see the year 2000 and hopefully the twenty-first century, but I did! In the twenties, the life expectancy of a Frenchman was 56 years. My father barely made it, he was 56 when he died! The four packs of cigarettes he consumed every day did him in. I learned of his passing one month after his funeral because at that time I was inaccessibly involved with an operation in a foreign country. After learning the cause of his demise it never occurred to me that I should sue Philip-Morris. Instead I decided to learn from his mistake and to stop smoking altogether which I did fifty years ago at the age of 29.

After landing in New York in May, 1939, it did not take long for me to realize that unless I knew what people around me were saying I would never know what was going on, and would never be able to make myself understood. My chances of getting anywhere in the USA would be rather slim. Even though at work the foreman and most of the employees spoke French, my first undertaking was to go to night school and study hard. After one year in America, once I mastered a good portion of the English language, I asserted myself, and asked my boss for a raise. I did not ask him in French, but in perfect, probably accented English, to which he said "no" or perhaps "Non!"

My only regret is not having taken advantage of the opportunity to improve my formal education the government gave me after the war. I had left France in May, 1939, one month before my high school graduation. Unlike my sister who finished her schooling in an American high school, I went to work and as a result have never graduated from any high school. As a civilian in the workplace as well as in the Army I had no trouble keeping up with my contemporaries. In the military, because of my IQ several of my commanding officers had suggested that I apply for OCS. I did not because I felt that my limited language capability would cause me to fail. I preferred staying where I felt comfortable, where my duty did not require much interaction with others. My wartime infantry experiences in Texas proved to me that I would have had a rough time with those I would command, particularly if they came from the south, specifically Texas.

I do not know if the British assessment program I went through showed this propensity, and if this was the reason they sent me alone behind the German lines! I always did better, and probably still feel that way, doing things by myself without the help of others.

I am still surprised that I reached the rank of major without having attended the required military schools, such as the Basic Officer Course, the Advance Officers School, and various other schools needed in an officer's personal file for his advancement. This did not prevent my assignment as an instructor at Army Intelligence schools, where I had graduate students under me, including some with doctoral degrees. In my various military assignments my lack of formal education was never a problem.Some of my associates even jokingly called me "doctor" knowing full well that I was no "PhD." If I had pursued an academic endeavor I might not have accomplished what I did and my life might have taken a different direction. Who knows?

In retrospect, my decision not to pursue an academic education, or to improve my formal education was wrong. I hope that none of my grandchildren will emulate this grandfather, and instead will amass as many academic credentials as they can even if they do not actually use them.

This said, I have mixed feelings concerning my involvement with Military Intelligence which is an oxymoron having originated in England with their MI-5 and MI-6. There is nothing intelligent about the military because whatever the military knows is very seldom used by the policy makers, the politicians. During WWI Clemenceau expressed it very clearly stating that, "War was too important to leave it in the hands of generals." The French have a more realistic term for that activity. They call it "Renseignement," or Information.

The reams of material produced by OSS and SOE agents in Europe could not predict the cold war. After reading *"Too Secret Too Long"* by Chapman Pincher, and *"C"* by Anthony Cave Brown, it appears that the Soviets had access to SOE reports, as we know now that the British had been thoroughly penetrated, long before the war. Until WWII the US intelligence was non-existent. With the help of the British and General Donovan's persistence, OSS was eventually created despite the reluctance of the JCS. Note how quickly OSS was disbanded after the war! Spying was a dirty word and still is in some quarters. Shortly after the war, the Delimitation Agreement was created so as to define areas of operation of the CIA, the FBI and the various military organization such as CIC, OSI, and ONI. The agreement was promptly violated by several of the signatories, causing all kinds of problems.

During the war I felt that agents and spies were doing a very important if risky job. Subsequently, as a counterintelligence agent, I became disenchanted with the caliber of those in authority. I soon discovered that one of the favorite jobs given to officers without leadership capability, including West Pointers, was the position of S-2, the intelligence slot of a battalion or G-2 for a division. Having operated as an agent during the war, I understood the spy business differently from those who had learned from others, or the book.

I soon discovered that, for an officer looking forward to a rewarding military career, an intelligence slot was not the most desirable assignment. This was not a command position and those unlucky enough to fall into it tried desperately to get out even if they enjoyed the job. As a result there was no leadership continuity. The officer in charge was only concerned with the results he could achieve during his short period of assignment, which was usually three years. Unlike the Soviets' KGB, or GPU who recruited for the long-range, our political and military leaders expected results the day after an agent or spy was recruited.

Some of our generals did not know the functions of the agencies under their command. Some confused CIC with CID, and some did not think that information collected for their use was worth their time. They blindly supported the administration they served, then criticized it when they retired. They did not have the guts to tell it the way it was to those who could make the difference.

Disappointed by my experiences as a CIC agent in CONUS, in 1950 when reporting to my overseas assignment I told my old OSS friend, Major Aaron Bank, the CO of the unit, that I wanted to go to the files where no one would make me do stupid things. He understood and shortly thereafter he was promoted to LTC and left for another assignment with the Special Forces.

I do not want to give the impression that I was surrounded with dunces. I served for and with outstanding officers, and top-notch agents, but these were few and far between.

In the Asia Theater during the war our field leaders had no idea who the people were they were dealing with. Ho Chi Minh was the individual who was one of the creators of the French Communist Party. This was no secret, the French newspapers had hundred of articles including pictures of Ho Chi Minh. Before releasing him the Chinese, our ally, had him locked up for eighteen months because of his communist activities. In 1945, into the IndoChinese jungle OSS sent a team whose leader thought that Ho Chi Minh was an agrarian reformer. After spending time with him this officer thought that perhaps he was a communist!

After that war I watched our prestige slowly dissipate. The USA, the leader of the world, the nation which overwhelmed the German and the Japanese armies, two of the best, could not manage a country the size of North Vietnam. Our military leaders, lacking the guts to tell our political leaders that they were wrong, should be held responsible for the Vietnam fiasco. The administration believed that what had succeeded in Europe would succeed in South East Asia. Guerrilla warfare is only successful if you are helping the people against an invading enemy. In Europe the enemy was well defined. In Vietnam, we were the invaders. Not a single North Vietnamese, left alive after Ho and Giap eliminated all opposition, wanted to be rescued. We should have learned from the French. The Vietnam Story of this book shows what did occur in Vietnam shortly after WWII. We were involved in a regional conflict dating back centuries. We had no business there.

When my successor at the Indianapolis CIC field office told me that strapped with a shortage of agents, they were sending postcards to the neighbors of subjects of personal investigations, I knew then that I had left this profession at the right time.

For additional information about the French Resistance, OSS, SOE, and CIA the author recommends the following:

Resistance Fighter by Elisabeth Sevier
Sunflower University Press

War Without A Front, by Elisabeth Sevier
Wesley Publishing company

Flames In The Field, BY Rita Kramer
Michael Joseph, London UK

F Section Soe, by Marcel Ruby
Leo Cooper, London UK

The Secret War Against Hanoï, by Richard H. Shultz, Jr.
Harper Collings Publishers

Secret Army Secret War, by Sedgewick Tourison
Naval Institute Press

Sisterhood Of Spies, by Elizabeth McIntosh
Naval Institute Press

The Very Best Men, by Evan Thomas
Simon and Shuster

Inside Camp X, by Lynn-Philip Hodgson

Acronyms

AFEES . . . . Air Force Escape and Evasion Society
AGAS . . . . Air Ground Aid Service
BAR . . . . . Browning Automatic Rifle
BBC . . . . . British Broadcasting Company
BCRA . . . . Bureau Central de Renseignement et d'Action
BOA . . . . . Bureau des Opérations Aériennes
CIA . . . . . Central Intelligence Agency
CIC . . . . . Counterintelligence Corps
CID . . . . . Criminal Investigation Department
CJCS . . . . Chairman, Joint Chiefs of Staff
CNR . . . . . Conseil National de la Résistance
CP . . . . . . Command Post
CWO . . . . . Chief Warrant Officer
DMD . . . . . Délégué Militaire Départemental
DMR . . . . . Délégué Militaire Régional
DZ . . . . . . Drop Zone
FBI . . . . . . Federal Bureau of Investigation
FFI . . . . . . Forces Françaisesde l'Intérieur
FTP . . . . . F Franc-Tireurs Partisans Français
GBT . . . . . Gordon - Bernard - Tan Group
HQ . . . . . . Headquarters
JCS . . . . . . Joint Chiefs of Staff
KIA . . . . . Killed in Action
MI-5 . . . . . British Counter-espionage Service
MI-6 . . . . . British Secret Service
MUR . . . . . Mouvement Unifié de la Resistance
NARA . . . . National Archives Records and Administration
NM3 . . . . . National Maquis Region 3
ONI . . . . . Office of Naval Intelligence
OPS . . . . . Operations Officer
OSS . . . . . Offices of Strategic Services
QSL . . . . . Message received and understood
RAF . . . . . Royal Air Force
SAS . . . . . Special Air Service (British)
SEATO . . . South East Asia Treaty Organization
SHA . . . . . Service Historique de l'Armée
SIPO . . . . . Sicherheit Polizei (German Security Police)
SIS . . . . . . Secret Intelligence Service (British)
SNM . . . . . Service National Maquis
SNR . . . . . Service National Radio
SOE . . . . . Special Operations Executive
TOE . . . . . Territoires d'Outre-Mer (Overseas Territories)
VNQDD . . . Viet-Nam Quoq Dan Dong
VOSS . . . . . Veterans of OSS
WO . . . . . Warrant Officer

Index

Achille   63
AFEES   71
AGAS-China   198
Air Force Academy   72, 113
Alessandri column   194
Alfred   133, 134, 135
Allen, Doctor   104, 112
American-Netherlands Foundation   7
Amerloque (slang)   30, 25, 35
Amicale Buckmaster   171
Amicale des Reseaux Action de la France
     Combattante   116
ANACR-Yonne   122
Anguille   (DZ)   26, 58, 91, 113
Annay   (village)   33, 58
Antoine   60
Aramis   168
Armored Division, 6th   108
Army Air Corps (Air Force)   14, 21, 71,
     75
Avrin, WO   188, 191

Bac Cam Qui   also Bak-Kham-Cui   177,
     198
Badaire   60, 140, 143, 144, 145
Badaire, Jean-Bernard   60
Bank, Aaron, Major   201
Barbillon   DZ   58, 113
Bartholomew, Wm. and Mary (Bart)   66,
67, 71
Bartram, Carl   69
Bassett,   Clive   69, 73
Battard,   Raoul   145
Bauchet, Guy   41, 49
Bauvais Castle   119
Bazooka   25, 37
BBC   24, 115
BCRA   62, 74, 113, 116, 166
Beaufort, Alain de   113, 166
Beauvais, castle   119
Beauvais farm   120
Belfort   63
Belleau , also Belleau Maquis   104,105
Bellot   167
Bellot, André   54
Benedictine monk   44
Bieler   119
Black Thai   177
Blandin, Serge   127

Block, Michel   61, 173
Bloit, Michel   61, 171, 174, 203
Blondet,   157, 158, 159, 162, 168
Blondet, Andrée   117, 119, 121, 122,
124, 154, 155, 156, 161, 163, 167, 168,
     170
Blondet, Robert   157
BOA   101, 109, 110, 113, 162, 163
Boches (Germans)   28, 30, 36, 44, 130
Bombardment Group Association,
801st/492nd   82
Bombardment Group, 492nd   74
Bombardment Group, 801st   74
Bon, Pierre   14, 161, 169, 170
Bourgoin, Colonel   41
Boutissaint   165
Boutissaint, Maquis of   122
Boyer, Louise   72
Bradbury, Lt. Col. (Brad)   72, 73, 74, 113
Bradley, General   172
Briare (also Briar Bridge)   106, 108
Brienon   122
Brisset, Pierre   20
Brisset, R.   54
British SOE   152
Brown, Anthony Cave   200
Buckmaster, Maurice   25, 60, 61, 137,
139, 148, 149
Bulge, Battle of   7
Burgert, Colonel   1 72

Cacane   119
Cagnat, André   117
Calvat, Vic (Capt. Dubois)   1, 20, 21, 22,
     23, 53, 61, 62, 65, 127, 130, 153, 157,
     159, 160, 170
Caron, Father (Norac)   19, 112
Carpetbagger (s)   73, 74, 77, 93,
CARPETBAGGERS , Directory listed   92
Cercle Interallié   60
Charanton (Village)   106
Charité, La   (Village)100
Chleus (French pejorative term for
German)   41
Churchill, Winston   62
CIA   61, 71
Clamecy (Village)   55, 107, 116, 121, 154
Clange   122
Clemenceau, Georges   200

Colby, Bill   68, 71
College Park   75, 76
Colon, Colonel   167, 168
Colt, Cal.32   117
Committee of Liberation   5, 42
Coolies-tram   188
Cordex (Cordtex)   112
Cornol (Village)   13
Corvel L'Orgueuilleux   54
Cosne-sur-Loire   3, 4, 5, 13, 14, 22, 116
Cosne Town Hall   33

Dédé (Butcher)   25, 101, 110, 120, 121
Dédé Maquis   119
Dairyman (Circuit)   114
Daniel (Julien) 13, 14, 30, 49, 96, 99, 101
Davis, Captain   41, 71, 107, 129, 146, 169
De Foe (Nicholas Solivélas)   (See Deux
Fouets)   167
de Gaulle   62, 135,138, 174
Deer Mission   82
Deer Team   74, 75, 198
Défourneaux, Marc, General   125
Défourneaux, René Julien Lt.   49, 50,
   51, 59, 78, 96, 101, 114
Delle (Village)   53, 126
Deo-Van-An   196
Deo-Van-Long   196
Deo-Van-Phat   178
Des Etages, Doctor   22
Des Vernes   120
Desfourneaux, Etienne B. General   125
Dessons, Max   54, 161
Deux Fouets (See De Foe)   102, 111, 167
DGER   145, 152
Diane (See Hall, Virginia) 24, 61, 96, 97,
137
Division, 75th   7
Dodds-Parker, Douglas, Sir   18
Donkeyman (Mission) 167
Donovan, Wm. General   200
Dorandeu, Lt.   191
Dubois, Captain (Vic Calvat)   16, 26, 58,
   59, 111, 114, 116, 134, 136, 137,138,
   146, 164
Dubois, Maquis   115, 154, 155, 167
Dufrene, Colonel   134
Duguet, Louis-Jean (See Léon)   96
Duplessis   35
Dupré, Lt. (See Léon)   114
Duval, Raoul   172

Egelee, Captain 137
Eglin, Lucienne   126
Eisenhower, General   64
Eliane   129
Elster, General   173
Ensminger, Tom   75, 76, 78, 82, 91
Entrains   20, 29, 37, 58, 104
Escalier, Jean   161
Eureka   32, 101, 109

Fairbanks, Charles   74
Fayen, Doctor   122, 123
Fayol, Pierre, Lt. Col.   60, 61,62, 171
FFI   54, 99, 104, 106, 110, 132, 134,
   138, 139,155, 166, 174
FFI/FTP   131
Fish, Robert W. Colonel   71, 72
Flames in the Field   94
Fort Ord   66, 67
Fougerat, Paul & Yvonne   46, 129, 130
François (Gestapo agent) 102
Freelance (Operation) 171, 172
Freeman, Roger   72
French Communist Party   143
FTP   104, 114,134, 135, 138, 139, 155, 160
FTPF   162, 174, 175

Gadoin, Mr.   101
Gadoin, Simone   4
Gaufillier, Madame   163
Gazo (Burner)   24, 29, 31
GBT   (Gordon-Bernard-Tan Group)   198
Geneva Convention   134
Geo   54
German spy plane   26
Gestapo   27, 31, 60, 63, 133, 134, 135,
   136, 142, 153, 172
Gilpin, Henry, Capt.   66, 67, 77, 80
Giordano, David 74, 75, 82
Golmar, Laura   125
goutte (Alcohol)   26
Grand Louis   46
Grandjean Maquis   54
Guillot, Armand   19
Guillot, Jean and Eugenie 19, 20, 24,26,
   30, 33, 34, 46, 111, 129, 130, 131, 132,
   137, 138
Gumbel, Bryan   94
Guyot, Jean   103, 111

Hall, Virginia (Diane)   24, 60, 61, 62, 94,
    167, 168, 171
Harrington Air Base   69, 76
HECKLER (Circuit) 113
Heddleson, James   68, 74, 82, 171,
Heflin, Colonel   79
Henri   46
Historia (Publication)   47
Ho Chi Minh   47, 195, 201
Hubert (Agent) 172

Jacqueline (Calvat)   22, 50, 51
Jarry   113, 166, 167
Jean-Marie (Circuit)   167
Jimmy le Chat   82
Joe (s)   66, 71, 72, 73, 75, 78
Joe Hole   72
Johndeux   24
Jojo   144

Kettering Park Hotel   69
Khau-Co Pass   178
Kiki   (see Roger Tartrat)
Kinnard, General   10
Koenig, General   97, 98, 134, 138, 166
Korrot, Roy   76, 77, 78
Kramer, Rita   94

Léré (Cher)   58
La-Thi-Kuen   193
La Celle-sur-Loire   55, 129
La Celle Saint Cloud   15, 19, 60
La Charité   105, 106, 107
La Pierre Qui Vire Monastery   40, 102
Labcuth   36
Laboué   102, 111
Lainsecq   101, 117, 162
Lambert, Major   182
Lane, Patricia   176
Laripette   143, 144
Lauzon, Russell J.   79, 80
Lavergne, Major   181, 182
Le Chambon-sur-Lignon sous l'Occupation
    60
Le Grand, Raymond   42
Le Jarloy   154, 156,158, 161, 162, 163,
    164, 166, 168, 170
Le Loup   114
Le Vengeur   144
Lenoble, Maitre   147

Léon   13, 24,26/30, 38, 53, 58-60, 93, 94,
    96, 99 ,100, 102, 104, 105, 107, 109,
    110, 111, 113,/115, 118, 131, 137,138,
    142, 145, 149, 163, 164, 168
Les Deux France   62
Levengeur, Captain 143
L'Hermite, Colonel   180, 196
LICENSEE ex-LOINCLOTH   (Circuit)
    82, 94
Licensee Mission   75, 91, 94, 139
List of crew members   82
Loincloth (Operation)   96, 100
London 104, 110, 111
Lord, Edwin, Major   172
Louisette   40, 44
Lucien   63
Lysender (Aircraft)   69

Méos (Tribesmen)   181
Mably   126, 127
MacCormick   161
Maco   161
Macomber, 2nd Lt. 172
Margrit, Princesse   10
Marie Louise   AKA Miquette   166
Mariet, Colonel   192
Mariet, Louise Maria   176,191
Mariet, WO   178, 184, 189, 192, 194
Marin, CWO   180
Marin, Marcel   180
Marty, Miss   49
Matriolet   144
Maxwell Air Force Base   74
McIntosh, Fred & Elizabeth (Betty)   75,
    76, 94, 176
Mic (Michel Pailler)   166
Michalowski, Corporal Chef   188
Michel, Ferdinand   176
Michel, Henri, Captain 176, 177,
    178, 179, 182, 184, 185, 203
Michel, Lieutenant   141, 148
Mick   119
Mike, Captain 101, 109
Milice   42, 171
Miller   79, 80
Miller, A.B.   79
Miller, Federick W. 79
Miller, George F. 79
Miller, Glen   42
Miquette   AKA Marie Louise   166
Miss Fitts   76, 77, 78, 79, 158

Licensee, Mission   24, 137
Lisencee, Mission   115

Mission Reports   109
Montemart, Duke of   20,36
Montespan, Marquise de 36
Montrevillon DZ   114
Moreau, Commandant   134, 135, 136,
    137, 138, 139
Moreau, Louis   163
Moriset   40
Moulin, Jean   138

Nadine   5
Napo   140, 142
NARA   74, 75, 82, 94, 113, 172
National Maquis (NM)   155, 162
Nazi   63, 132, 136, 140
Nevers   38, 58, 105, 106, 133, 137
Nguyên-Dinh-Tan   183, 187, 189,
    190, 194, 192, 195, 196, 197
Nguyên-Dinh-Tu   197
Nguyên-Dinh-Van   193, 194
Nicole   129
NM3 National Maquis   167
NM3 Badge   155
Norac, (Lt.)(See Father Caron) 19, 40, 44,
102, 104, 111, 112

Oberg, Marie-Jane and Harold   65, 66
OCM   115
O'Connor, Mary, Capt. 72
OSS   16, 18, 60, 61, 74, 116
Ouroux   167

Pailler, Mic   162, 163, 167
Pain   113
Pair   166, 167
Pam-Van-Duong   193
Parnel   74
Party of Moscow   151
Pasquet   132
Pasquier, Yves   123, 124, 155, 159, 160,
    161, 162, 163, 164, 168,169, 170
Patis   30
Patriotic Militia   143
Patti, Major   195, 198
Patton, General   39, 41, 42, 49, 58, 108
Pavie, August 194
Pere, Captain 178
Perrisian, Jerry   166
Petrenko, Igor (Pete)   74

Petti, Jean   54
Peuchot, Dr. Lt.   184, 188
Pham-Van-Duong   197
Phillipe, Mr.   102, 111, 167
Pichard, Michel   113, 166
Pincher, Chapman   200
Pompel   37
Ponsard   27, 41
Pontiche, Monsieur de   178
Pou, Charles D. 79
Pouilly   31, 55, 100
Prevost, Léon   114
Puig, Corporal Chef   191

Quilichini   195

Radio-London   26
RAF   98, 107, 138, 164
Rake, Denis   167, 168
Rebeka   109
Rendall, Richard   82, 171
Rendall, William   171
Revére, Captain 145
Revenue Office of Cosne   136
Rhin/Danube Association   7
ricain (Slang for American)   29, 36
Roberts, James   79
Roche, Colonel   108,139, 140, 142, 144,
145, 150, 152
Roland   104, 167
Rondenet   166
Roosevelt   62
Rouget DZ   58, 113
Rouquine   101
Royal Air Force (RAF)   98, 107, 116,
138, 164
Ruby, Marcel   62
Ruh, Eugene   76, 77, 78, 80

Salan, General   189
SAS   71, 105, 106, 108
SEATO   176
Seccafico, James   76, 79, 80, 91
Secene   46
Secret Army   133
Service Historique de l'Armée   114
Setting Europe Ablaze   18
SHA   114
Siamo   24
Simone   4
Singlaub, John K. Major General   94
SIPO   167

Sisterhood of Spies   94
Sitting Duck Pub   94
Sizemore, Richard and Bernice   71, 79
SOE   16, 18, 60, 61, 62, 70, 71, 74, 94,
        109, 113, 115, 116, 152, 159, 160, 161,
        166, 168, 172, 200
SOE, F-Section   94, 100, 159, 166
SOE/OSS   109, 113, 168
Solnon, Mr.   126, 127
Soubielle, CWO   183, 190, 191, 192
Soulage, Madame   180
Special Forces Club   70, 71
Spy plane, German   26
SS units   107
St. Benoit Monastery   19, 112
St. Laurent Bridge   55
St. Satur   40, 106, 108
St. Thibault   58, 100
St.Germain-Laval   126
St.Mère Eglise   18
St.Paul Clinic   189
St.Satur   154
St.Thibault   39, 154
Steel, John, Lt.   18
Sullivan, Robert Colonel   72
Suppliciau, Marcel Sgt.   33, 34, 40, 44,
104
Switzerland   13, 126

Targets   99
Tartrat, Janine Mrs.   123
Tartrat, Roger   (Kiki)   23, 74, 93, 113,
        116
Tatoué   104, 112, 167
Taylor, John   74, 75, 94
Testard, Dr. 13
Testard, Colonel   6, 13, 14
Thorez, Maurice   147
Thu, WO   191
Tournaire, Joseph   126, 127
Traction avant   35, 36
Traigh House   70, 71
Trancart, Monsieur   196

U.S. Air Force   116, 138,164
U.S. Army Air Force   93
Unified Movement of the Resistance   138

V.N.Q.D.D.   195, 197
Vaissereau, Colonel   137
Val-de-Salm, Chalet   7
Valençay   159
Verity, Squadron Leader   69
Vichy police   60
Viet-Minh   also Vietminh   190
Vilnat   54
Vogué, Arnaud de   167
Vo-Nguyên-Giap   47, 195
Vomécourt, Odile Boulot de   60
Vomécourt, Philippe, Baron de   60
VOSS   60

Wersell, Harold   78
Wilkinson, Andy J.   79
Wilson, Captain   112
Wright-Paterson Air Force Base   76

Yvonne   129, 130

Zidore   123, 124